THE
WITCHFINDER
GENERAL

THE

WITCHFINDER GENERAL

GENERAL

A POLITICAL ODYSSEY

⋘•⋙

JOYCE GOULD

Biteback Publishing

First published in Great Britain in 2016 by
Biteback Publishing Ltd
Westminster Tower
3 Albert Embankment
London SE1 7SP
Copyright © Joyce Gould 2016

ISBN 978-1-84954-975-2

10 9 8 7 6 5 4 3 2 1

A CIP catalogue record for this book is available from the British Library.

Set in Sabon LT and Flenja by Adrian McLaughlin

Printed and bound in Great Britain by
CPI Group (UK) Ltd, Croydon CRO 4YY

To my dear daughter Jeannette

ACKNOWLEDGEMENTS

David Marsh and Joanne Chambers, *Abortion Politics*

Betty Boothroyd, *The Autobiography*

David Denver, Colin Rallings and others, *British Elections and Parties Yearbooks*

Richard Heffernan and Mike Marqusee, *Defeat from the Jaws of Victory*

Giles Radice, *Diaries 1980–2001*

Eric Shaw, *Discipline and Discord in the Labour Party*

Tony Benn, *The End of an Era: Diaries 1980–1990*

Barbara Castle, *Fighting All the Way*

Jimmy Allison, *Guilty by Suspicion*

John Golding, *Hammer of the Left*

Harold Wilson, *The Labour Government, 1964–70: A Personal Record*

Eric Heffer, *Labour's Future*

Peter Kilfoyle, *Left Behind*

Michael Crick, *Militant and The March of Militant*

Dennis Skinner, *Sailing Close to the Wind*

John Grayson, *Solid Labour*

Lucy Middleton (ed.), *Women in the Labour Movement*
Labour History Museum Archives

Particular thanks for memories:
Terry Ashton
Charles Clarke
Neil Kinnock
Gus McDonald
Sally Morgan
Richard Taylor
Larry Whitty

Peter Mandelson for recommending me to the National
    Democrats

Merlyn Rees for being a friend and sponsor

Roger Hough for my wonderful leaving party

Betty Lockwood my friend and mentor

To my staff at head office and in the regions and colleagues
who guided me through twenty-four years

The legal team who guided me: Derry Irvine, Alan Wilkie and
John Sharpe

My House of Lords colleagues, who were a snapshot of my
political life

ACKNOWLEDGEMENTS

To all those people in Leeds who were dear friends and
colleagues
To the fantastic Yorkshire women

To Sally Cline for her advice

To Lee Butcher for his research

To Jean Corston and Sally Morgan for their reminders

To Bernadette McGee, who spent many hours typing and
re-typing – a very special thanks

To my family, Kevin and Jeannette, who put up with my
impatience when I was not getting it right

And to many others who I have failed to name, but they
know who they are

CONTENTS

A Socialist believes that all human beings, however differ-
ent in gift and achievement, are equal in importance and
dignity. That society shall be so contrasted, and incomes so
distributed as to give everyone an equal chance of an active
and enjoyable life.

Extract from *This Is Our Faith*, Labour publication (1950)

PRELUDE

Mae West said it, and I believe it: 'You only live once – if
you do it right that is enough'.

I sat on the couch in John Smith's office one day in February
1993. I was there to tell him that I intended to retire at Easter
from my post as director of organisation of the Labour Party.
He asked me, 'Will you be able to manage financially?'

'Yes,' I replied.

Then he said, 'Joyce, would you like to go in the House of
Lords?'

Six months of silence followed, six months of evasive answers
when people asked me 'What are you going to do with your
retirement?' I did not know and could not answer them until I
learnt what my future was to be. The rules are absolute, everyone is sworn to secrecy until the official announcement is made.

On 31 July 1993 I returned home late at night from speaking
at a conference in Madrid. There were four messages on the
answerphone from John. 'Ring me urgently tonight, no matter how late – going on holiday tomorrow.' With trepidation I
dialled his number. His opening words were, 'I asked the Prime

Minister, John Major, for ten new Labour peers but he has only given me three.' Then he paused for what seemed a very long time. I steeled myself for disappointment. I thought he must be working out how to let me down gently. Then he uttered thirteen magic words: 'And I have decided you are going to be one of the three.' The announcement would be in *The Times* the next day.

Next morning early I made several urgent phone calls to my family, before they read it in the press. Seeing the announcement in print I still could not believe it was true. Was it real? Was I really going to be a baroness? Why me? Why did I deserve this honour? I knew that my work for the party had not been easy – that it had meant long hours, late nights and sometimes scary moments – but I had a job to do, so I got on and did it. Sometimes I don't always understand the impact I made.

I found the answer four years later on the night of the Labour Party's landslide victory in May 1997. At the celebratory party a young man, a stranger, crossed the room to speak to me. He said, 'We would not have achieved this victory if you had not made the party electable.' Then he disappeared into the crowd. I never discovered who he was – but, my goodness, did it make me feel it had been worthwhile!

I have always worried what the future might bring, what to expect, what opportunities might come my way, what challenges I might face.

When I served behind a pharmacy counter in Leeds and when I worked with wonderful Labour women in Yorkshire I never imagined that one day I would be in the House of Lords, that I would be Baroness Gould of Potternewton or that I might be addressed as 'my Lady', for what I had done seemed simple. I had felt passionate about several significant causes and worked to bring about change.

So I found myself moving into a completely fresh environment. I hurtled into the front room of politics. As the *Yorkshire Post* wrote, I went from Boots Girl to Baroness.

INTRODUCTION

◄<┼>►

EIGHTY YEARS
OF CHANGE

Over the years in the centre of the political arena I heard many racy stories and saw many personal incidents. I was offered a great deal of money to tell all, dish the dirt, and say where the bodies were buried. I could not do that. For me it would have been out of character, an alien act, so I said no. Perhaps I was naive for it would have made me a rich woman.

I did not feel relaxed about a decision to write a book until I suddenly realised that I was an octogenarian. Although I did not feel old, my age made me re-consider my decision not to put pen to paper. I decided to write a personal story. Not only, as you might expect, about the disruptive and fraught days of the party in the 1970s and 1980s but about me. About the stages of my life, my origins, coming from intellectual Jewish stock, surviving a traumatic birth and a lonely childhood, growing up in a Jewish family with no money, run-of-the-mill school years, employment opportunities, being a mother and the events that followed joining the Labour Party. And ultimately my becoming a Labour peer.

Volumes have been written by politicians that cover my sixty-three years as a Labour Party member, through ten party leaders. But whilst many academics have put their own interpretation on that period, it dawned on me that there was no chronicle written by an insider: someone who had played a prominent role at local level in the Labour Party; someone who became a senior member of staff at head office; someone whose beliefs and passions were always intertwined with the women's agenda. This last has been a winding thread throughout my life. Very few politicians, men or women, have written about the Labour Party's attitude to women and their struggle for change.

Writing my story made me think not only about my history but also about how I define myself. How do others perceive me? What has made me who I am? Is it my heritage, my childhood? What have I done with my life? Have I used the years sufficiently wisely? I have of course been influenced by people I have met, but even more than that, what has driven me to take on so many challenges and how did I handle them?

As I mused about these questions the memories came flooding back, the changes, the disappointments and successes, the opportunities and the experiences. I thought about the great diversity of people I have met. I had the opportunity, whilst vice-president of Socialist International Women, a post I held for nine years, to meet and work alongside international socialist presidents and prime ministers. I learnt from women across the world about the challenges they faced, how they were campaigning for their democratic rights, for their freedom and justice. Those wonderful sisters were still battling for equality in spite of having experienced degradation and suffering, just because they were women. At the same time I recall the many wonderful moments when I joined with women in celebrations of success, to achieve the right to be a part of the decision making in their countries and the right to own a small piece of land. Importantly women achieved reproductive rights to determine the size of their family.

One day I was having a conversation with a friend, and I remember her reaction when I told her about my meeting with the first woman in space – 'How many people can say that?' she said. Valentina Tereshkova, who was president of the Soviet women's committee, had been our hostess when I had headed two delegations of Labour women to the Soviet Union.

There was a further key question I had to try and answer, which everybody asked me: 'Why do you feel so strongly, so passionately about the causes you have been involved in?' It might have been my childhood environment which strongly influenced me. I recall the occasion as a seven-year-old evacuee when I lived in the maid's quarters of a vicarage in Lincolnshire. We were never allowed in the rest of the house. Eventually we were asked to leave as the vicar decided it would be inappropriate for two young girls to be living in the house when the son of the family came home from Eton for his Christmas vacation.

At Roundhay High School for Girls, a girls-only grammar school, the divide in society became even more real to me. There were the posh girls who were the majority and there were the others who lived where I lived, downtown.

Those childhood experiences had a negative effect on me. Having two intelligent and very clever older brothers made it worse, not to mention a bevy of aunts who constantly asked me 'Are you going to be as clever as your brothers?' The consequence was that I felt inferior and insecure. I had a terrible lack of confidence which stayed with me for many years. It even manifested itself in my behaviour patterns. If I was late for a meeting I would not go in, I would turn round and go home. Even today I am obsessive about never arriving late.

I did not appreciate how important a moment it was when I paid my first sixpence to become a member of the Labour Party. Slowly I developed new skills, how to organise, arrange events and evolve my own views, thoughts and independence. When I told my friend Lewis Minkin that I was considering my memoirs, he said he had thought I would be just another wimpish wife always supporting my partner, irrespective of the issue. 'How wrong I was,' he said.

The Labour Party gave me a purpose. I could not know, of course, that it would take me up a ladder to the top of the party. I developed a real understanding of how deeply entrenched were the discriminations and injustices in society, against women, against those of colour. I recognised the enormity of the barriers that had to be climbed to establish the legal and cultural principles of equality. I was sure that through the Labour Party those cultural and prejudicial barriers could be overcome, exposed and challenged, and I fully committed myself to try to make that happen.

I was supported and encouraged by a wonderful group of Labour women, all fighting for the same causes, irrespective of where their politics placed them in the political spectrum of the party. What I did not appreciate was that it would take so long. I never believed that when I reached the age of eighty, equal pay for women would still be a dream, violence against women would still exist, and the concept of women's rights as human rights would still not be understood.

What I was absolutely clear about was that to achieve these aims Labour had to be in power, locally and nationally. How true that turned out to be. Labour governments have been responsible for bringing about some fundamental political, societal and cultural change. To work for that Labour government as a volunteer I spent many hours and days and months, footslogging, leafleting and door knocking. I held every office at local level, both in the women's movement and in the party, eventually going on to organise the party in the city of Leeds. These experiences gave me the ability to work with party members. They enabled me to lead a team. They showed me how to direct the work, whether it was on the doorstep or in a committee room or organising a public meeting, and how to make difficult decisions. Most of all I learnt how to stand my ground with the politicians on whom the future of the Labour Party rested.

I need to go back, back to my contemplation of the passage of time. Through the relentless pace of change both globally and here at home, the technological revolution that has transformed almost every aspect of our lives. There are 35 million cars on the road yet I never learnt to drive. Foreign travel is the norm, and credit cards have taken over from saving up or hire purchase. Men and women have been to the moon and walked in space. The speed of communication today means we rarely write letters, rather we use the computer, mobile phone or iPad. We send emails, texts and tweets, we Skype and use Facebook, in order to see and speak to each other across the world. We exchange our views by writing blogs, and gain our information from Google.

The structure of families has changed. Divorce has trebled since my childhood, marriage rates have declined, more than one-third of parents with children are cohabiting couples, lone parents or same-sex couples. This development of new partnerships, the growth in the number of step-families and more intricate family arrangements now shape the income and working patterns and living standards of families. Life for both women and men is now more complex.

The world is unrecognisable as the one I grew up in. That bastion of the past, the British Empire, has disintegrated. The geography of the world is different. Countries have exerted their independence, names of countries and towns have changed to bring back their original identities. We have seen the first woman prime ministers and the first black President of the United States. I am proud that as an active member of Anti-Apartheid I played a small part in supporting the years of struggle and the bravery of men such as Nelson Mandela who challenged and finally outlawed the evil of apartheid in South Africa. Europe has been re-defined; the symbol of the divide between East and West, the Berlin Wall, has been torn down, ultimately bringing with it the demise of communism and the introduction of democracy. The old Soviet Union has become Russia and has given independence to countries it had previously controlled. In the late 1980s and the early 1990s, I spent three years visiting many newly democratic countries, including South Africa and Russia, helping with the writing of their constitutions, and explaining the concept of democracy and the conduct of the free and fair elections.

These memories set me on the trail of the many ways in which key moments in my life had been inextricably linked with a range of social changes here at home and abroad. Recollections take me back to a time when my parents had to pay a few shillings each week to be on the doctor's panel. If they hadn't done, I doubt if I would be here today. Those payments were to be no more. The 1945 Labour government introduced a free health service for all, and on 5 July 1948 the National Health Service was born, becoming responsible for 480,000 hospital beds and the work of 1,125,000 nurses and some 5,000 consultants.

One year after I started grammar school as a fee-paying student, the 1944 Education Act made secondary education free for all. My parents were relieved of having to scrape together £25 a term to keep me at such an awful school.

My mother, and many other women who had no control over their own fertility, found their lives transformed by the advent of the contraceptive pill in 1961. It was still restricted, however, not free, and at that time only available to married women. Thirteen years later Barbara Castle introduced free family planning for all. For most women today taking the pill is a daily routine like brushing your teeth. The Family Planning Clinics, previously run by the Family Planning Association, of which I am now president, were taken over by the NHS. My first intervention into family planning services was to campaign across Yorkshire to ensure the retention of clinics in danger of being closed down. My second intervention was the long and arduous campaign to ensure the retention of the 1967 Abortion Act.

Women got the right to vote, and steadily advancements were made but the 1970s were the decade that fundamentally changed women's aspirations and hopes. The Equal Pay Act provided equal pay for work of equal value. The Sex Discrimination Act was designed to remove sex discrimination on the grounds of employment, goods, services and education. My dear friend Betty Lockwood, then chief women's officer of the party, was instrumental in making these fundamental improvements to women's lives. The replacement of the Family Allowance with Child Benefit, moving payment from wallet to purse, was one of the most important social welfare advances at the time.

Unfortunately, a change of government in 1979 meant it was to be another eighteen years, following victory in 1997, before we were able to continue the progress started in the 1970s. Victory brought peace in Northern Ireland, the minimum wage and civil partnerships and devolution in Scotland and Wales.

These few examples identify for me how my dreams of so many years were beginning to come to fruition. But history shows how easily those fragile achievements could be weakened and overturned. However, my determination has not waned. In a different role I still want to help and encourage others to carry on. I am very delighted at my age when I am asked, as I frequently am, for advice and support by young women on how best to continue raising awareness of the challenges women still face.

I go back to the central question: what has prompted me to be involved in these causes. My mind goes to my paternal grandfather, whom I never met, although history records show his many achievements in improving the lives of others. Did he pass his genes to my father, and did I inherit them?

CHAPTER 1

⊰⟨⊹⟩⊱

WHO I AM

I have always had the urge to know who I am. Where did I originate from? Was there someone amongst my forefathers with whom I can feel an empathy?

My four grandparents were émigrés, part of the Jewish exodus from Eastern Europe. They all left Lithuania in the late 1800s, but at different times; they left to escape persecution and the extremes of poverty. They came with the hope of a better and more secure life.

When they arrived they embarked on different paths, paths that were ultimately destined to come together. My paternal grandfather, Joshua Aric, later known as Simon, son of Solomon Manson, was the first to arrive. He came in 1874 at the age of nineteen. The census in 1881 records him as a tailor, but his ambition was to be a rabbi, a Jewish minister. Interestingly, the 1908 Kelly's Directory lists him as a rabbi and a grocer.

Before he could become a rabbi he had to prove his credentials. This meant he had to receive a testimonial from the Jewish community in the home town he had left behind. Five years later it arrived, written in Yiddish, from the Jewish

Ecclesiastical Church Court in Darishinishok. A copy now sits on my wall; its translation shows that Joshua Aric Manson was descended from a long line of rabbis, Jewish judges and theological students.

Simon's great-grandfather Menachim Manele of Kalvera was famed throughout Russia and Poland for his teachings. His great-great-uncle was the chief rabbi of the Jewish Ecclesiastical Church Court of Dineberg and author of a definitive work called *Judah of Calvara: The Ethics*, published in Lithuania in 1800, copies of which now reside in the Bodleian and the British Library. Simon was following a family tradition.

Simon had settled in Leeds. He became a respected rabbi of the new Belgrave synagogue in Briggate, the main shopping street in the centre of the city. How exciting it must have been that the first wedding to be held in his synagogue was his own! He married the slightly younger Kate Frieze. Kate came from affluent Lithuanian peasant stock and had been with him on the boat from Lithuania.

Simon's salary of £3 a week was probably enhanced by the generosity of his congregation, enabling his family of thirteen children, seven boys and six girls, to live in a substantial four-storey house, 8 Elmwood Street. It was in the heart of the Jewish settlement in Leeds, in the parish of Leylands St Thomas, locally known as a ghetto without bars.

My grandfather was a remarkable man of his time whose interests and good work centred on the Jewish people but embraced the whole community. This is particularly remarkable because in those days Jews had little contact with non-Jews and the close-knit community did not generally participate in civic life.

The majority of Jewish people tended to vote Liberal. Grandpa Manson was an active member of the Leeds Liberal Party, canvassing door to door in local and general elections. That kind of political activity was unique for a rabbi. I have followed him in his belief that only left-wing politics was the means of improving people's lives.

The level of Simon's charitable work was formidable. He was one of the founders of the Jewish Work People's Hospital Fund and became its first president. He was a key participant in the Jewish Board of Guardians and was the first Jewish minister of religion to pay hospital and prison visits. He had a real commitment to improving health services. He was a member of the board of Leeds General Infirmary, where he launched a kosher kitchen so that for the first time Jewish people could have kosher food in hospital. He was also on the board of the Women's and Children's Hospital and became president of the Friendly Societies Medical Association and of the Jewish Sick Aid Society. The renowned surgeon Sir Berkeley Moynihan, later Lord Moynihan, was his close friend.

When Simon died at the age of sixty-nine, his obituary in the *Yorkshire Post* highlighted his many achievements, extolling his commitment to the development of the Jewish and non-Jewish communities in Leeds with the words 'his loss will be felt by all sections of the community in the city'. On the day of his funeral the streets from his house to the synagogue were crowded with people from all faiths, watching the cortege pass. Many members of his congregation walked with the family behind the hearse.

My cousin Rose recalled him as a tall, fair-haired man with blue eyes that my father inherited. I regret that I never met him;

this influential, inspirational man, for curiously I feel a connection with him. He was a man with a social conscience – did I inherit that from him? Nor did I meet Kate, my grandmother, as she, like Simon, died before I was born. I know little about Kate, maybe because the role of women is seen as of little significance in family history.

It is strange that when Simon came to England he was called Manson, a north Scots name, the surname also of his father Solomon. Jews in Lithuania in the first part of the nineteenth century did not have surnames so where did Manson come from? Perhaps some Scottish engineer had wormed his way into the family, or more likely the name had been the German Manssohn, or son of man. Wishing to find out, my brother consulted a genealogist, Professor Ludwik Finkelstein, pro-vice-chancellor of City University, London. He suggested that the old family name Manele, which appears on Simon's grave, was a diminutive of Emmanuel or 'Son of God'. I was not entirely convinced, but it did bring a little light to a corner of a rather overgrown graveyard, in which Manele had been misread as Manela with its misleading suggestion of sunny Spain rather than grim Lithuania.

My maternal grandparents, Harry and Jenny Schneider, were anglicised to Taylor, a decision perhaps made by the customs officer as they landed. They were both born in 1872, and came to this country as children. Grandpa Harry Taylor was accompanied by his parents, younger sister and grandparents. When his mother died, his sister Bessie emigrated to New York with their father and grandparents. Through all the intervening years, Harry and Bessie kept in touch with each other by correspondence and the exchange of pictures.

On 17 January 1948, at the age of seventy-six, Grandpa Taylor set sail on the *Queen Elizabeth* to visit Bessie at her home in Tennsville, Florida. This was a big event in a very small town. 'Man meets sister here after 62 years' was the headline in the local paper. Evidently, Grandpa was pleased to find goods so plentiful; maybe in response he told everyone that there were no empty stomachs in Britain. He indicated that unlike the period after the First World War rich people and poor people had the same opportunities to buy the necessities of life. How I wish that was an accurate statement. Until this visit, the family in the UK were unaware that Harry Taylor had two half-brothers living in the states and as a consequence we had found another family of cousins.

My memory of Grandpa and Grandma Taylor is of a couple who had a happy and contented marriage. Their home was the centre of the family. Through our young teens I would go there after school with my sisters Cynthia and Heather and my cousin Gerald. It was where our mothers were gathered. My brothers David and Louis, being older, were exempt from the ordeal of these daily visits. Our first duty was to pop in to say hello to our grandma, a clever lady, but who through illness was confined to bed. I remember this little old lady lying there, with the longest plait I have ever seen. Grandpa was a stocky, round man with white bristles on his chin which he rubbed on my cheeks, affectionately, to greet me.

Their house was a wondrous place. There was always the aroma of fruit being dried over the vast kitchen range, tied to long lines of string stretching from one end of the large kitchen to the other. The scent of apples, pears, plums, cinnamon and ginger pervaded the house. I waited eagerly for the time when the fruit was dry enough for us to eat. The large garden was full of crab apple trees, constantly scrumped by the local youths.

The great excitement was when Grandpa Taylor would bring home American and Canadian Jewish servicemen for a genuine Jewish meal. They always looked handsome in their uniforms, and arrived with their pockets filled with Chiclets chewing gum, chocolate and other goodies. This was when sweets were rationed.

How did the Mansons' and the Taylors' lives become entwined? The story goes that one day Kate Manson met Jenny Taylor, who was wheeling my mother Fanny, her first-born, in her pram. Kate peeped into the pram and announced there and then, 'She will be for our Shamie,' my father, her eleventh child.

My father Solomon Joseph (known as Sydney), born on 23 June 1893, was small in stature but a smart, dapper, sociable man, always conscious about his appearance. There are many differing versions of his ambitions as a young man: for instance, why when he was at grammar school did he never gain the matriculation certificate? My cousin Rose suggested that he wanted to be an actor. He was intelligent and literate, wrote plays and took part in amateur dramatics. At the age of twenty-one, Sydney joined the army where he was an orderly in the Royal Army Medical Corps, stationed at the limb-fitting centre in Roehampton. He may have been on the front line in the war, but I have found no evidence and he never talked about his war years.

My father's only vice was that he smoked sixty Woodbines a day, maybe a throwback to the days when part of his job as an orderly was to dole out cigarettes to the convalescent soldiers.

He left the army without a trade and without a job. How he earned a living over the next few years, I do not know.

My parents' arranged marriage, which to many of us today seems extraordinary, took place in Middlesbrough in 1921, where Grandpa Taylor, a master painter and decorator, ran a successful paint and wallpaper business. Not everyone was happy; members of the Manson family saw it as an unsuitable match. Indeed Kate wanted my father to escape by emigrating to America to join his younger brother Leslie, but Grandpa Manson would have none of it. The *shiddach* had been arranged, and it must be honoured.

What appears not to have been honoured was the promised dowry and the job Grandpa Taylor would give my father; neither transpired. So started the antagonism between the two families, who were never seen together again. Grandpa Taylor did, however, persuade Alderman Morris, owner of Morris's Wallpaper Store and the first Jewish Lord Mayor of Leeds to give Dad a job as a commercial traveller. The great luxury was the car that accompanied the job. The disadvantage was that being a commercial traveller meant moving away from Leeds. First my parents moved to Dundee, where my brothers were born: Julius David in 1926 and Louis Joshua two and a half years later. Next came Nottingham, and a bungalow my mother loved. Finally they returned to Leeds, where I was born, on 29 October 1932 in Mexborough Street. As children there was an enormous contrast between my brothers. David had straight black hair and Louis, the pretty one, a mass of blond curls. Now that they are both grey-haired they look like brothers.

The late 1930s saw my father unemployed until 1939, when he became a full-time air raid warden, a well-known person in the neighbourhood. He was always there to help our neighbours, giving advice, drafting letters, sometimes to my mother's annoyance for he spent too little time at home and too much assisting others. He was a man of routine. Each night he would have his cocoa, set the fire ready to be lit the next morning and polish his shoes. My mother used to say I was a father's girl. I helped him on his allotment in Potternewton Park, and on a Friday night we would go to see a man who sold sweets. I came home with more than any ration allowed. Rummaging through old papers, I found his certificates qualifying him to give first aid and to be a firefighter. His handwritten ARP book described different types of bombs and the actions that had to follow an air raid. Part of it I had used for pasting in recipes I might make one day. I have always felt that it is a tragedy that his abilities never achieved a better life for him.

Mother was eighteen months younger than my father, but to me she always appeared older. She was small, 4 feet 11 inches tall, dark with a sallow complexion, and shy. She was often ill, spending time in hospital with severe colitis, which dogged her adult life.

At just short of forty years old, my mother had no knowledge that she was pregnant. I suddenly appeared on 29 October 1932, premature and weighing only one and three-quarter pounds. My Aunt Kitty, one of my mother's younger sisters and a nurse who happened to be in the house at the time, later proudly told my friends, 'Joyce just dropped into a chamber pot.' My brothers remember the midwife, Nurse Ness, appearing quickly, as our neighbour had run out into the street to find help. She also found Dr Pearce, our family doctor, who rushed up the stairs to my mother's bedroom. Had they not arrived so quickly, I would not be here today writing this memoir. Louis said he hid in his bedroom just opposite to where I was being born, wondering what was happening. David remembers my father sitting at the foot of the stairs and crying. It took six weeks before my birth was registered – why? Unfortunately there is no one still alive who can give me the answer; even if I wasn't expected to survive I still had to be registered.

My mother was the eldest of nine, six sisters and three brothers. Because of her illness my brothers and I spent much of our childhood living with relatives. My aunts spent whole afternoons gossiping, sometimes malevolently, about their neighbours, friends and other members of the extended family. Mother took little part in this gossip, for she was a quiet, timid, fragile woman who I know would not have been able to respond to their often nasty comments, some directed at my father. The sisters were quick to blame him for my mother's ill-health and her perceived unhappiness; I am not sure that was true but to me she always seemed sad.

My abiding memory of my mother is that she spent her life in a constant round of cooking and cleaning. My daughter Jeannette's memory is of 'Little Grandma', as she was called, teaching her to make rock buns. She was extremely superstitious. She would never refuse to buy heather from a gypsy at the door, and always remembered which shoulder to throw salt over for luck. But she did have a wicked sense of humour, describing the woman who lived next door as 'red hat, no knickers'. She hardly went out except for the daily walk the one block to her father's to meet up with her sisters or take our dog Nelly for a walk. On occasion

I would persuade her to put on some make-up, wear a bra and come with me to one of our local cinemas, the Gaiety or the Forum, which was the first cinema to show the much-awaited *For Whom the Bell Tolls* starring Gary Cooper and Ingrid Bergman. We went to the first performance.

My parents kept a Jewish house. My father went to the synagogue most Saturdays with Grandpa Taylor. In a book on Jews in Leeds, I found a photograph of them both walking up Chapeltown Road returning from their prayers. My mother prayed on the candles every Friday on the eve of Sabbath. We then sat down to traditional chicken soup, a chicken dinner and, on special occasions, strudel to follow.

For the week of Passover the special pots were brought out, carefully washed ready for use, and the cupboards where the Passover food was to be stored were scrubbed clean. The first two nights were celebrated in the traditional grand Seder style at Grandpa Taylor's. I wore my best dress and proudly walked with the family from our house to his. The large table with its gleaming white tablecloth was laid with the best china and glasses. My father led the service that accompanied the meal. The meal started with a small piece of onion or boiled potato dipped in salt water, to represent pleasure and freedom with the family. Five cups of kosher wine were drunk to symbolise joy and happiness, giving me my first taste of alcohol. It was late at night that, very tired, I walked with the family the block back home, and so the meal went on at my grandfather's house, accompanied by the prayers for salvation.

In school, the few Jewish girls were exempt from daily prayers. We ate packed lunches, school lunches not being kosher. This isolated us from the rest of the school.

Judaism was present throughout my childhood. I went to B'nai B'rith and joined the Judean Club, both groups for Jewish teenagers. I attempted, unsuccessfully, to learn Hebrew, and had mostly Jewish friends. But only my historical past is Jewish. Nevertheless my becoming a member of the House of Lords was reported in all the Jewish newspapers. It is a great sadness to me that my parents were not alive to read their words. I think they would have been proud.

My mother died at the age of sixty-six, during an operation for her colitis. Her younger brother Barney woke me up in the night to tell me in person, as I did not have a telephone. Ten years later, whilst I was at my first Labour Party conference in Brighton as a full-time official in 1970, my father died. Dad had been ill for a while in Donisthorpe Hall, a Jewish old people's home, but despite this, I had been assured by the doctor that I should go to the conference. At the conference on the Sunday morning Alderman Raymond Ellis, who was a trustee of Donisthorpe Hall, came to find me to tell me. Immediately after, Jeannette phoned me. I caught the first train from Brighton to Victoria, crossing in London to King's Cross, but I was too late for the funeral. Jewish funerals are held twelve to twenty-four hours after a person has died. It is something I have always felt guilty about. The job should not have come first.

Although I do not believe in fate that one's destiny is ordained, life is full of coincidences. There have been links, even if somewhat tenuous, to the Labour Party since the day I was born. That tenuous connection arises from the coincidence that nineteen years later Alec Baum, the son-in-law of the helpful neighbour who found Nurse Ness, signed me up as a member of the Labour

Party, and Dr Pearce's brother Solly was the Labour Party's kingmaker in Leeds. I worked closely with Solly for many years. During our many policy disagreements he was known to mutter, without malice, 'It's all my brother's fault'. Dr Pearce was no doubt of a different political persuasion to his brother for he refused to join the NHS, setting up a private practice in the nearby town of Harrogate.

I have very little memory of my early years, almost a blank. My brother David has suggested that I may have blocked them out, because of my mother's illnesses and her many stays in hospital. Unlike my mother I have been extremely fortunate that my early birth has not affected my health. Photographs show me as a chubby child, with my dresses going straight down over my tum from collar to hem. Dr Pearce found that unbelievable.

Because of my lapses of memory up to the age of seven I only recollect two short stays in hospital. One was in the dark dreary Leeds Dispensary where I had my tonsils and adenoids out and the other was in the Infectious Disease Hospital with measles. My mother was also in hospital at the time and I was put in a cot bed in the centre of the ward as it was the only place I could go. This was extremely humiliating and scary for a little girl of five.

In 1939, when I was six, war broke out and the big evacuation of children from danger zones began. And so started a new chapter in my life.

CHAPTER 2

❮❭

FORMATIVE
YEARS

At nearly seven years of age I was standing in a long line of boys and girls at Leeds City station. I carried a white pillowcase that contained my clothes and over my shoulder a cardboard box holding my gas mask. The Second World War had been declared and the children of Leeds were evacuated to places where supposedly we would be safe.

I did not know what was happening. I am sure I felt excitement, definitely bewilderment and a lack of understanding. I had no idea where I was going as I waited to catch a train supposedly to safety. As it turned out I was being sent to the Lincolnshire countryside, surrounded by American airfields. This was not the most sensible thing to do, as I discovered when my bedroom ceiling came down when the village I was living in was bombed. When I returned home from Lincolnshire eighteen months later, if the sirens went off we rushed to take cover in Grandpa Taylor's cellar.

Paradoxically Pamela Saltman, who became my closest friend, and her family moved from Hull to Leeds, seen as a safer place to spend the war. They never returned to Hull. It was even more ludicrous that in our small house in Leeds we looked after Jewish families escaping the bombing in London. My memory is of a tallish, fair, wan and depressed-looking woman and her young son sleeping in our front room.

Television programmes which today show children being evacuated assume that it was only children from London who were sent from their homes and families. There has been very little account of the many thousands of children from other parts of the country who were separated from their families, to live with strangers in strange places.

I have a memory of being put on a bus outside my school, Cowper Street Infants' School, to travel to Leeds City station. I had never seen a railway station before. Families were split up, segregated into groups according to age, and I was separated from my brothers. David and Louis ended up in Lincoln, whilst I arrived at a village eight miles from Newark called Brant Broughton, where I was told by the locals to pronounce it 'Brooton'.

Still bewildered, I was ushered into the old Quaker Meeting House where I stood in a row with other boys and girls of my age. We stood like little orphans waiting to be picked out by some kind person willing to take one of us to their home. Eventually I and another Jewish girl, Ruth Rosenthall, were chosen by a dear elderly woman – at least she seemed old to me – whose name I cannot recall. We lived in a typical country thatched cottage, all so different and strange. I had never been in the countryside before. It was awesome seeing these very different, beautiful houses with gardens filled with flowers. I was used to houses in terraces, maybe with a narrow strip of grass in front or with the front door opening straight onto the street. I was fascinated by the pond in the centre of the village. I was warned not to go too close. I still have pictures of the village that show the black-smith's shop, the School House and the wide main street. It was a street where many of the houses dated back to the eighteenth century. They were country retreats for the London gentry, who worshipped in the church of St Helen, reputed to have the most elegant spire in Lincolnshire.

My stay in the thatched cottage was short. It proved too much for this kind elderly woman to look after two small girls. Ruth and I moved on, to the impressive stone-built vicarage, where we lived in the servants' quarters. We were not allowed in the main house, with its wood-panelled walls and big pictures. At Christmas Ruth went home back to Leeds and I went to live with the parents of Eileen Watson, one of the maids at the vicarage. Eileen's father was the village blacksmith, and there were pigs in the back garden. Another new exciting experience: I had never seen a pig before and I had certainly never heard one grunt, but I soon realised they were harmless and I adored feeding them. There was an apple orchard. I was fascinated by the rows and rows of trees with fruit hanging off them. We lived on apples, baked, stewed or in pies, and for the following eighteen months, I was very happy. It was a completely new life which I loved.

A great excitement for me was to be carried on the shoulders of John, the farm labourer who lodged with the Watsons. He appeared big and handsome and I adored him.

During those eighteen months living this new life family visits were infrequent. My father came once with my brothers and stayed overnight. Mother also only came once, travelling on the train to Lincoln and then on the bus. She was delighted to go home with a bag of apples from the orchard, a real treat as fruit was scarce. My brothers left Lincoln and went home after a few months.

Before I returned home, Mr Watson retired and the family moved to an even smaller village, Scragglethorpe. I missed the pigs and big John but we still had apple pies. I stayed for a few months. For several years I kept in touch with Eileen, who married a policeman and moved to Lincoln.

I vowed I would never go back to Brant Broughton, afraid that all my memories of this pretty village would be shattered and that it would have been filled with little box-like houses. But many years later, on a holiday in Lincolnshire with a dear friend, Jill McMurray, travelling in her little Beetle, I did go back. To my delight nothing had changed. Although the vicarage was no longer the vicarage, the vicar now living in much more modest accommodation, the blacksmith's was just as I remembered it minus the pigs. Visiting the graves of Mr and Mrs Watson was a moving experience, for they had been such kind and loving people.

My brother David recalls my coming home. I walked in and greeted my parents in a full-blown Lincolnshire accent: ''Ello Maister, 'ello Missus!' I don't think it was long before I returned to my usual Yorkshire brogue. Number 25 Hamilton View was a smallish house and I lived there with my parents and brothers until they departed and I got married. It was an end-of-terrace house next to a vacant lot. It should not have been the last one in the street but the builder went bankrupt and a spare piece of stony ground was left unbuilt upon. The thin outer wall of our house was a great place to bounce a ball. The thud, thud of the balls caused endless frustrations and despair to my mother. Pamela and I and other youngsters spent hours playing on this small piece of ground. One of those youngsters, Gerald Kaufman, who lived in the next street, was later to become an MP.

Downstairs was the Best Room, rarely used, with a monstrous ebony cabinet covered in cameos, and one other large room where everything happened. We sat by the fire, listened to the radio, did homework, and ate meals on a large table protected by a brown plush tablecloth, and where later the black-and-white television became the focal point.

I went back to the primary school at Cowper Street for a year or so before I sat the 11-plus examination. The school was on a hill, the girls in the upper building and the boys down below. A typical school of its time, it had classrooms round a big central hall, the floor of which was made of glass. Punishment for bad behaviour meant standing on the glass, much to the enjoyment of the boys down below. We were well looked after, with school milk and a teaspoon of malt each day. The school nurse regularly made sure we didn't have nits and that we looked after our teeth.

I was told that my chance to go to grammar school was to pass the 11-plus examination, but that I had only one chance. The exam was held in another school, which meant crossing the major Chapeltown Road. I was with my cousin Cynthia, I was ten and she was eleven and a half. With either nervousness or excitement I walked into the road and was knocked down by a passing car. I picked myself up and went on to the exam, unaware of any injury I might have done to myself. I failed and later learnt my writing was illegible as I had injured my elbow.

I swore Cynthia to secrecy, my parents only being told of the accident when it was too late for me to re-sit the exam. I went to grammar school as a fee-paying student, which was financially a burden for the family. They were released from that burden by the 1944 Education Act, introduced by the coalition government of that time.

Then loomed my future for the next six years at Roundhay High School for Girls. Not a school of my choice, my parents chose it because my brother Louis was already at the boys' school. It was the wrong decision, as it separated me from most of my friends, particularly my friend Pamela, who went to Allerton High School for Girls. The decision was purposeless as I was not permitted to talk to anyone in the boys' school – not even my brother.

One's school days are said to be the best days of one's life. For me that was a myth, as they were merely days I had to get through. School was a necessity, not a pleasure. I felt insecure and unhappy for the whole of my years at the school I did not choose. However, the six years passed largely uneventfully, although I found sport difficult, being very left handed. It was impossible for me to play tennis or hockey holding a racquet or stick with my right hand, which was insisted upon. I was happier playing the lowlier games of netball and rounders.

My time at Roundhay started badly. As a paying pupil from the 'wrong side of the tracks', I had a pre-school interview with Miss Hilda Nixon, the headmistress. She asked me, a nervous child of ten, a completely ridiculous question: 'How would you set a table for tea?' I am not sure whether I got the cutlery in the right order but when she asked, 'Would you put a bowl of flowers on the table?' I replied that my mother did not like flowers on the table when we are eating. That was clearly not the right thing to say, and defined where I sat in her social scale.

Roundhay High School for Girls was in the affluent part of north-east Leeds, which is where most of the fee paying pupils came from. The scholarship girls came from the more working-class area where I lived. I never joined the Old Girls' Society, I had no desire ever to go back, but perhaps I should have done so as a baroness.

After school my only meeting with Miss Nixon was some twenty years later. Then secretary of the Yorkshire Vegetarian Society, she appeared on my doorstep to discuss a possible joint meeting with me as Yorkshire secretary of CND. I hoped she wouldn't recognise me, but of course she did. Jeannette was moving to secondary school that year. She asked the inevitable question: was I going to send her to Roundhay Girls? The answer did not please: 'No, she is going to Allerton Grange', the first comprehensive school in Leeds. I never heard from her again.

One of the nine School Certificate subjects had to be a language. I chose French, in which I just managed to scrape a pass. It was a pity that I had such difficulty getting my tongue round foreign languages because of my speech impediment (I cannot distinguish between my Ls and Rs), for the French mistress was my favourite teacher.

After only one year in the sixth form I left school. I worked at the Inorganic and Physical Chemistry Department at Leeds University as a junior laboratory assistant, earning 27/6 a week, whilst waiting to take up a pre-degree course at Bradford Technical College. Bradford was the only college that provided the pre-degree course I needed for a pharmacy apprenticeship. Twenty years later Jeannette travelled to Bradford to take advantage of a similar course. We were both fortunate that within reasonable travelling distance there was a college that provided opportunities for a wide range of age groups and flexible learning. Bradford was only eight miles from Leeds but was unknown territory. I knew little about the city, although I discovered in due course that my French mistress at Roundhay lived a few doors from my aunt Kitty, in Manningham Lane, and I used to visit her for tea. The two cities were separated by the Borough of Pudsey. I had to get two buses, one from Leeds to Pudsey Bottom and another from Pudsey to Bradford. There was a through bus by the time Jeannette made the same journey.

I never went back to finish my pre-degree course. During my two-year pharmacy apprenticeship, at Boots the Chemist, I got married. My friend Pamela also worked at Boots, as did her mother, whom I called Aunt Minnie. It was a great place to work. It is a pity that pharmacists no longer have the pleasure I had of making up medicines from scratch or counting pills by running them through my fingers. I had forgotten that references were required before I could be taken on as an apprentice until, going through old papers, I found two accreditations. Evidently, the department at the university saw me as a 'pleasant and conscientious worker' and Bradford Tech found me industrious and hardworking and would recommend me to any pharmacist seeking a suitable apprentice.

Many years later, I valued those days working behind the chemist's counter at Boots, then at Timothy Whites & Taylor (which was opposite the Chemistry Department where I had previously worked, and which later became a part of Boots) and for a private chemist, Watson's on Roundhay Road, for they gave me an insight into the world of sexual health, a subject that has become an important part of my life during these last fifteen years.

We do not always appreciate how pharmacies have always had a history of being involved in sexual health provision, 'French letters' or 'johnnies' were kept in the lowest drawer under the counter and wrapped in a brown paper bag before being handed over. Men would blush or run out of the shop when they saw a woman behind the counter. Now condoms can be picked up from a shelf in the supermarket.

Women wearing curtain rings or borrowed wedding rings that didn't quite fit came in for the contraceptive pill, which at that time was only available to married women. Gonorrhoea bags were sold for venereal disease and mercury ointment for syphilis. Widow Welch's Pills were sold ostensibly as a tonic, but both customer and chemist knew they were in fact an abortifacient – an alternative to gin and hot baths. It is a pity that generations of young women do not know how women suffered before the 1967 Abortion Act and the introduction of the contraceptive pill on 9 May 1960. Together they gave women for the first time some control over their lives, over their fertility. The Pill has become the symbol of economic independence for all women.

Within a few years of joining the Labour Party, it began to play a big part in my life and Saturday's activity became important. Saturday was the day meetings were held or we were out on the streets delivering, knocking on doors, running street stalls and holding social activities. As I worked on a Saturday, I was not able to participate. I gave up my job as a dispensing chemist, and Saturday working, and immediately set about looking for a nine-to-five, Monday-to-Friday job. I applied for a job as a clerk with a potato distributor, but was turned down as I had no experience as a clerk. This fascinated me for I believed I was of average intelligence, and I did not believe that having to learn how to be a clerk would have been a problem. My Jewish contacts helped me to get a job with Pioneer Women, the women's section of Poale Zion, the Jewish Labour Party. It meant travelling to London and Manchester, the towns with the biggest Jewish communities. I soon realised the job was not for me. I had difficulty relating to these very pleasant middle-class women whose lifestyle was very different to my own. I moved to work nearer home for Montague Burton, the tailors, becoming a section head in their mail order department.

Working with almost two hundred women, many with young children, I felt comfortable and content. I enjoyed their company and our social occasions together. I enjoyed evenings having a drink, and when we hired a bus and went out as a group for an evening meal. They were women I felt I had an affinity with, ordinary women. They became my friends. I became the department's representative on the company's United Nations committee, where we discussed ways in which we could help people in other countries.

I was keen to get my colleagues active in supporting the relevant organisations in the city, and I became their unofficial voice in negotiations with our trade union, the National Union of Tailors and Garment Workers, a union far too close to management. This led me to my first foray into trade union negotiations. It came about when we discovered that Kay's mail order firm in

Leeds was allowing its staff to leave at 4 p.m. on a Friday. I was duly despatched to ask our union to negotiate with management for us to have a similar arrangement. The trade union officials met management and by mutual agreement refused our request. After unsuccessful efforts to try and get them to change their minds, there seemed to be only one action to take: to remove our membership from the Tailors and Garment Workers and, en bloc, join another union. No trade union wants to lose 200 members, so – surprise, surprise – our request was promptly granted and 4 p.m. became our leaving time on Fridays.

Orders for clothes and household items came in from all over the country, and my responsibility was Leeds. The rules were clear that I should refuse orders from a part of the city where customers were reported to be bad payers, a rule I ignored. It was the area in which I lived. This was still the time when in order for a woman to get credit, she had to have the agreement signed by a man. That was another rule I attempted to ignore but to my frustration it wasn't always possible. Certainly not when I had a senior manager looking over my shoulder.

After five years I left Burtons, to work for the Leeds party full time on a voluntary basis. It was a working environment I had enjoyed and was sorry to leave. The past sometimes does come back and many years later when I became president of the British Epilepsy Association, a letter arrived from a man whose son had epilepsy to ask me if I was the same Joyce Gould who had worked in Burton's. 'Do you remember me, as the young ginger-haired office boy?' I did. I was offered a job as an organiser for the Union of Shop, Distributive and Allied Workers (USDAW), which I declined, for two reasons. I wanted to put my efforts into the Labour Party and they had refused my membership when I was working part time. They did not accept part-time members, who would of course been mainly women.

During my school days, and my teenage years from twelve to nineteen, I earned spending money working after school and at weekends. This meant going alternately to Uncle Alf's wallpaper and paint shop and Uncle Barney's television shop next door, or working the printing press for Uncle Joe across the road. Uncle Joe was my friend Pamela's uncle and had married my Aunt Ruth, my mother's youngest sister. I was fortunate that a side of my family were shopkeepers as they were a source of pocket money.

These three businesses were at Sheepscar, at the junction of Chapeltown and Roundhay Roads, next to my public library. The closeness to one another made it easy to move between them as one of them would always want help. Then sometimes at weekends I went to help Aunt Marie, one of my mother's sisters, in her sweet shop, which was most exciting of all. I loved weighing out all the multi-coloured sweets and tipping them into the triangular bags. When I was sixteen I worked three evenings a week in the ice cream parlour higher up Chapeltown Road. I made fantastic banana splits. I felt smug when the young man who owned the parlour picked me up from school in his grey Jaguar to take me to work, much to the chagrin of the 'posh' girls.

It was at this time that I made my first visit to a restaurant, to celebrate my brother David qualifying as a dentist. We went to Jacomelli's, then one of Leeds's most expensive restaurants. Going down the stairs was a bit scary, with the dimmed lights and waiters in fancy suits. David established his practice at 168

Chapeltown Road, opposite the ice cream parlour. On a Saturday morning I sometimes became his dental nurse. It was a frightening experience when a patient from the ex-servicemen's hospital on Potternewton Lane reacted to the anaesthetic. He kicked out and shattered the light in front of him. More peacefully, David's upstairs room was used for Labour Party meetings.

My uncle Barney, who owned the television shop, was friendly with the then Leeds United football team. On a Monday evening, many of the players would come to my grandfather's house. We spent the evening playing bagatelle, cards or musical instruments, and it was there that I met the great John Charles, a Welsh international, the gentle giant of football and to many the world's greatest footballer. I became an avid Leeds United fan. No one could head a ball like John Charles. It was a pity when he left Leeds to go to Juventus. His fame in Leeds lives on as the Queen's Hotel in City Square has two conference rooms named after him. With dismay I found whilst speaking to a group of younger people at a conference in one of the rooms in 2008 that I was the only person who had ever heard of him. In these days footballers existed on a very poor wage – not the ludicrous amounts many footballers earn today. Jobs had to be found on retirement, and men who had been stars became a milkman or a plumber, or if lucky a publican. A memorable sporting occasion was when Pamela and I queued all night with her father to see Don Bradman play at Headingley Cricket Ground. At that time I was not very interested in sport but Pamela was an avid cricket fan.

Pamela and I went everywhere together. We were inseparable. I went on holiday to Bournemouth with her parents, and later being very adventurous we went on our own to Butlins at Clacton. I realise I never had a family holiday. We went to Blackpool for the weekend, where we stayed with a relation of Pamela's, and went dancing to Joe Loss at the Winter Gardens. Pamela was taller than I was, thin and dark; she took after her father in appearance. Her mother was plumper, with a lighter complexion, more like me. We were often taken for sisters, Pamela looking like our father and me her mother.

Pam's parents ran a market stall selling second-hand clothes. I would go through their stock looking for things I could wear. I found my first pair of high-heeled shoes, brown leather with a cut-out rosette on the front. They went with my New Look maxi-length coat. I was up to date with the fashion of the moment. Amongst their treasures I also found a lemon silk pleated dress, great for dancing as it spun round as I twirled.

Recently I listened to a young woman talking, from ignorance, about the days of the maxi. She told her mainly young audience that the long skirts were imposed for the sake of modesty. I wanted to stand up, and tell her she was wrong, I wanted to tell her that I had felt a real fashionable bobby-dazzler in my brown high heels, maxi coat and matching box handbag. But I didn't. The new look was a reaction to the lack of material during the war. How history gets misinterpreted.

Going dancing was the fashion. It was Wednesday night at the Mecca, when Jimmy Savile was the compere, Saturday night at the Capital Ballroom in Meanwood, and Sunday night at the Hare and Hounds at Menston. This meant walking over a mile through the countryside to get the last bus home. On one occasion, I think we were sixteen, without any sense of fear or danger, we set off to walk the two miles home from a dance at Leeds Town Hall. With no concern Pam and I accepted a lift home from a lorry load of military policemen – Red Caps. They took us safely home and we became friends. A spare Sunday evening would find us at their camp at Oakwood, near to where I went to school. We played cards, went for walks and drank non-alcoholic drinks. We had little money, and none of the luxuries of teenagers today but we had a sense of freedom, of not being overprotected, almost of innocence, whilst at the same time there was without doubt a serious level of parental control.

It was at the Capital Ballroom that I met Harry Patterson, later to be known as Jack Higgins, the author of *The Eagle Has Landed*. Harry and I, in his words, became an item. Although not a horror movie fan, most Sunday nights I went with him to the Harehills Picture House to see Dracula films. He liked them and I liked him. He was tall, lean, handsome and dark haired. He regaled me with stories that I believed, but now I wonder how many he made up. Four weeks after the announcement that I was to become a baroness, Harry sent me his book *Memoir of a Dance Hall Romeo*, a fantasy written about a young man of twenty. Having read the book of this young soldier's sexual coming of age, I certainly could not see myself, although his inscription might lead others to think so: 'Joyce with love and fond memories'. Before his success as an author our paths first crossed again when he taught Jeannette English at Allerton Grange. After his first successful blockbuster he moved to Jersey, believing he would never write another one, but he became an international best-selling author, writing over sixty books and selling more than 300 million copies.

As I mentioned in the previous chapter, I joined the Judean Club, a club for Jewish teenagers. My brother Louis had earlier been the chairman of the club. I was not a very active member, until I met Kevin Gould, who ran the football team, I then found myself taking the gym class. The club members used to congregate outside our local Jewish fish and chip shop, Cantor's Corner café, before crossing the road to the ice cream parlour where I worked.

Kevin was one of the boys from the club, whose only interest was in the latest football match they had played. Each move was analysed, and the way they had won or lost because of the referee's short-sightedness. We were introduced by my then current boyfriend, Michael. The future was determined, and after twelve months we married, in 1952, with our daughter Jeannette being born just over a year later in the Maternity Hospital at the other side of the city in Armley. She weighed 7 pounds 12 ounces and was a week late, unfortunate as it now affects when she can draw her pension. I put on very little weight whilst pregnant, and was able to get into the green pencil skirt that Kevin brought for me to wear to go home in. Because I had met a lovely young woman called Benita, that was my choice of name. However, my father objected strongly. It was too much like Benito, as in Mussolini, so she became Jeannette after the skater Jeannette Atwegg and Rochelle after a great-aunt Rachel.

Kevin Gould came from a political background in Liverpool. His uncle Ernie, his mother's brother, was chair of Bessie Braddock's constituency, and his mother Lily had been a militant trade unionist. We were told that she had been born on a Liverpool tram (trams in those days had curtains) and that she was given the freedom of the city. We never were sure if it was true, but Jeannette researched and found the evidence to prove it. Although her mother was Jewish, Lily married a Catholic and moved to Ireland, where Kevin was born in the Rotunda Hospital in Dublin. Then they went back to Liverpool before coming to Leeds, which is where Kevin's grandmother Bobbie lived.

Remarkably, for a well-brought-up Jewish girl, Bobbie had been a Tiller girl. She was tall and straight backed even in her old age with the most beautiful pair of legs. A true matriarch, she terrified me. I told her I loved her aspic jelly dish, but I hated it. It was frequently part of the meal when we went for tea. I took to taking a paper bag in which I scraped the plate when she wasn't looking. The problem was that there was always a second helping. When I was pregnant, we arrived late for our tea, having stopped off for a drink, I was told with great force that pregnant women should not drink. We think that is a new finding but that was sixty-two years ago.

Kevin had a sister, Myrtle, and two half-brothers, David and Allen. Myrtle died in her thirties of leukaemia, and both brothers now live in Florida. Allen, the younger brother, was only eighteen months older than Jeannette. At school together, he took his responsibilities as her uncle seriously. One day he came to ask my advice because he said she would keep walking in puddles even though he had told her not to get her feet wet. He had told the teacher, who refused to believe he was Jeannette's uncle, and accused him of lying. I sent her a note to let her know he was telling the truth and I was happy for him to look after his niece.

After being at a council nursery, Jeannette attended the Selig Brodetsky Day School for Jewish children. Not because I wanted

her to attend a Jewish school but because it was conveniently near
enough to my mother for her to collect Jeannette from school.
She had tea with my parents, 'Little Grandma and Grandpa',
until either Kevin or I picked her up from work or from some
political activity. It was only because of the support we had
from my parents, Kevin's mother and his sister Myrtle that we
were able to be so fully active in the party. When Kevin and I
had a Monday night free we would go to the Leeds Empire or
the City Varieties, sitting in the gods, where tickets were two for
the price of one.

Kevin played football, and I ended up washing eleven muddy
shirts and pairs of socks. When we could we watched Leeds
United and Hunslet Rugby League Club. It was a pity I never met
my uncle, who became the head of the Rugby League Association. We went to a Leeds–Manchester United game just after the
Munich air crash that had killed so many of Manchester United's
young players, the 'Busby Babes'. We really were the enemy. I took
off my scarf and rosette and stayed silent for the whole of the
match, unusual for me, for I could be very noisy. Kevin used to
pretend he was not with me. The greatest excitement was going
to Wembley for the Leeds United versus Sunderland cup final in
1973. Leeds lost. I had never before seen grown men sitting on
the Tube crying over a football match.

CHAPTER 3

-<-<-→->-

BECOMING A LABOUR
ACTIVIST

I asked my brother David why he had joined the Labour Party.
He replied, 'With our background it was the natural thing
to do.' So it was for me. Having paid my sixpence membership
fee and signed the membership form, I had no idea that I was
going to play a major part in decisions that could ultimately
change people's lives.

My father was not a party activist, although he was a highly
political and compassionate man. Like so many of his generation
he thought the Liberal Party was the answer. He gravitated to the
Labour Party in the 1920s, when it became a serious force in the
politics of the country. The *Leeds Weekly Citizen* reported in 1924
that 'the Labour Party is now a political machine of great power.
It is the expression of working-class opinion'. Eight years later,
the year I was born, the Labour Party was sufficiently confident
to run a campaign to try and achieve a million new members.

I am writing these memoirs having participated in seventeen
elections since 1945. It was long before the days when the media

influenced elections as they do today, although my father always said if the media was with us, we would have a permanent Labour government. They were fought on the streets. The ringing of bells would announce that the candidate was in the street or on his or her way. The bell ringers were followed by a decorated car with a loudspeaker through which the candidate would appeal for support. The candidate could not be everywhere so supporters walked up and down the street repeating the message through a loudhailer.

My young friends and I would go from street to street shouting at the top of our voices 'Vote, vote, vote for George Porter'. George Porter was our MP in Leeds Central for ten years. After boundary changes our constituency became Leeds North East, where I lived until I left Leeds. Alice Bacon when a candidate reckoned she addressed meetings in every street and on every street corner in her constituency, never missing an afternoon or evening. All this hard work had its effect for she became the first woman MP in Yorkshire.

Public meetings created great excitement. Candidates spoke to huge audiences, meetings my father and uncles never missed. The subjects were discussed for weeks after, what had been said and what should have been said.

I was confused as to why my father always seemed to invite the Conservative candidate in for a chat and a cup of tea. He was not going to be converted. My father told me that it was a delaying tactic. Whilst drinking tea they could not be knocking on other doors. When I was a party organiser I would say to new canvassers and candidates, 'Never take time off drinking tea.' It was clearly a lesson learnt, for my daughter Jeannette recalls when she was the Labour candidate in Canterbury in 1983 she was told never when out canvassing to accept an invitation to a cup of tea. When it couldn't be avoided, after five minutes or so she would be called away for an urgent meeting. Kevin and I were delighted that Jeannette became an active member of the Labour Party. We were anxious not to put pressure on her to join the party, but at fifteen she announced that she had joined. I was proud of her response to my question why she had joined. She said, 'It is wrong that so many people live in poverty.'

In 1951, the time I joined, the party was not at ease with itself. There were divisions and conflicts. So much so that Clement Attlee, who is the longest-serving leader of any political party, leading the Labour Party for over twenty years, acted to prevent any possibility of there being a party within a party. How those words came back to haunt me many years later. Nevertheless under Attlee, there was a radical programme. Britain was transformed, industries were nationalised, full employment provided, the welfare state and the NHS created a large public sector.

For the next thirteen years, the wilderness years, the party turned inward. It was a period of reflection, examination and intense national and local debate. There were rows over the party's commitment to nationalisation, the Common Market and unilateralism, with big divides between the Gaitskellites on the right and the Bevanites on the left. Many learned and some not so well-informed descriptions have been written about those days.

Of course the biggest dispute for me was the question of 'the bomb'. I never had any doubts about where I stood. I firmly felt that the use of nuclear weapons was wrong, although I do appreciate that the arguments of today are very different. Another continual debate centred on comprehensive education. I was convinced that that was the way we could ensure that everyone had an equal opportunity. Jeannette passed her 11-plus but opted to attend the first comprehensive school in Leeds.

In 1964, with Harold Wilson as leader, Labour won the general election, but only with a small majority of thirteen. Wilson had been elected leader after the untimely deaths of both Hugh Gaitskell and Aneurin Bevan. He called another election eighteen months later, which gave Labour a majority of 110 over the Conservatives. Now I was sure that we were to be the party of government. It was assumed that he called that election because of our success in the famous Hull North by-election. It is more probable that the announcement of the long-awaited Humber Bridge influenced the result. Harold Wilson himself in his book *A Personal Record 1964–70* says, 'I had decided on an early election quite firmly, before Hull polled ... I interpreted the Hull vote not as a decisive vote of confidence but as a vote telling us to get on with our job.' Kevin and I were proud to receive this important book from Harold with the inscription 'For Joyce and Kevin with the writer's best wishes. Harold Wilson, 29 October 1971' – my 39th birthday. Before his retirement Harold and his wife Mary invited us for dinner at No. 10.

Hull North was a highly marginal seat which Kevin, our close friend Dennis Matthews and I went to frequently. Our commitment to the party meant we regularly travelled to many other by-elections in all parts of the country. We could sense victory in Hull. The media misjudged the result, stating on the eve of poll that they predicted a Tory gain.

My friendship with Dennis showed that irrespective of differing political positions you could still be friends. Dennis was a senior figure locally, a long-time councillor, on the right of the party. I used to say to him, 'Dennis, you are so far to the right you will drop off the edge.' Together we spent many days writing a paper titled 'UDI for Yorkshire'. We felt we had all the necessary natural resources and plenty of agricultural land, and were an economically sound area. Our own concern was that what would make us complete would be to have two coastlines. At that time Yorkshire's western boundary was only eight miles from Morecambe Bay and the Irish Sea. We pondered but came to no conclusion on how we might take over that piece of land. Shortly afterwards boundary changes took a swathe of Yorkshire into Lancashire, taking us further away from the coastline we wanted.

Many of the aspirations that I felt passionately about were achieved by the Labour government under Harold Wilson. It was a period of social liberation, legalisation of homosexuality, the abolition of capital punishment and a woman's right to choose. Campaigning for the abolition of the death penalty was the only demonstration that Dennis ever took part in. Our views, however, came together on the importance of remaining in Europe. We were both absolutely committed and campaigned hard for a 'yes' vote. It did mean sometimes being on the doorstep with some strange bedfellows and political opponents of the party.

I left Leeds to come to London as the party's chief women's officer in 1975, and have since only made infrequent visits, mostly to see my friend Pamela. The most recent return was when the

Lord Mayor gave me a reception to celebrate my 80th birthday. It was a great surprise and pleasure for it gave me the opportunity to invite friends I hadn't seen for a very long time. I was disappointed that Pam and her husband Ian were on holiday and couldn't celebrate with me.

I also had to go back to Leeds to recall my many years of party activity there. I had looked forward to spending time in the West Yorkshire archives in Sheepscar library, which when I was a girl had been my local library. It stands on an island in the centre of the various shops where I had worked for my uncles, but to my disappointment the archives had moved to Morley.

Leeds is now a very different city, but to me it always was a great place and still is. Now as the second major financial centre in the country, it is more vibrant and lively. New buildings, shopping malls and hotels have sprung up across its expanded centre, but to its great credit its famous arcades and grand buildings, and the indoor market and the Corn Exchange have been retained. The Black Prince on his horse in City Square and the lions sitting majestically outside the Town Hall are still there to protect the city. I was told when small that the lions walked the streets at night and I was terrified the first time I was taken across the town in the dark, after a family wedding.

Boots in Briggate where I did my apprenticeship is no more. This main shopping street is now pedestrianised, and shoppers are entertained by buskers, offers to have their portrait painted and a variety of stalls. I never expected that one day I would sit on a bench outside Harvey Nichols watching all this happen whilst eating a Mr Whippy ice cream.

In the days in the archives, I spent my time going through

the pages of the *Leeds Weekly Citizen*, the Leeds Labour Party paper which was first published in 1911 and survived until the mid-1980s. Each week it dealt with and made comment on local and national issues and events, on the actions taken by Leeds City Council, women's and youth activities, local sporting fixtures and titbits in its gossip column. How the memories came flooding back, pictures of people portrayed when they were young, names I had forgotten and now remembered. So many friends from the past, comrades no longer with us. It is a great tragedy that since the closure of the *Citizen* the history of the Leeds party is now not being told and will not be available to future generations.

Solly Pearce was influential in the selection of Hugh Gaitskell, his successor Merlyn Rees and Denis Healey, as well as Alice Bacon. Following the re-distribution of parliamentary seats in 1955, 'kingmaker' Solly Pearce was responsible for putting pressure on George Porter to resign. He became a peer in order that Alice Bacon could take his seat and did not end up as a candidate in an unwinnable seat. Solly's motivation was not only to ensure candidates on the right, but he wanted Leeds to be the best represented in the House of Commons. All our four MPs became ministers: Denis Healey, Merlyn Rees, Alice Bacon and Charles Pannell, something we were all proud of. They were all hardworking and responsible members. I was happy to sell photographs of the four of them to raise funds for the party. I doubt if any other city had such a group of high fliers at any one time.

I was surprised to see how often I had written for the paper, articles about subjects which are still not yet resolved: women's equality, equal pay, race relations or employment rights. It is

with a wry smile I read and recalled my anger at the Labour
government's attempt to kill Ted Bishop's Matrimonial Prop-
erties Bill, which was designed to give equality of property to
both partners in a marriage. The article showed that I had contacted a number of ministers and National Executive members
to express my views at this travesty. In his home town of Bristol
it was known as Ted's His and Hers Bill, and it sensibly became
law in 1969.

Kevin Gould, my future husband, was even more prolific,
penning articles on the importance of day centres for the mentally ill, vandalism in Potternewton Park, and many aspects of
housing as chair of the Leeds City housing committee. He also
wrote the weekly sports column and the gossip column 'Albion'
along with Bernard Ingham, an activist in the Labour Party
before becoming a part of Margaret Thatcher's team. Kevin took
over as editor when Solly Pearce retired. As he was chair of the
housing committee of the Association of Municipal Authorities
attempts were made to influence him through me. This happened
at a dinner organised by the *Leeds Weekly Citizen* to celebrate
its seventy years of publication. The dinner was chaired by Kevin
as its editor with Woodrow Wyatt as the speaker. When I was
dancing with a director of the local gas board, I was offered
free central heating and a new kitchen. I was horrified to realise
how easy it would have been to accept. At the same dinner I was
wearing a new dress from Richards, which had cost more than I
could afford, and I was shocked to find another woman wearing
the same dress. I decided it suited me better.

There were many articles written by me and others on the
subject of race relations. In the 1950s Leeds became home to

many families from the West Indies. I headlined in the *Citizen* that it was only the Labour Party that could break the odious bar that precluded people of colour from having the same freedoms as the rest of the population. Nobody should be treated differently.

It was a time when there was little recognition of the more subtle and insidious forms of discrimination, alongside the obvious ones of 'no blacks welcome here'. There was no protection under the law. Many had difficulty in finding accommodation and took on lowly jobs often below their abilities.

Rupert Charles and his family, who came from St Kitts, became dear friends. Rupert got me into trouble with my constituency party when I was their delegate to a party conference in Blackpool. I was expected to attend every session of conference and present a full report of proceedings to the next meeting of the party. On the Monday evening, Rupert plied me with cocktails which looked like fruit juice but which turned out to be lethal. The consequence was that I missed the Tuesday morning session. On giving my report, Laura Verity, a visitor to conference, said she had to inform the members of my non-attendance, and gave them a report of what had happened in my absence.

It was Rupert who introduced me to Dr David Pitt, later Lord Pitt, who I firstly joined in Campaign against Racial Discrimination as the Yorkshire representative and later as the official representative of the national party. Another St Kittian friend and colleague was Diane Phillips. I was delighted to play a major part in her becoming the first black magistrate in Leeds.

The Labour Party was on the right side of this debate. Hugh Gaitskell vigorously opposed the 1962 Conservative

Commonwealth Immigration Act. It was disappointing that Merlyn Rees's 1968 amendments to that Act were discriminatory. They made me consider tearing up my party membership card. Now I am glad I was persuaded not to. I was stunned that such racist action could be taken by a Labour government. I found it difficult because I considered Merlyn a friend, having worked with him since he became an MP, even though he caused me embarrassment at a meeting he was speaking at in Leeds, when he asked me why I was wearing a chair back. I had a slipped disc and I had that day been provided with a corset with metal bars up its back, and had not yet learnt not to lean forward. The corset, which I wore for two years, also had strings to pull reminiscent of Victorian days, which gave me for the only time a wasp-like waist.

Attending party conference as a delegate or a visitor was the event of the year. It was the time when I saw and heard and sometimes met the hierarchy of the party. Most importantly it was when I met comrades from other parts of the country.

Speaking at party conference for me was an ordeal. In 1968 the party held one of its many reviews on the organisation of the party, the Simpson Report. It included a recommendation for the abolition of the then five women's places on the National Executive. As a member of the national women's committee I was called to the platform at the end of the morning session by the formidable Sara Barker, the national agent, and told to prepare a speech over the lunch break to oppose that proposal. She also told me to change into something brighter and asked, 'What colour will it be?' 'Blue,' I replied. It was the early days of conference being televised, the lights were so bright that the people on the platform could only see the front rows. I was called to the rostrum by the chair pointing in my direction and saying 'The woman in the blue suit'.

My words may have had some effect for no decision was taken at conference and the proposal was quietly dropped. Certainly it was a speech that I was pleased with, getting applause for high-lighting the small number of women at conference; 'particularly amongst the trade union delegations, hardly a woman to be seen'. I went on to say, 'There are areas where women are discouraged from attending their own local general management committee. One would have thought those Victorian ideas would have died long ago. I fear, and the women's movement knows, that they still exist. Let us not be fooled by the glib words of Bill Simpson [a member of the National Executive Committee]'. And finally making the point that the party still had a long way to go, I remarked that it still had different coloured membership cards: pink for women and blue for men.

The following year, as a delegate from the Leeds City party, I spoke against the Maud Report on local government re-organi-sation. It was first thing Monday morning, a time when conference delegates haven't yet settled down. I felt it was a good speech but was very nervous. I was greeted as I came off the rostrum by a member of the Maud committee who used to be an agent in Leeds with the words 'I am ashamed of Leeds'. It did nothing for my morale, but I was relieved it was the content he objected to, not my presentation.

During my speech there was a little confusion over the lights. The red light goes on when time is up, but it was lit too early. The chair apologised and I was allowed to continue. A similar situation happened at a later conference, when it was my turn to get it wrong.

I frequently spoke at the annual women's conference without too much apprehension except for the one time in 1967 in Southend, when I was asked to move the vote of thanks. I am not good at telling jokes but I was told that there always had to be a joke. Finally Joe Haines, who was Harold Wilson's press officer, came up with one for me. It must have been alright for dear 'Auntie' Laura Verity wrote a letter to the *Leeds Weekly Citizen* praising my speech, including my ability to tell a joke.

Nerves can never fully be overcome and have been with me through all my years. Whilst moving a controversial resolution at the Yorkshire regional conference, I was conscious of Sara Barker looking down at me from the platform. My anxiety was made worse by the microphone standing on its own in the middle of a wide space in front of the platform. There was nothing to hold on, nothing to support me. I am sure Sara could see my knees knocking. I was quaking in my boots. I made my speech and I felt such relief when it was over. Because of that experience I have always insisted even today that there be something to hold on to and somewhere to put my notes.

How can I ever forget these wonderful Leeds women, little dynamic Laura Verity (Auntie Laura) or Jenny Siddall? Jenny had exhausted herself physically and mentally through her work as Leeds North East constituency party secretary, and moved to live near Howes in North Yorkshire to plant and save flowers that were nearly extinct. Councillor Jean Bell had two autistic boys and moved to Cumbria to open a home for autistic children, I cannot leave out the kindness of Mrs Knipe and her daughter, Beryl, or those elder stateswomen such as Alderman Mrs Hamilton and Alderman Mrs Shutt. But most of all I could not have survived without the advice and support of my friend Jill McMurray. Jill died of breast cancer in her forties. I shall never forget my last visit to her in the hospice; when she said goodbye, I walked down the street in tears.

CHAPTER 4

≺‹•›≻

THE SNOWBALL ROLLED

The first offices I held were as secretary of the Potternewton and Allerton women's section and secretary of the Potternewton ward. This second job should not have happened, because at the time I was not living in Potternewton but in the neighbouring ward of Harehills. It was a complete breach of the rules of the party: you could be an officer or attend meetings only in the ward in which you lived. But Potternewton was without a secretary and could not find anyone to take on the job. I think it is ironic that many years later I had to not only enforce the rules, but actually write the rules that I myself had broken. We did move to Potternewton shortly afterwards, so the position was rectified.

Kevin informed the party that I would be willing to do it and then came home and told me. He was due to be away for a year doing a party-sponsored course at Fircroft College in Birmingham and thought it would keep me occupied whilst he was away. My reaction was one of horror: no way was I competent or confident enough to take on such a job.

Going to my first meeting of Potternewton ward, I was firmly convinced I would get it all wrong. To me being a secretary of a ward party was daunting. However, it turned out to be an invaluable experience, for it gave me the confidence to open my mouth and utter words, mainly to an audience of men, confidence gained through having to read out the minutes of the last meeting and the correspondence that had been sent to the ward. It also taught me how to write minutes and to take responsibility for the decisions the members had agreed to. I was grateful to Victor Zermansky, chair of the constituency and council candidate, who guided me through the first meeting.

The political snowball started to roll. I felt almost breathless as I read and realised the level of non-stop activity, as my involvement increased year by year. Each day was different, whether it was meetings of the local ward party, the women's section, the constituency party or the city council; attending working groups, special committees or the council Labour group; fundraising; or out on the doorstep, canvassing or delivering leaflets. There were conferences and training courses, social activities, and the important end-of-day meeting in the pub, talking out the events of the day, having a lot of laughs. It was an exciting time. Life was certainly not dull.

There had to be two of me on this roller coaster, me as a political activist and me as a mother, balancing this chaotic lifestyle with running a home. I never neglected the needs and wishes of my daughter. As a young mother, I panicked when Jeannette went to nursery at eighteen months old. Leaving her in tears, I was assured by the nursery nurse that immediately I was out of the door, the crying stopped. Jeannette reminds me of so many incidents in her childhood; I would meet her after work on a Saturday lunchtime at Watson's chemist, and we would go to Hernando's for a knickerbocker glory and then buy her two favourite comics, *Bunty* and *Judy*. I also spent a lot of time arguing with her physics teacher. It was not a subject of Jeannette's choice and she was not very good at it. He made it clear that in his opinion girls were not equipped to do sciences. I had matriculated in sciences and told him in no uncertain terms how wrong he was. As Jeannette grew older I embarrassed her by always being at the bus stop to meet her if she was coming home after dark.

It was also important to me that Kevin and I had a social life outside the party. We managed to fit in visits to the Theatre Royal, where we saw the early Morecambe and Wise when they were bottom of the bill, or to the famous City Varieties. Sunday afternoons tended to be the time for staying home and having friends visit. It was an open house. I would prepare a buffet, never knowing who would come. One thing didn't change: every Sunday Dennis Matthews brought his slippers. We were also fortunate to be frequently invited out for meals at the homes of party members, including at the Yellands', the Siddalls' and the Taylors', until Percy was deselected as a council candidate and joined the Tories. There were also many social events and parties to attend.

I shall never forget the first time I knocked on a door to ask an elector how they might vote. I went on my own, armed with my canvass card, to be filled in 'for', 'against' or 'doubtful', membership application forms, 'sorry you were out' cards and a pack of leaflets. With trepidation I knocked at the first address on my canvass card, and my trepidation was justified. The response was short and sharp: 'If it is anything to do with bloody elections, get off my doorstep.'

I ran down the path and stood on the street corner. Should I go home or should I try again? Potternewton ward had a substantial Jewish electorate, and in the main they voted Labour. Finding what looked like a sympathetic Jewish name, I walked two streets, and knocked on the door. My instincts were right, nice people who voted Labour. So back to my planned route, having learnt the lesson never to go out canvassing on your own.

There were many other lessons that I learnt, lessons I was able to pass on. Never make assumptions that Labour voters do not live in big houses or in posh areas. Whilst out canvassing in one such area when Bernard Ingham was fighting a hopeless seat for the party, I quietly banged the wrought iron knocker, and the butler answered the door. He looked at me down his nose and in response to my question gave a resounding 'No'. Then the owner's head appeared over the butler's shoulder and to the surprise of both of us, said, 'That is not so, I have always voted Labour.'

Canvassing, however, had its funny moments. I knocked on the door of a large house on Chapeltown Road, and a voice shouted 'Come in'. In I went to see four women sitting in the hall. It was only after speaking to them I realised that the house was a brothel. This was the second occasion that I fled from a doorstep.

One of my aspirations was to ensure that the party was seen as a part of the wider community, part of the life of the city. We shouldn't just attend community or third-sector meetings but engage people in the activities of the party. It was the women members that led the way.

The Labour Party bazaar was the major event, held each year in November in the iconic Corn Exchange in the very centre of Leeds. A painting of the Corn Exchange hangs on my wall at home. As the co-ordinator of the bazaar committee, for me it meant many months of preparation and promotion, getting pre-publicity brochures printed and distributed. Important too were the discussions with the press to ensure that the date was in their schedule. There were over fifty stalls to be organised with different-coloured awnings for each stall. Who does what? What are they selling? The decorations inside and outside the building had to be designed. Little disputes had to be resolved as they arose, which was time consuming. It was necessary to be eagle eyed to make sure offence could not be caused, such as stopping Charlie Pannell, our Leeds West MP, from putting South African wine on the French wine stall. He had bought it by accident, but sales were boycotted because of the apartheid regime. Appeals were sent out for raffle prizes, one of the most successful raffles being when Harold Wilson sent up one of his pipes.

The dates of some events stay in the memory throughout one's life. One date that certainly stays with me is 22 November 1963. It was the eve of that year's bazaar and I was standing on a stall putting up its awning when Barrie Pepper, deputy leader of the council, rushed in with the news that President Kennedy had been shot. The shock was visible as in disbelief everyone left whatever they were doing. We huddled together going over and over how it happened, where it had happened and when, and had anyone been arrested.

As social secretary part of my job was being responsible for our concert party 'Singing thro' the Ages', but I could not have a singing part. I still cannot sing in tune. In the name of the party we took our concerts to hospitals, old people's homes and to charitable events to help them raise much-needed funds. It became so popular that the requests came flooding in. Every time I hear 'Winter Wonderland' I remember Kath Lloyd, our star turn, wearing a bright blue dress and singing beautifully.

I was, however, happy to take part in our fashion shows, held at the Co-op store. I thoroughly enjoyed strutting up and down the catwalk, and Jeannette enjoyed it as much as I did as she accompanied me on the catwalk wearing pretty dresses. Other activities included arts and crafts exhibitions in the Civic Hall and whist drives. I ran the Leeds Labour women's luncheon club, which was our attempt to introduce non-members to the party. It was strange going back as their guest speaker when I became the regional women's officer. We produced our own *Labour Women's Cook Book*, with recipes from senior women in the party, which I edited and still have a copy of.

For the 50th anniversary of women's suffrage, I organised an exhibition of suffragette memorabilia in a window of the main Co-operative store in the city centre. Our aim was to celebrate not only the anniversary but also the part played by our very own suffragette, Leonora Cohen CBE JP. Leonora had been the leader of the tailoresses' union in Leeds. Antonia Raeburn in her book *The Militant Suffragettes* records that Leonora Cohen was one of a delegation of suffragettes that visited the Treasury. At the meeting she told of the Leeds tailoresses who worked for 3½p an hour whilst the men were paid 6½p an hour for the same job. When the delegation failed to show any interest, Leonora decided her journey would be in vain unless she took some positive action. The book described in Leonora's own words how she took the decision to steal the Crown Jewels, and did so by breaking the protective glass cover. Leonora was duly arrested but after deliberation by the courts her case was dismissed as long as she paid £4 19s. 6d. to have the cover repaired.

It was an honour for me to meet Leonora and hear her story first hand. She moved to Colwyn Bay and attended the Labour women's conference in Llandudno. I treasure the beautiful letter she wrote to me to thank me for the photograph of the exhibition. In it, she said: 'Now I have passed my ninety-fifth year and wonder how much more I can do towards talking to women, to carry the torch of progress for England's loftier race ... The frailty of humans must be strengthened to reason, the wars of enmity overcome by the fraternal spirit of Brotherhood.' What a wonderful woman.

Our concentration on the suffragettes means we all too often forget the activities of the suffragists, who campaigned just as vigorously but were opposed to breaking the law. In July 1913, determined to show how serious their demands were, they organised the great Suffrage Pilgrimage. Both men and women walked for over a month, following one of eight different routes and converging on Hyde Park, where Millicent Fawcett addressed more than 50,000 people. A hundred years on, to commemorate the event women from Brighton and Hove walked the routes from Brighton to Hyde Park. Speaking as the patron of the Brighton and Hove Women's Centre before they set off, I recalled how in the early 1860s major changes were made to the law. The words 'male person' were changed in legislation to 'man', but panic set in when it was realised that five years earlier the word 'man' had been declared to include woman, meaning that anything that men could do, so could women, including vote. A quick dash to the male-dominated courts put it right: they declared it didn't apply in this instance. What a difference that would have made! There would have been no suffragettes. Preparing for that speech made me realise that in 1918, my mother, aged twenty-five, would not have been able to vote, being under thirty and not owning property, and that universal suffrage only happened four years before I was born.

Throughout my eighteen years as a volunteer in the party I continued to attend my own women's section, Potternewton and Allerton. For me these women were the bedrock of the party. The section usually met on a Monday evening. Jeannette would go to her friend's mother, Mrs Knipe, straight from school, where she had a fish supper before the meeting started. There were occasions when it was easier to meet at my home, but that idea got abandoned after my dog Pepe cocked his leg on Mrs Gertrude Hickton JP's brogue shoes.

Twice a year I would go with women from across Yorkshire to the Women and Children's School at Cober Hill, near Scarborough, piled into a bus driven by the brother of the regional women's officer, Betty Lockwood. Cober Hill was a large house in extensive and beautiful grounds. I would take Jeannette with me when she was still a baby. During the day she and the other children would be looked after by a group of older women, who organised their own schedule. At mealtimes and in the evening I would take over so Jeannette and I had playtime before bed.

Opportunities like this were a bonus, enabling me to combine my political development, learning from prominent speakers, with my role as a mother. Many years later when I was chief women's officer, women campaigned and won the right for a crèche at the annual women's conference.

As chair of the propaganda, education and membership committee in Leeds, which ran a variety of policy and organisational training courses, I believe that I made one of the first attempts by a political party to break into the world of public relations, discussing how to use personalities and ideas to promote the party. The discussions were based on a paper written by Jack Ashley, 'How to Win Votes and Influence People'.

The Leeds City party was an extremely effective co-ordinating body that campaigned across the city. Without it we would not have won a by-election in 1968 in the Tory stronghold of Round-hay ward. We beat the Tory Chief Whip. The hours spent going door to door were all made worthwhile on seeing the headline in the *Yorkshire Post* the next morning: 'Duggie Thomas Miner wins Roundhay'.

About 200 people regularly attended city meetings and voting was usually close. Nobody wanted to miss a meeting. The intensity of the challenge to win a vote was illustrated at one meeting I was chairing when one councillor, George Murray, arrived late. The door was locked after apologies for absence and not re-opened until the minutes had been approved and matters arising dealt with. He broke the glass in the door with his fist and sat through the meeting even though he had cut his hand badly and blood flowed.

The different political strands within the Leeds party were complicated. Not only was there the difference of stance between the Gaitskellites and the Bevanites, but we also had the involvement of two Trotskyist groups, the Socialist Labour League (SLL) and the Socialist Workers' Party (SWP). They vied with each other for dominance but neither represented a real challenge to the party. The SLL was generally the more dominant of the two, having almost complete control of the Young Socialists – the 'Tiny Trots'. The SLL in Leeds was led by party members Cliff and Barbara Slaughter and John and Mary Archer, and the very busy George (Jack) Gale.

I was targeted by Mary Archer, a pleasant but an extremely fearsome woman. I was terrified of seeing her walking up the garden path, then having to listen to the litany in her attempt to influence me into participation. I did not accept that the revolution was imminent. Jeannette was a friend of Cliff and Barbara Slaughter's daughter Kathy, who was in her class at school. Serious attempts were made to draw her into the fold but she remained ideologically sound.

One incident always makes me smile. At a ward meeting being held in the home of the party's full-time agent in Leeds, Dick Knowles, a very middle-class Tiny Trot known as 'Black Leather', because that is all she ever wore, was asked to leave the meeting for being disruptive. She did, only to return a few minutes later, open the door and say, 'Please thank Mrs Knowles for the tea.' I wonder what happened to this polite girl and how she feels now about her days as a 'revolutionary'!

At the party conference in 1947 Laura Verity called for action to be taken against the Trots in Leeds. It was like Liverpool in the 1980s. During the times when I was leading the fight to rid the party of the Militant Tendency in some constituencies, I was reminded of Laura and what she would have said. She would probably have turned to her two Walters, Walter Preston, Dick Knowles's predecessor as party agent, and her quiet but very supportive husband Walter, and in her wise way said, 'Good on her – the lass did good.'

During this period we took in two students to lodge with us, Mike Hyam and Chris Harman, who both turned out to be members of the SWP. It was through them that I first met Gus Macdonald, now Lord Macdonald of Tradeston. Together with Paul Foot he was travelling from Hull to Liverpool via Leeds, setting up aggregate meetings, and they slept on my floor for the night. We were frequently seen as a stopping-off point. One evening Kevin's sister Myrtle was babysitting Jeannette. She was 'invaded' by a group of shipbuilding apprentices, who were on strike and hitchhiking their way from London to Glasgow. They had been told 'Stop off in Leeds, the Goulds will put you up'. I arrived home to see my five-year-old daughter sitting in the middle of the floor, surrounded by sleeping bags, drinking lager and thoroughly enjoying herself. They were great lads, and they did not expect me to feed them. Next day they went out and bought packets of bacon and eggs and made their own breakfast.

Although I was a member of the city council Labour group as a party representative I never became a councillor. As a representative of the local party I was there to ensure that the councillors heard the views of the rank and file during their deliberations. I was, however, a council candidate many times. I stood in Potternewton ward three times, following Kevin, who had previously been the candidate. He moved across the city to fight the safer Labour seat of Stanningley. Potternewton was one of those areas that should have been Labour but never was. It is sad for me that re-distribution of the wards means it no longer exists.

There was one time that I was convinced that Potternewton was going to go Labour. My Conservative opponent was Irwin Bellow, of Bellow sewing machines. He later became Lord Bellwin. As a prominent member of the Jewish community he won over the traditionally Labour Jewish vote and had the largest majority ever. I learnt later that this was in spite of one of my Asian colleagues, never to be named in print, telling me he had voted for me nine times. I was disappointed but that is the nature of politics.

Normally a third of the council was elected each year, but after the boundary re-distribution in 1968 there was an all-out election for a completely new council. I was one of three candidates in the Kirkstall ward, where Dennis Matthews was the sitting councillor, now fighting alongside me to win the seat again. The election turned out to be a disaster. The party ended up with only four wards in the whole of the city – thirty wards in total. 'We was robbed' was my headline in an article on the re-distribution, in 'a Tory stitch-up'.

A major factor that caused the defeat was that three days before election day Dick Crossman, the Minister of Health, announced an increase in NHS charges. Challenged about the timing, he said he regretted that he had forgotten about the local elections. I was appalled. How could a Cabinet minister be so divorced from the party?

Not to be deterred I tried again the following year, again with the expectation that this would be my turn. It was in the apparently safe ward of Burmantofts. I lost by 113 votes, robbed by the Communist candidate's 126 votes. Was I jinxed? The following year I was selected again in Burmantofts, but before the election I had to resign, having taken up a post as a regional officer. George Murray, the chair of Burmantofts ward, was so annoyed that he rang head office to complain. He recorded his dim view of the ruling by the National Executive Committee that prevented me from continuing as the candidate. He said, 'Both personally and on behalf of the ward, I would like to express my sincere regrets about Joyce having to withdraw her candidature. She has proved a most excellent candidate, has put a great deal of work into the ward and we are indeed sorry to lose her.' The restriction on organising staff taking public office was imposed because of the advantage that full-time agents and party secretaries had taken in promoting themselves to be parliamentary candidates in 1945. The ruling, which included not being on any committee outside the party, was eventually removed by Jim Mortimer when general secretary.

My thoughts had also turned to trying for a parliamentary seat. I wasn't sure I wanted to be an MP but it seemed a natural progression. I tried twice and got shortlisted by both constituencies. At my first selection meeting in Barkston Ash, a Tory seat situated between Leeds and York, I was met at the door by a male party member. 'Whose wife are you?' he asked. Maybe he could not possibly imagine that a woman could be a Member of Parliament. At the second selection, in Haltemprice in the East Riding, I lost by just one vote. A man came over to me and said by way of apology, 'You were by far the best candidate but you looked so fragile.' I have never looked fragile in my life; at that time I was a size twelve. Had I been selected when the party started to seriously understand equal opportunities, it might have been different.

My own constituency, Leeds North East, was a safe Conservative seat. Keith Joseph was our MP. The first time I met him was at the 1964 general election count when Kevin was our candidate. In my mind I saw a coat of many colours. He came up to introduce himself, clicked his heels and said, 'I'm Joseph.' I had the presence of mind not to reply, 'I'm Gould,' but I was tempted. In 1966 I was election agent, and although we did not win I was excited to win the national award for best election address. After boundary changes, Leeds North East is now a Labour constituency.

Outside party activity, as secretary of Yorkshire CND I went on Aldermaston marches and marched from Hull to Liverpool. The radar base at Fylingdales in North Yorkshire was a key target for opposition. After work one Saturday, I travelled to a demonstration there, to be met by SLL member Jack Gale with the words 'Your stupid husband has been arrested'. It wasn't for me to agree with a member of the SLL but this time I did. I thought it was a daft thing for Kevin to do. He spent a week in Armley jail scrubbing floors. At a public meeting shortly afterwards with Alice Bacon, minister of state at the Home Office, he stood up and registered his complaint at the standard of prison food.

I was chosen to be one of the three British women to go to the United Nations at Geneva for a Women for Peace demonstration. My colleagues were Anne Kerr MP and a local friend, Ann McIntyre, partner of the philosopher Alasdair MacIntyre. We visited embassies and marched through the streets led by a hundred-strong American delegation. I became friendly with June

Brumer from California. We had daughters of the same age. They became pen pals and Jeannette spent a year with the Brumers in Oakland. I still have the letter she wrote me as part of her creative writing class: she said, 'Although you were not always there you brought so many interesting people into our home and I was part of so many interesting discussions.' Fifty-three years later Jeannette and Leah are still in touch.

One incident made me realise how easy it is to get things wrong, even when what you are doing has the best intentions. One of the many houses we lived in was in Spencer Place, a wide tree-lined avenue. Behind the façade it was a red-light district, with cars constantly crawling along the kerb. As a resident, I joined a committee working with the police to get rid of this nuisance, but it all went wrong. I was wrong to get involved. One evening the police stopped an elderly black man who was travelling slowly in his car. He got cross and they arrested him. It turned out that he was the head of the local West Indian church and was looking for the house of one of his parishioners. This heavy-handed approach by the police made me realise we had not got the right answer to solving the problem of kerb crawling and prostitution. The police also challenged a Tory councillor who had to explain to the chief constable why he was travelling slowly up Spencer Place. He explained that he went along the avenue on his way home and had slowed down to pass pleasantries with me, when I was out walking my dog after work.

The party in Leeds had always employed a full-time agent. Dick Knowles took over when Walter Preston retired. Dick and Dorothy came from Kent, where he had been the party agent in Dover and Sevenoaks. At first he found our northern bluntness difficult to cope with. At his very first meeting, Dick arrived full of bright ideas, but was faced with the forthright comment from Sylvia Murray: 'Do not bring your southern ways up here.' He was bluff and frank with a strong southern accent. He would always tell it as it was. I fully supported his view that he regarded candidates as a distraction from the real work of electioneering. It wasn't long before his experience and judgement was recognised and he fitted in with our ways of working.

Dick left us six and a half years later to become the Co-operative organiser in Birmingham and ultimately became leader of Birmingham Council. He was knighted as Sir Richard in 1969. For the first time we found ourselves without the resources to pay for an agent, so I took over as the full-time unpaid organiser of the Leeds party. At Dick and Dorothy's leaving party, Dick welcomed me as his replacement, saying, 'No one is more familiar with our local party, the administration and its problems. The job Joyce has taken on is not an easy one and I hope she will get all the support she deserves.'

I did the job until I moved to the party's regional office at 13 Queen Square, two doors down from the city agent's office. Queen Square had been an impressive, elegant address to have with gates that opened to let Her Majesty's carriage through. I am told my father's oldest sister actually lived in number thirteen, where I was now to work.

I would have happily continued as an unpaid full-time organiser but realism meant I had to get a job that paid. I could have done that by cutting back on party activity, or applying for a full-time post in the party. There was no contest. The Labour Party had to come first. It has been that absolute belief that only the Labour Party can make a genuine difference to people's lives that has been the driving conviction in my life, a conviction I still hold today.

I have never been ambitious. I didn't go on the staff with any thought of further promotion. Barbara Castle once berated me for not pushing myself. She thought I should have been general secretary and although I never achieved such heights, I find it fascinating that many people I now meet think I was.

I look back with nostalgia on those eighteen years as a voluntary worker for the party. I appreciate that they took me from being someone lacking in confidence, shy and diffident to someone who could say she had achieved a great deal not only for the party but for herself.

CHAPTER 5

LEAVING LEEDS

Perfect your organisation, educate your fellows, look to the register, 'spread the light' and the future is yours.

James Keir Hardie, first leader of the Labour Party

Keir Hardie's words became my mantra when I eventually became a party official. I say 'eventually' as I had applied for the same post, that of regional women's officer, eighteen months earlier. I never found out what happened to that application, which was not even acknowledged. I assume that it went straight in the bin. I was very embarrassed when Leeds councillor Barrie Pepper returned from a meeting in London and said to me, 'I gather you were not shortlisted.' My embarrassment was made more acute because I was having a drink with friends, in the bar of the City Varieties Music Hall, all of whom heard what he said.

Although the language has changed, the words of Keir Hardie having been written some sixty years before I joined the Labour Party, their significance still applies, and still has relevance, Harold

Wilson quoted them in a message to the organising staff in January 1970 which was later printed in the *Labour Organiser*, the Labour Party's full-time organisers' journal. These words identify the fundamental philosophy to which all of us in the regional units of the Labour Party worked. They call on us to make sure that the party is well organised, that the rules are followed and that members understand the policy of the party. The reference to the register is an indirect way of checking that the views of individual electors are being canvassed and their responses recorded on the electoral registers which are used for knocking up Labour voters on the day of an election. The regional organising staff are the custodians of the party in its regions.

I was surprised when the post went to Marian Craythorne, the personal assistant of the national agent, Sara Barker. Marian had no organising experience nor any connection with Yorkshire. A colleague told me that Sara thought it would be good experience for her. At the time I thought that it was to ensure that the post was kept 'in house'. I had mixed feelings, but in some way I was relieved. I loved my work as a volunteer but at the same time I was furious that nobody had had the decency to tell me.

The vacancy had arisen when the then holder of the position, Betty Lockwood, became chief women's officer at head office, a post she had held for the past fifteen years. Betty had been only our second women's officer; the first had been Sara Barker, who had got the job when the region was established in 1941.

In spite of that rejection and my disappointment I continued in my role as the chair of the Yorkshire regional women's committee, and worked alongside Marian. I introduced her to key Labour women throughout the country, advising her on what they expected of her. This was important due to her lack of background in the women's organisation. At times I found it frustrating, as I am sure Marian did. Whilst the Yorkshire women were always pleasant and kind they were clearly not happy about the appointment. They were aware of Marian's lack of knowledge about what was expected of the women in the party, and the many activities she was expected to know about and participate in.

Marian had been told by her boss, the regional organiser, Harold Sims, that she should not get too friendly with party activists. It was not good advice and made her life more difficult as they were the people she was having to work with every day. How else was she to make friends and motivate and encourage members? I made sure she was invited to events held across the regions and went with her to the many social activities held throughout Yorkshire. She was staggered by the amount of food at all the events, something she was not used to.

It soon became evident that Marian was not happy doing the job, and felt 'isolated' from friends and family. I also think she had a problem with the bluntness of Yorkshire women, and didn't always understand the Yorkshire sense of humour, which could at times be unintentionally hurtful. I was not surprised when after eighteen months she resigned and went back to head office. Later at head office I again worked with her closely, organising party conferences, in her new role as conference officer. We were jointly responsible for both the national women's conference and the main national party conference.

The post was re-advertised, which created a big dilemma for me. Did I have another go and possibly have the humiliation of being rejected a second time? Once again it was Betty who encouraged me to apply. She was sure I should try again, so with her support behind me, I did, although I felt unsure and anxious.

There was a long time lag before I got a reply. I became more and more convinced that I had made a mistake, but eventually a letter arrived saying I had been shortlisted. I was later to learn that the delay had come about because Sara Barker, now retired but still influential, and Alice Bacon MP had been to visit the officers of the regional executive to persuade them not to appoint me. Alice Bacon was a senior member of the party's organisation committee and together with Sarah was an important participant as a supporter of Hugh Gaitskell. I assumed that they thought I would impose my dangerous views on the women in Yorkshire, clearly unaware that I had had plenty of opportunity to do that as a key player in the women's organisation throughout Yorkshire. Betty of course knew how farcical that concept was, having worked with me for so many years.

I was interviewed by the officers of the regional executive, whom I had worked with for a number of years as a member of the executive. The chair of the interviewing panel was Ernest Hayhurst, treasurer of the regional party and regional secretary of the Transport and General Workers' Union. It was more a friendly chat than an interview. There was no point in asking me what I had done in the party. That was irrelevant as they knew of my level of activity over the last twenty years. Appointing me was almost an automatic decision. In spite of such powerful opposition I was appointed and I was delighted even though I would miss the frenetic activity of the last few years. So began my career as a full-time official of the Labour Party. Although I had the advantage of having been chair of the regional women's committee and therefore knew many of the women across the county, I knew that it would not be easy to follow Sara Barker and Betty Lockwood, who during their time as chief women's officer had built a formidable organisation and were respected by the women in the region.

I was so pleased, however, that my friends in Leeds missed me; they were happy for me personally but regretted my moving on. A piece in the *Leeds Weekly Citizen* said, 'What has been a good year for Joyce has become a bad year for the Leeds Labour Party.' I was also anxious as to how my new colleagues on the regional staff across the country would react to my appointment. I hadn't come into the post through the usual channel, that of being a paid full-time trained party agent. Somehow for some doing the job voluntarily didn't seem to count. So I was delighted and relieved to read their welcome in *Labour Organiser*: 'Joyce Gould, the appointed regional women's organiser for the north-east, is already well known to Yorkshire Labour women. Ms Gould is well equipped to carry out the duties of the important post to which she has been appointed, bringing a combination of experience at local, regional and national level.'

Labour Organiser was a monthly publication which updated the staff on changes to the law and party rules and which gave examples of good organisational practice. It was key in providing us with up-to-date information. It ceased publication in the 1970s as new technology took over.

I held the job for six enjoyable but sometimes difficult years before I followed Betty and became chief women's officer. Betty became the first chair of the newly created Equal Opportunities

Commission. Betty was an inspiration to me and it might seem that I have been destined to follow her in my professional career. Later I was to join her in the House of Lords, become a deputy Speaker, as she had been, and take her place as chair of the equalities committee on the Council of Europe. We are still firm friends although I regret that she no longer comes to the Lords, to sit next to me on the red benches.

It was a privilege for me when Betty asked me to lead the tributes to her at her 80th birthday party given by the University of Bradford, where she was chancellor. I had been immensely honoured that she had recommended me to receive an honorary degree on the day she became chancellor in 1997. There were four graduands that day, and I was asked to express the thanks of us all for being recipients of such an honour. I was anxious as this was such a big occasion, and preparing the speech made me realise how little I knew about the rival city just ten miles from my own, even though I had attended Bradford Technical College. I discovered that it is a city with a great history, starting with the entrepreneurial German immigrants who brought with them their skills and their own heritage, which made Bradford a cultural centre of the north. I was pleased to discover that in 1916 the Bradford Trades Council produced a programme for educational reform, so powerful for its day that it was adopted in its entirety as Labour Party policy under the title the Bradford Charter. Following that tradition Bradford was the first university to establish a course in peace studies and resolution of conflict.

Jeannette, my brothers and their wives Hilda and Jan came up to Bradford. It was the first time they had heard me speak in public, so I had to do it well. I received a great deal of praise so I must have done.

I was fascinated to learn that there had also been controversy when Betty was appointed to the regional staff. On that occasion it was not about questioning her politics but because there was objection to her title as Yorkshire women's organiser. This implied that she would only work with the women in the region and not take on general party work. Irrespective of the title, that was not to be the case. Clarity was established with my appointment, which carried the title of assistant regional organiser and women's organiser.

Joining the staff meant that I could no longer participate in any outside activity. For instance, I had just been asked to join the Lord Chancellor's committee on the appointment of magistrates, an important job as there were few Labour magistrates. I was told by Ron Hayward, the general secretary, I had to resign. I could also no longer take part in the political, sometimes controversial debates that took place at the party meetings I attended as an official. Sometimes I was tempted, sitting there at the top table listening to inaccurate statements being made. This was particularly frustrating. I wanted to intervene, but I was very disciplined and knew my place.

Having been involved for so long in discussion on policy, I needed an outlet, so I continued to attend the meetings of the Fabian Society. The society met once a month on a Friday evening in the Metropole Hotel in the centre of Leeds. Barbara Castle's sister, Marjorie Brett, was the secretary and always arranged for high-level national speakers with the help of the party's 'kingmaker', Solly Pearce. It was a pleasure to be able to meet up with old colleagues and take part in a lively and sometimes heated debate. The discussion would continue at the hotel bar where we gathered after the meeting.

There had always been a tension between Yorkshire regional office and the Leeds office, so on my first day at the regional office I was stepping into what had been hostile territory. This tension was partly due to the independent attitude of the party members in Leeds both organisationally and politically. The city had its own full-time organiser, Walter Preston, who had organised activities for nearly twenty years from 1949 to 1967 and had in spite of his own views established a working machine that crossed the political divide. He was a quiet man who never got involved in the political debate but simply got on with the job of making sure the party machine was running well. I have no doubt that he did report to head office of the political differences in Leeds and who was involved.

Walter was a Quaker and a conscientious objector during the war and served some time in prison. His compassion was shown when Jeannette was very small and he loaned his caravan at Reighton Gap, on the coast near Filey, to me, Kevin and his brother Allen and Jeannette when we could not afford a holiday. It rained continually, and over and over again we listened to and taught Jeannette the words to 'Little White Bull', made popular at the time by Tommy Steele.

John Anson was the regional organiser most of the time I was a volunteer in Leeds. John was a bluff, frank northerner, and he had a serious mistrust of anyone who did not always support every aspect of the party line. He was very close to the Gaitskellite Campaign for Democratic Socialism (CDS), which had been set up to challenge the Tribune group on the left. In 1961 John Anson foolishly declared that all active unilateralists in Leeds who appeared to be working in close association with the Socialist Labour League (SLL) and Bevanites should be proscribed. We all attended the same meetings and even the same social evenings but a close association it was not; yet John felt it necessary to keep files on us all in locked filing cabinets. I wish I had seen what he had written about me, complimentary or not.

It was a surprising thing to do, not least because two years earlier John had attempted to expel a number of members of the SLL as well as a Leeds solicitor, Ron Sedler, on the alleged grounds that he was a supporter of the SLL. The legal wrangling that surrounded this incredible affair rumbled on, concluding when it was unproven on a technicality. The complete vindication of Ron Sedler made the national party cautious about the use of proscriptions and led to their gradual liberalisation of party discipline.

Such actions could have alienated a large number of hardworking party members, but loyalty to the party prevented that happening. There were, however, frustrating moments, such as when the regional office organised a tea party for Hugh Gaitskell to meet all the constituency party officers at the Metropole Hotel. Kevin as chair of Leeds North East constituency was the only one excluded, as he was a Bevanite, although he was one of the most active members in the city. This resulted in a demonstration outside the hotel where the tea party was being held. I got annoyed and hot tempered and had an altercation with the policemen who kept us walking round in circles. Kevin calmed me down before I got arrested.

John's successor, Harold Sims, who was the regional organiser until 1981, had a much more tolerant approach. One of his first actions on becoming regional organiser was to open the locked files and discard their contents. It was during this more tolerant period that I moved two doors down Queen Square to number thirteen. We were a team of three organisers and an administrative assistant. Harold was the senior officer and Bert Twigg was responsible for the youth organisations in the region. For the next six years I think we worked well together, I cannot recall one serious altercation.

Bert Twigg had joined the team a year earlier, originally coming down from Tyneside to be the agent in Brighouse & Spenborough and ultimately going back north to be their regional organiser. He was pleasant to work with, unassuming and anxious to get on with the job. From my own experience as a Young Socialist, the youth movement of the party was always seen with a degree of suspicion, but in reality at that time they had little influence. More time was spent making sure that they behaved well. At weekend schools I would join Bert in supervising their night-time activities, ensuring there was a clear divide between the bedrooms for the girls and the boys, and sending them back to bed when they attempted to sneak across the corridor.

Team working was essential for the apparatchiks of the party as we were not always the best loved of personalities, sometimes viewed with suspicion. We were machine politicians, the party's firefighters, there to ensure that the party machine was functioning well and that the rules were not broken. We were responsible for seeing that campaigning was on the agenda as well as checking that the local party finances were in order. There was the impression that the closet activities of the machine took place in an aura of secrecy, and to some degree that was true.

I was shocked by the hierarchical structure of the regional staff, and the absolute rigidity of roles. The regional organisers (ROs) saw themselves as the 'kings' – for they were all men – and the assistants (AROs) like myself as minions who were expected to listen and learn. To be fair this did vary from region to region and was dependent on the characters of the people involved. Although my own office was fairly relaxed this changed when the ROs all got together, whereupon they vied with each other to show their level of authority.

I realised that the power some of the ROs gave themselves was to cover their own weaknesses, weaknesses that on occasion resulted in a level of harassment. This is not something I experienced but I know it was real for some of my other regional women colleagues. A classic example was the attitude of Paul Carmody, the north-western RO, to the woman officer in his region, who he summoned into his presence by banging on her office wall.

Twice a year all the regional staff and the senior staff from head office came together. The meetings would discuss the state of the party and new developments on the way we should be working. We looked at any changes to the rules of the party or to its structure and what they expected of us over the coming months. The meeting room was so arranged that each region had its own table; on our table my RO, Harold Sims, sat in the middle with Bert Twigg and me on either side. Only the ROs were expected to intervene in the discussion with the senior officials at the top table, who they presumed were the only ones in the room who had the knowledge to express a view. On one occasion it all went wrong and there were no set tables, so we were able to sit anywhere. Not having Harold watching over me, I expressed my point of view on a new ruling from head office, which was seen as an outrageous thing to do. What I said might or might not have been relevant, but it was frowned upon by the ROs. Nonetheless, we never again returned to the rigidity of the past, we all participated in the discussions. Without doubt it improved the quality of our decisions; the experiences of all the staff were invaluable. Working as a team is by far the most effective way of achieving the right result. Some years later when I became director of organisation and I was responsible for these meetings, everyone was equal and could express their views as individuals. Tolerance and loyalty to your colleagues were for me the important factors.

In spite of my long experience as a voluntary organiser I had to learn many different ways of working. I had to oversee a number of parliamentary target seats, intervene in disputes, ensure that the rules of the party were being adhered to as well as running women's activities and visiting as many local groups as possible. This could mean that I would be visiting a women's meeting in South Yorkshire in the afternoon and dashing to catch a train to York for an evening meeting of the constituency party.

To become a parliamentary candidate the person chosen by the local constituency party had to be approved by the National Executive Committee (NEC), who vetted the procedure. I had to ensure that the procedures as laid down by the national conference of the party had been followed absolutely. That was my role but everyone suspected my regional organiser would also report the political views of the successful candidate to the NEC, which could affect their decision whether or not to endorse them as a candidate. Had I ever been a regional organiser, I would have found that hard to do, but I was never put in that position.

Two of my eight target seats were Doncaster and Halifax. Doncaster never caused me any great anxiety. It was frustrating that they met at six o'clock on a Sunday evening, so on two Sunday evenings a month I would catch the train to their meetings in Doncaster Labour Club, which fortunately was situated next to the station. The timing and venue for the meeting meant the members could start their evening's entertainment at the club and then simply move into the next room for the meeting.

I dreaded my first visit to Halifax. Sara Barker had retired back to her home town and was a member of the Halifax general committee. The meeting was held in a large old-fashioned school hall, and sitting on the high stage, I saw her in the front row just below me. It took real courage for me to stand up and speak. My role was to give sound advice to experienced members of the party, many of whom were well seasoned on how to organise their general election campaign in their own area. I sat down nervously. First on her feet was Sara. I was expecting her to tell me what I should have said, but much to my relief she congratulated me on my presentation. She instructed the delegates to listen to the wise words of their regional officer. I so appreciated her loyalty.

After the meeting she invited me to visit her for tea. I did so on several weekends, and found her to be friendlier than I had expected. She displayed a wicked sense of humour, as she recalled her own days in the party. At the same time she offered me good advice on how to react when a meeting got difficult: keep calm, but make your position very clear.

I did not drive but was being pressurised to take driving lessons. Sara's advice to me was not to do it if I didn't want to. She had never driven and neither have I. It did mean that I had to plan my journeys around the region carefully. I am not sure I could do it now as transport services have deteriorated. I would travel by train or bus, which meant on some occasions having to ask for a lift from or to the station or bus stop. Only once did I ever have to stay overnight. Bert and I did the costings of our travel and we discovered that I was saving the party a fair amount of money because I was losing out by only being able to claim for the price of the tickets whilst Bert got a substantial mileage payment. There was nothing I could do about it as it had been my choice not to drive.

It was a seven-day-a-week job, which meant I had to work to a strict timetable. I had to work out how much time I had in the office, how much out in the region and how I could fit in some time at home. I also needed time to relax and enjoy myself, to go to the theatre, the cinema and visit friends. If I was not working on a Sunday I would have open house. After lunch I would make a buffet for friends who would just pop by.

There were local parties where there had to be a high level of supervision, which I sometimes felt was a waste of my time. Because of conflict in the Barkston Ash constituency, which no longer exists, the NEC decided a regional officer had to attend every meeting. The chair, Lord Popplewell, who was a senior member of the House of Lords, no doubt influenced this decision. Unfortunately, I was chosen to take on this tedious and

time-consuming job. It was a Conservative constituency, mainly
rural but including two rival mining villages. The conflict between
them was intensified by a boundary change that amalgamated
Garforth and Kippax, the two mining areas. Kippax, the smaller
village, had the smaller party membership and the members felt
that they would be completely taken over by Garforth. I looked
at the membership lists and was amazed to see that every member
was a man. I reminded them that women could also be members.
Women were duly enrolled, and the party's membership nearly
doubled overnight. Having always been in a party where women
were prominent I was appalled that no women had protested
and that such a position still prevailed in the party.

The next time I was confronted with this problem was when
I was going to a party meeting on a Saturday morning in one of
the small towns outside Barnsley. The meeting was being held
in a working men's club which did not admit women except on
'ladies' night'. On attempting to enter the premises, my way was
barred by a large burly man who said, 'No women allowed.'
I explained who I was and why I was there, but this was irrelevant to him; I was a woman. Clearly he had to obey the rules
of the club. After a long and heated altercation, we came to an
agreement: I could sneak in through the back door. Such incidents
opened my eyes to the strength of those South Yorkshire women
in making their voices heard and challenging such discrimination. The Labour women's conference passed many resolutions
calling for equality for women in Labour clubs. It took time, but
we did win in the end.

There are many reasons why I am grateful to the party. One
of the most significant and unexpected was when I came home

early one evening from a meeting that was inquorate. I switched on the television and saw a programme on the effect on lungs from smoking. At that time I smoked about forty cigarettes a day. People used to say they saw me behind a cloud of smoke. I realised how stupid I was being, and never smoked another cigarette. I left the packet of cigarettes in my handbag. It was my will against this thing in my bag that was turning to dust. Never did I say I was stopping smoking; I would tell myself I would not have a cigarette until a certain date, then another date, a birthday, a holiday and finally after some months until Jeannette came home from America. But in fact I never smoked another cigarette after watching that programme.

Regional staff from all over the country were expected to work in all parliamentary by-elections. Within weeks of starting at regional office I was summoned to the Louth by-election in Lincolnshire. There was a strict limit on the amount that could be paid for bed and breakfast, which meant I stayed together with my colleague in a rather cheap miserable boarding house, for three weeks. John Prescott arrived proudly in his grey Jaguar. I wryly smiled when I heard that it had broken down on his journey home and limped its way back to Hull. The result of the by-election, on 4 December 1969, was a victory for the Conservative candidate, Jeffrey Archer. He held the seat until he stepped down at the October 1974 general election and turned to writing paperback novels.

I was very surprised when I had joined head office to get a letter from a Mervyn Watson, telling me that he was currently producing a television version of Jeffrey Archer's *First among Equals* for Granada Television. He went on to say:

I am currently producing a television version of Jeffrey Archer's *First among Equals* for Granada Television. You may have read the novel. It features a character called Raymond Gould and his wife – Joyce!

I neither want the public to be confused over reality/fiction of 'Joyce Gould', nor do I wish to cause you embarrassment. So this coincidence, (heightened by your recent promotion and publicity) worries me. However, I am very loath to change the name, as it is a very good and appropriate name.

Would you kindly reassure me that this coincidence will not in fact trouble you, and that you will not be suing us for our millions?

Despite the obvious political polarity between yourself and our author, I hope you will eventually enjoy the series. Joyce Gould is a strong and sympathetic character in it. And I look forward to hearing from you.

Having not read the book I was completely taken aback by this coincidence, even more so as Raymond was a parliamentary candidate in Yorkshire as Kevin had been. I was staggered, we negotiated, and I withdrew any objections I might have had as long as there was an honest representation of Joyce as sympathetic, loyal, organised and with a natural grasp of politics.

To avoid any confusion her name was changed to Brenda; Brenda happens to be my second name. I think I made a mistake in not suing for millions, as tentatively suggested by Mervyn Watson.

Visits to other by-elections followed but one of my most memorable was being sent to assist in the Dundee East by-election in

March 1973, where I ran the campaign in the Broughty Ferry ward. This was the part of Dundee where my parents had lived and where my brothers were born. The only thing my mother told me about those days was that they pulled the beds down from the walls. I was told by head office to keep a low profile as the English were not welcome, even though our candidate came from Sheffield. As it turned out I could not have been more conspicuous, as my committee room was a caravan stationed on the grass in the middle of a roundabout.

The party members tended to be elderly, they were happy to canvass, but leafleting was more difficult. To make sure every leaflet was delivered I 'tempted' a team of youngsters to deliver them. Each day they queued for their Cadbury's Penny Chocolate bars, not something I could claim on my expenses, but it was worth it. It helped the party get the job done.

I was surprised and delighted that on my departure the ward party members had a party and showed their gratitude by presenting me with a nightdress case. The well-used nightdress case is no more but I still have the card, which says, 'To Joyce from your friends in Ward 5 in grateful appreciation for all your help and support, you will always remember "Bonnie Dundee".'

My first experience as a full-time party official working in a general election came in 1970. It was very different from when I was working in elections as a volunteer. My first job was to supervise the parliamentary selections of my eight marginal seats. The rest of the time I was to give them my advice and support and to check on their canvass returns. I had to ensure that doors were being knocked on, that posters were going up in gardens and in windows and that all the leaflets were being delivered.

I was sometimes a little sceptical at the number of promises I was given. Were they being exaggerated? I doubted that a particular number of houses had actually been canvassed. This scepticism arose from my experience of working in by-elections, when the figures sent to head office could have come out of the telephone book.

Prominent figures in the party toured the country, addressing big meetings and large public rallies before such meetings became ticket-only events. Another part of my job was to determine the best places to visit, book the venue and liaise with head office about who the speakers were to be, when they would be arriving, and any foibles they might have.

George Brown was the star of old-style campaigning. His capacity to draw a crowd was phenomenal. Over his two-week tour across the country, including Yorkshire, he addressed between five and eight meetings a day: no speech was identical. He made ninety-eight speeches, sixty-five of them in the open air. I spent a week with him travelling through Yorkshire, and although I enjoyed his company, he was not an easy man to work with. He rarely ate, but drank a lot. I felt great sympathy for his ever-patient wife Sophie. I have more recently had the pleasure of working with their daughter Freda in the last three general elections in Hove.

Every aspect of the rally was minutely planned. One evening George was feeling particularly belligerent and impatient. I had him at the side of the stage of a very large hall in Huddersfield waiting for the introductory brass band to finish. He decided to wait no longer, marched onto the platform and started his address. The stunned band stopped playing. My panic was, how could we get the band off the platform? I found the curtain cords, pulled, and drew the curtains behind George. They quietly crept off.

Very different in style but equally effective was Harold Wilson, the Prime Minister. For him precision was essential. Harold reacted to his audience and was brilliant at dealing with hecklers. He sometimes even encouraged them. They were a gift to him and his sharp responses were legendary.

Until 2005 I was the campaign co-ordinator for general elections after entering the Lords and I know the valuable role of my Labour colleagues at election time. Tony Blair acknowledged this in a letter to me in 1997: 'I wanted to write and express my appreciation of all your work during the recent election campaign. Please pass my thanks to your colleagues.' So different today from the October 1974 election, when two bowler-hatted Labour peers arrived at the regional office and offered their help. Of course I was pleased to see them, but the dilemma was what to do with them. Definitely not canvassing! I found the candidate and proposed they accompany him, shaking hands with the electorate. I hope they felt that their visit to Yorkshire had been worthwhile.

Maintaining the history of the party is essential for future generations: the trials and tribulations as well as the good times. It was very disheartening to discover that all records relating to the Yorkshire region had been destroyed. David Robertson tells me there was no such documentation when he took over as regional organiser in 1981. None has been placed in any of the archives I have contacted. I am therefore particularly grateful to John Grayson for his book *Solid Labour: A Short History of the Yorkshire Regional Council 1941–1991.* It covers the early years of the party, party discipline, the youth movement and the women of Yorkshire.

One of the interesting stories that the book revealed is that even Sara Barker, who became the matriarch of the party and its rule book, had had her moment of opposition to the NEC. In 1935 she gave her support to the Home Counties Labour Association, which was calling for the rank and file to have more influence in the national party's decision making. She was then secretary and agent of the Halifax party. After strong opposition from both the trade unions and the NEC, Sara was quickly won over and continued to be a loyal, rigid supporter of the establishment.

The book tells that Yorkshire was a powerful heartland for the party, and that many key figures in the party originated from there or gravitated to the county. The cover of the book has pictures of two leaders, Harold Wilson and Hugh Gaitskell; the high-ranking parliamentarians Barbara Castle, Denis Healey, Roy Hattersley, Roy Mason, Alice Bacon and Ann Taylor; and two senior national officials, Betty Lockwood and myself. But added to that list could also have been Merlyn Rees, Len Williams, general secretary during the 1960s, and Sara Barker, as well as Betty Boothroyd, the lively and renowned former Speaker of the House of Commons. There is no question that organisationally as well as politically Yorkshire has played a powerful role in the party.

Yorkshire can also take credit for the establishment of the women's organisation of the party. Betty Lockwood and I both feel strongly that without the time spent working with Yorkshire Labour women neither of us would have had the experience that followed.

A resolution at the Railway Women's Guild conference in 1905 requested the National Labour Representation Committee to form a national women's Labour committee. More influential, however, was a letter from a Hull dock labourer's wife, Mrs Cawthorne, to Ramsay MacDonald, then secretary of the party, asking for a Labour Party organisation for women to be set up. MacDonald called a meeting of senior figures in the party, who granted the request. She must have been a very determined woman, for never having been to school she persuaded her children to teach her how to read and write.

An inaugural conference was held in Leicester on 26 June 1906. Mrs Cawthorne attended and became a member of the new women's committee. In the three months since the original decision was taken eleven groups in different parts of the country had already been established. In her opening speech, Margaret MacDonald, Ramsay's wife, said, and I quote:

> We want to show the wives of trade unionists and co-operation, particularly who they have not yet fully discovered that the best way of looking after their homes is by taking an interest in the life of the community, to improve their conditions it is necessary to take up their cause with earnestness on the same lines as men have done and if it is to be anything the Labour Women's Movement must be international.

The Women's Labour League, as the organisation became, was a semi-independent group working alongside the official structure of the party, with an advisory committee of women from the regions. It had its own journal, *Labour Women*. Seventy years later it was incorporated into a section of the party's newspaper, *Labour Weekly*.

In 1955 I attended a special Yorkshire regional women's conference in Hull to celebrate the 50th anniversary of the sending of that important and influential letter that led to the establishment of the party's women's organisation. From that day Yorkshire has had a long history of strong and influential women, and the Labour movement in the county was built on the efforts of women as well as men. They include the formidable Jessie Smith, who was the first woman chair of West Riding County Council and devoted more than forty years to local government, holding a variety of roles; Violet Satterthwaite, from Edlington, near Doncaster, who was chair of Edlington Town Council, my companion on the national Labour women's advisory committee and a writer of short stories; Irene Faulkner, who was a councillor in York and a well-known educationalist; and Doris Kenningham, from South Elmsall, near Pontefract, who left school at fourteen and through determination and commitment became a councillor in Wakefield, chairing the social services committee. These were women who fought their way up for recognition. I was fortunate I never found it a struggle but I did find it hard work, and I had to be endlessly persistent and absolutely determined.

Jessie Smith reminded me of the part that Labour women contributed during the Second World War in voluntary support services, at the same time as keeping the party functioning. All that effort was lost as men came back from the forces and took over again. The quote from the TUC General Council Report of 1948 sums up the attitude of the day:

There is no doubt in the minds of the General Council that
the home is one of the most important spheres for a woman
worker and that it would be doing a grave injury to the life of
the nation if women were persuaded or forced to neglect their
domestic duties in order to enter industry particularly where
there are young children to care for.

It took another sixty-five years for the TUC to appoint its first
woman general secretary, Frances O'Grady. Women in the
party were being encouraged and expected to go back into
the home, and many did. 'Know your place' was the slogan that
stifled women.

Women were fighting in a man's world not only in the workplace but also in politics. When I was at a meeting of the South
Yorkshire women's advisory committee in Barnsley, the MP, Roy
Mason, arrived and asked, 'Who's making me a cup of tea then?'
I pointed out to him that it was a women's meeting. I suggested
that he put the boiler on so we could all have tea together when
the meeting was over, which to his credit he did. Teatime was a
big event, it was not a time for losing weight. There was great
rivalry amongst the women's sections as to who could put on the
best spread for their regional women's officer. The tables were
covered with home-made cakes, scones, freshly made sandwiches
and sausage rolls, and I was encouraged to eat; not sampling each
item in this great spread could be seen as an insult to the cooks.

The *Yorkshire Labour Year Book* in 1946 identifies that 'the
Labour Women's organisations has never been a feminist movement'. I am sure that was true then and the question of the 'place'
of Labour women remained a tension for many years. Throughout

the 1970s and 1980s, consequently it was often difficult to build relationships with other women and equality organisations. In 1971 the Women's Liberation Movement conference produced a statement for consideration by the national conference of Labour women. There was no question but that we were a very long way yet from achieving equality within the party. A year later the party produced its own examination of the position of women, 'Discrimination against Women'. In many ways our thinking was more radical than publicly perceived. Being part of a political party acted as a barrier, it prevented us from being as forthright as we might otherwise have been.

Alice Mahon when she became the MP for Halifax in 1987 described the forms of discrimination women faced in the House of Commons: offensive comments about appearances, class or regional background. But it was not only in the Commons that appearance was taken note of. I worked hard always to conform, and I thought I was doing so when in 1970 I bought a very fashionable brown trouser suit. Wearing it for the first time at a meeting in Rotherham, I was firmly told that women should not wear trousers, women wore skirts. Twenty-three years later on entering the House of Lords the Labour Chief Whip, Ted Graham, re-iterated those words and added that I should not have bare arms. Today women do wear trousers and have bare arms.

I had little time for those women who didn't support others, and made my feelings known to a woman councillor who said, 'I have made it; so can they.' She was not prepared to give any support and encouragement, or to help other women to take on political roles. The Regional Forum for Education held seminars and sessions based on confidence building and training, so enabling women to take on responsibilities in the party, be representatives of the party and get involved in organisations within the community. Each September we held our annual week's training school, which Betty Lockwood first attended in 1946, the first training school.

We were at the forefront of women's activities throughout the country. In 1971 I held the first ever regional women's conference, in which women's sections and councils submitted resolutions and women were able to express their views without feeling dominated by a male audience. The Yorkshire women's rally was held every year, attended by up to 2,000 women; no national politician ever turned down the opportunity to speak. But the highlight was the singing of our choir, made up of women who had rehearsed in their own homes and only assembled on the morning of the rally, to bring all their voices together. I used to have a recording of one of their performances, on an old 78. Their repertoire included well-known songs such as 'Greensleeves', but also Yorkshire songs, and never missed was their rendition of 'Prattie Flowers'.

When chair of the Yorkshire women's organisation, I presided over the rally held in Leeds Town Hall. I wore a black suit and a big red hat. I had never worn a hat before, and I was so nervous I couldn't eat my lunch. Roy Jenkins, then Home Secretary, was our key speaker. I have never forgotten the advice he gave me: 'If you are not nervous, you will not do it well.' He took me to the front of the curtained stage, pulled back the edge of the curtain, so I could see the gathering crowds, all 2,000 of them, and said to me, 'They are thinking how brave you are – prove it.' At least I got his name right when welcoming him, unlike Violet Satterthwaite the previous year, who had introduced that year's main speaker, Tony Crosland, as Tony Greenwood.

At the same time fundamental developments were happening nationally, such as the Equal Pay Act in 1970, for implementation in 1975, and the legislation on sex discrimination. Betty Lockwood, chief women's officer of the party, played a big part in persuading the Labour government how important such legislation was, if there were to be real advancements in women's equality. The Equal Opportunities Commission was established, to provide the mechanism that would make the legislation real. Betty was appointed its first chair and resigned her post with the party. The post of chief women's officer was therefore now vacant and it was Betty who encouraged me to apply for it. We had long conversations about my ability to do the job. Betty strongly persuaded me that I could, so I applied.

It was a difficult decision to take. Did I really want to leave Leeds? Did I want to live in London? Was I capable of doing the job? We examined the changes it would make not only to me but also to Kevin, who would have to give up his career on Leeds City Council as chair of the housing committee. Did I want to move away from our friends? Would we be happy in London? After lots of discussion I decided to apply and got on the shortlist. For the occasion I bought a new suit, midnight blue and very smart and more than I could afford. I spent the morning in London with Jeannette, who was at university there reading history, and went for the interview. Not expecting to get the job, I decided to be absolutely outspoken about my ideas on the ways the party should improve the position of women both organisationally and politically.

A few days later the letter arrived offering me the post. Now the decision had to be taken. Should I refuse or should I accept this fantastic opportunity? The family decision was yes, I should go to London.

The next question was where should I live? That problem was solved when Fred Mulley, the MP for Sheffield Park who was the then chair of the party, offered me the basement flat in his home in Maida Vale, where I stayed for nearly six months until Kevin joined me. On 1 November 1975 I again started a new phase in my life.

≺◄►≻

OVER THE
THRESHOLD

On 16 October 1975 I was appointed. Two weeks later on 1 November 1975 I stepped over the threshold of the Labour Party head office as a senior national officer with the grand title of chief women's officer and assistant national agent. The general secretary, Ron Hayward, and the national agent, Reg Underhill, gave me a warm welcome on the doorstep of head office. I was full of trepidation but at the same time excited.

The Labour Party offices were scattered throughout Transport House. It was in Smith Square, Westminster, the home of the Transport and General Workers' Union. I was guided to my office on the third floor by Ron's secretary Mary Griffiths, a small, dark and demure woman I had never met before. I came to realise how important she was, not only as the confidante of the general secretary but also as his gatekeeper.

My small room had one desk, a filing cabinet and two chairs with an internal window overlooking a white-tiled inner court. I imagined it was like looking down over the white tiles of a gents' toilet. In spite of the smallness of my office, I felt as though I had entered hallowed ground. Even now when I go through Smith Square forty years later, I still remember that feeling.

That sense of awe was accompanied by the fact I hadn't quite accepted that I was there and the doubts overcame me. Did I have the ability to do the job as efficiently and effectively as my predecessors Sara Barker, Constance Kay and my close colleague Betty Lockwood? But more than that, my new job had two distinct roles: firstly being responsible for the women's organisation and all that that entailed, and secondly as an assistant national agent working on general party work under the direction of the national agent. I was apprehensive about whether I could cope with both roles and carry them on satisfactorily.

I heard from Bryan Stanley, the Post Office Engineering Union representative on the National Executive Committee, who had chaired the eleven-strong interviewing panel, that the decision to appoint me had been a unanimous one. He said that they had been impressed by my relaxed manner and by how outspoken I had been about the future of the women's organisation, the need for development and the dramatic changes that were needed to strengthen its role. It was not what they had expected to hear. That was indeed praise from Bryan for he was a tough negotiator, a persuasive speaker and a man of very definite views. At the interview I had only been able to get over my normal nervousness because I felt I had nothing to lose, having been told that someone else was lined up for the job. Although I was delighted, I realised how disappointed my colleague must have been when she heard the news of my appointment.

I soon became aware of how much I had to learn. I was

enormously grateful to Isabel Guichard, my secretary, and Dasha Masrani, her assistant, who had kept the women's committees functioning for the three months since Betty Lockwood had left. I was completely reliant on their support. Dasha was to become my secretary when Isabel retired, and stayed with me for many years, before resigning to go on a trip round the world. Dasha now works in the Commons for Mike Gapes MP.

My first job was to bring the women's committees back to life and build excitement into their work. To do that, I had to find out how the women's organisation fitted into the structure. How did it liaise and work with other departments? The women's unit, that is the three of us, were isolated and to a degree divorced from the general work of head office. We were left to organise ourselves, running two national major women's committees, and organising the annual women's conferences. It was daunting but to be effective I needed answers. That led me to ask questions. I had to, in order to fill in the gaps in my knowledge, whether about policy, administration, promotion or publicity. How else could I learn?

Some colleagues clearly did not understand my approach. Walter Brown, the national youth officer, and Don Storer and Pat Kavanagh, both administrators in the organisation department, asked me if they could have a private word. We moved into a space in the corridor behind the filing cabinets. They advised me that it was foolish to ask so many questions. I was told, 'It will be assumed you don't know.' My response was, 'But I don't know and I have to know.' For them it was seen as a sign of weakness, but for me just the reverse. I was determined to show that the NEC had made the right decision in appointing me out of the many applicants to become a member of the management of the party.

The management team at head office comprised the general secretary, the national agent and the eight heads of department: Geoff Bish, head of domestic policy; Jenny Little, international secretary; Percy Clarke, head of publicity; John Pittaway, who ran the party finances; Roger Robinson, in charge of personnel matters; Donald Ross, editor of the party's newspaper, *Labour Weekly*; and Walter Brown and myself from the organisation department. We frequently met at heads of department meetings, strategy meetings, directors' meetings or on the financial management team. For me there were too many meetings, too much talk and not enough action, and no structured process of decision making.

I was immediately struck by the male domination of this party machine. It had to be broken. Jenny and I were the only two women round the table. As so often happens in such situations our contributions were repeated by a male colleague who then took ownership. We attempted to overcome this by immediately intervening to make sure that credit was given to whichever of us had come up with the proposal.

This was a time of low morale amongst the staff. There was a high level of in-fighting, suspicion and genuine dissatisfaction. It hid a level of incompetence by some whilst for others it caused great feelings of frustration. Some of the staff saw working for the party as a sinecure. I do believe, however, that the majority irrespective of their motivation were proud to work for the Labour Party. I certainly was.

The disputes and feelings of unrest were exacerbated by the

appointment in 1977 of Andy Bevan, an acknowledged member of Militant, as the party's youth officer. Bryan Stanley as chair of the organisation committee was against the appointment but his view was opposed by Tony Benn and Ron Hayward. Militant soon took over the Young Socialists (YS), giving the YS a seat on the NEC. In the words of Derek Hatton, the YS were the youth wing of Militant. This was a situation that continued until Tom Sawyer reduced the age limit for YS membership from twenty-six to twenty-three. Militant's next aim was to take over the party's student body, the National Organisation of Labour Students (NOLS). Fierce battles raged, but Militant underestimated the ability of the students to organise against them.

Sally Morgan, then student officer, recalls how attending the NOLS conferences were terrifying experiences of verbal and physical abuse. The NOLS had to use their imagination to keep control. At one conference they used striking miners as stewards, knowing that Militant would not challenge them. The students also knew how to use the rule book effectively. It was important to find out what the Militants were up to. It was not unknown for a glass to be pressed to the wall to hear what was happening in Andy's office, and I am sure he was aware of it. That is an example of the atmosphere in which we all worked.

In spite of all their efforts Militant never took control of NOLS because of the determination of NOLS members and student officers. Many of them became political advisors to Labour MPs, ministers and shadow ministers, including people such as Tom Watson, who had been chair of NOLS and the party's student officer. Sally had been on the staff for well over a year before I discovered that her father-in-law was Edward Lyons, a Bradford

MP. I had grown up with Edward. He was a very close friend of my brothers.

When Dasha left me, I appointed a seemingly pleasant young woman from Peacehaven, near Brighton. She disappointingly turned out to be a Militant Tendency plant. She was efficient in her job and gave me no official reason for sacking her. I had to resort to not giving her any work of consequence, or any information which would be of value to the Tendency. This must have been very frustrating and it wasn't long before she resigned the post. I did not know then that I would play a major part years later in the removal of the Militant Tendency from the party. The Peacehaven Militant was replaced by Sylvia Clovey, who helped me through many difficult situations, and was with me until I retired. She left shortly afterwards.

The frustrations of the staff continued to boil over, and the shortage of money meant we did not always get paid on time. The staff decided that they had had enough. Action had to be taken to express their discontent. Not long after I joined head office, they went on strike, a strike that lasted for some weeks. Meanwhile the NEC dithered about how to resolve the party's financial problems.

Along with my other management colleagues I would not, as a principle, cross the staff's picket line. We came to an agreement with them that each morning we would be allowed to enter head office and collect work we needed for that day. We then assembled at Percy Clarke's flat to discuss how negotiations were progressing and if there was anything we should be doing. We then moved on to a committee room in the House of Commons to settle down to our day's work.

For many years I had wanted to have my ears pierced but thinking about the procedure terrified me. I was teased about my fear. I had some free time on my hands because of the strike and was urged by my colleagues to get it done. I plucked up my courage and went to Selfridges on Oxford Street. I approached the desk only to be told to come back in two hours. This was the excuse I needed to escape, but that would have been sheer cowardice. I could not go back without holes in my ears, so I drank tea, went back and had the deed done. I proudly arrived at the Commons to show off the gold rings that rested in my ears.

The strike was over. Promises of better conditions and prompter payments were made by the NEC but the in-fighting continued, made worse by the political divide between the two trade unions that represented the staff: The Transport and General Workers' Union, which was represented by Andy Bevan, and APEX (the Association of Professional, Executive, Clerical and Computer Staff), with Barrie Clarke as its shop steward. Andy became chair of the overall staff committee, the joint trade union committee, which did nothing to ease tensions. I was fortunate that I could divorce myself from all this controversy, shut my office door and concentrate on other, to me, more important things.

In 1982 Ron Hayward retired, and was succeeded by Jim Mortimer. They could not have been more different in style and temperament. Ron had started as a full-time agent, then was promoted to regional organiser for the southern region, before becoming national agent of the party and ultimately in 1972 general secretary. It was not the most popular appointment, which he achieved by one vote, that of Tony Benn. Ron was passionate about international affairs and a strong advocate of the abolition of apartheid. He had a spontaneous way of speaking, and although his language was not always precise, we knew what he meant. Surprisingly to me, on his retirement he became a boxing promoter.

Politically Ron and Jim were both on the left. Jim was a formidable left-wing trade unionist who had successfully chaired the conciliation service ACAS before becoming general secretary. Colleagues said that he owed both of these appointments to his friend Michael Foot. He faced the same financial and political problems as Ron, unrest in every section of the party, low morale amongst the staff and a million-pound overdraft. In 1983 Jim even had to break the agreement to pay the staff for their extra work during a general election.

Whilst Ron was general secretary, the decision was taken to move out of Transport House to our own headquarters in Walworth Road, near the Elephant and Castle in south London. Ron proudly announced that our base was now amongst our own people. The move was expected to be paid for by asking party members to each buy a brick. The response was derisory and we had to get the trade unions to bail us out. The move caused me enormous inconvenience and a great deal of wasted time. The party van took me back and forth to Westminster. It was not always at the most convenient times or coinciding with the many meetings that were held in the Commons. I wasted time waiting for buses or I had to pay for a taxi out of my own pocket.

I realised that there was a different hurdle I had to overcome, another barrier. That was the attitude of my regional now ex-colleagues. I had to gain their confidence. I was aware that not everyone had been happy at my appointment, that now I had become one of their senior officers sitting at the top table. To them I had at least two flaws. Firstly I had never been a full-time agent and secondly, muttered but not openly said, I had a left-wing background.

I was determined that at the first meeting of the regional staff, I would not sit silent. I would have a slot on the agenda, speaking from that top table. I told Reg Underhill, who chaired the meetings, that I wanted to present a paper on my future plans for the women's organisation, nationally, regionally and locally. Reg questioned my judgement. Was it too soon? Was I sure I should not be in the job a little longer? I made it clear to him that I was sure, that I genuinely wanted to face them. He conceded.

When the day came I nervously stood up. I appreciated what I had to overcome personally. I also knew that the women's agenda was not their main priority. I made my speech, sat down and waited for reactions. I heard Paul Carmody, the north-west regional organiser, who saw himself as the spokesperson for his regional colleagues, say, 'She'll do.' I am not sure I was meant to hear that comment, but I was glad I did. It was a pivotal moment. It was a moment of acceptance by my regional colleagues. The moment when I felt able to start to promote and put into practice a women's programme for the future.

My greatest pleasure was working with the wonderful women on the women's committee. It could not have been a more exciting time. Women's policy and development was high on the agenda. This was the age of women's liberation. There was recognition of the campaigns for equal pay and economic freedom, of battered wives syndrome, and of divorce reform – the so-called Casanova's charter.

The United Nations General Assembly formalised 8 March as International Women's Day and had designated 1975, the year I went to head office, as International Women's Year. Nationally it was a particularly proud time for Labour women, as Barbara Castle's Equal Pay Act, enacted in 1970, came into effect. Barbara Castle had been influenced by two strikes: the Leeds clothing workers strike, when 20,000 women from forty-five factories came out on strike because of the low wage rate, and the strike of the Ford machinists in Dagenham. The year 1975 also saw the introduction of the Sex Discrimination Act and the establishment of the Equal Opportunities Commission.

These Acts, together with the Employment Protection Act, provided an income policy which favoured the low paid – mainly women. They were all commitments made in the Labour Party's 1974 general election manifesto. That was the first and only time a Labour manifesto has included a charter for women. Many women's organisations were campaigning for these advancements, but it is unlikely that without the hard work of Labour women, the party and the government would have promoted such a forward-looking women's rights agenda. To celebrate and commemorate these great events, one of my first acts was to organise a photographic exhibition in head office portraying the history of women's struggle for equality and identifying the Labour women who had been a part of that struggle.

In spite of this high level of activity and many successes in policy terms, I realised it did not result in changing fundamental attitudes and the built-in discrimination against women within the party itself. Getting equal rights and equal representation proved to be a hard and uphill slog. Men were still in charge.

The party didn't suddenly wake up to the realisation that it was discriminatory. The slow process of change started in 1971. The women in the party called for parity with men at all levels of the party structures. A Green Paper was produced in 1972. The party was then in opposition, so it lay on the table and a period of inaction followed. Eventually the NEC came to realise that the voices of the 'sisters' could no longer be ignored. These included women with vast experience, such as Millie Miller MP, previously the leader of Camden Borough Council and as such the first woman leader of a London borough, who died tragically at the age of fifty-five on my birthday in 1977; Dame Judith Hart (later Baroness Hart), who was the first woman to become a dame whilst being an MP, as well as the first mother to become a Cabinet minister; and Joan Lestor, with whom I worked closely on race relations and who lived near me in Tooting Bec. We became close friends. Then there was Lena Jeger, who was the first politician to raise in the House of Lords the terrible practice of female genital mutilation, sadly still performed today; and the three redheads, the firebrand Renee Short MP, the unforgettable Barbara Castle and Jo Richardson, who has been described as the 'dynamo of the left'. Jo was clear about whom she was put into Parliament to support, saying, 'I am not all that interested in high-achieving women. I am concerned about all the women with expertise and wisdom who never get to first base.' A philosophy I fully endorsed. All these doughty women, who for many years had been at the forefront of women's empowerment on the women's committees, gave me an enormous level of support.

It was Judith Hart who taught me how to keep up to date with areas of policy as they developed. She kept a pack of cards each covering a different aspect of policy, and carried it with her at all times. They could be easily updated. Copying this initiative I created my own pack of cards which proved invaluable.

The powerful lobbying by Labour women led to an investigation by the NEC on discrimination in the party. The outcome was the production of a 1978 paper entitled 'Obstacles Facing Women in the Party'. We then started to make some progress. However, the executive rejected giving more weight to the work of the women's committee that consisted of representatives from the regions by not being prepared to remove the word 'advisory' from its title. That decision was overturned by the national party conference. Whilst these important changes were being made, I could sense if not hear the groans each time I raised the women's agenda. 'Not women again!'

In the NEC report to the 1978 conference I wrote a section covering the work of the women's committees, regional and local women's activity, and my international role. Conference referred the report back. I think that was the first time such a thing had occurred. The delegates felt that the NEC were not taking sufficient notice of the views of the women in the party, nor giving them sufficient resources financially or organisationally. I was delighted. My involvement in making that happen was never proven but highly suspected.

Little progress was being made in increasing the number of women in Parliament. Rather they were in decline. There were two lists of would-be candidates, the party list (list A) and the trade union list (list B). In 1981, list A was made up of 101 men and five women whilst list B had 175 men and six women. When I challenged these low numbers of women, I was invariably told that it was the women's fault. They were not putting their names forward.

So began my campaign for one woman on every constituency's parliamentary candidate shortlist, for more of those women candidates to be selected and for the party to re-define its collective leadership to include more women. This proposal was originally agreed at the women's conference in 1981, and opposed by the NEC, but carried by the annual party conference. Unfortunately it became a 'token', and did not have the effect I had hoped. I then proposed 50 per cent women on a shortlist. That was also agreed, and led to a slight improvement in the number of women selected. Finally I put forward the more controversial proposal of all-women shortlists, a step too far for the time, but one which re-surfaced and was implemented after I retired. Now over 40 per cent of the Parliamentary Labour Party are women.

The reluctance by the executive to endorse any real form of positive action was illustrated by the fierce debate around the proposal for a national spokesperson for women's rights by Jo Richardson and myself. We wanted a minister for women as they had in France. Jo and I went to France to learn more about how to further the policy. Michael Foot, the then leader, was supportive but the NEC rejected it by nineteen votes to eight. Those voting against included Michael Meacher and David Blunkett, to the dismay of the women members of the party, who had expected their support. Had the proposal been accepted Jo would almost certainly have been the first person to occupy that post. But it continued to be opposed even when Neil Kinnock became leader. Jo also introduced a private member's Bill on sex equality looking at loopholes in the current discrimination law. To gain support for the Bill I initiated a campaign amongst Labour MPs. The Bill was blocked by the Tories.

As a gesture a working party was established on positive discrimination. I co-chaired it with Liz Atkins, the women's policy researcher. Our well-evidenced report on the subject was presented to the NEC. We were not surprised when they decided that it should lie on the table. There seemed to be no understanding of the impact this negative attitude was having amongst women electors. A similar attitude was adopted by the National Union of Labour Organisers, the organisers' 'trade union'. It rejected the concept of part-time organisers, a move which would have enabled more women to become party agents. A delegation from the NEC women's committee persuaded them that their attitude was indeed discriminatory and so changed their policy.

Established in 1906, the National Joint Committee of Working Women's Organisations was a committee that I had previously been a member and now as chief women's officer I was its secretary. Its power lay in its membership, made up of strong and knowledgeable women from the wider Labour movement who could not be ignored. The TUC was represented by the formidable duo of Ethel Chipchase and Marie Patterson, senior members of the Women's TUC. The committee also included five members of the NEC and representatives of individual trade unions, socialist societies and the Co-operative Party. My daughter Jeannette was the representative from the Co-operative Women's Guild. Three of my colleagues in the Lords were at one time members of the committee, Glenys Thornton, Anne Gibson and Brenda Dean.

The value of the committee was that it brought together these different women's organisations in the Labour movement. It was an effective means of challenging a Labour government, sometimes when it was difficult for women in the party to do so directly or publicly.

The women in the Labour movement believed it was absolutely essential that women had economic independence. They argued vigorously for the replacement of the Family Allowance, paid to the father, with one paid to the mother. Even after it had been agreed in principle by the Labour Party, there was a point when the Prime Minister, then Jim Callaghan, started to waver. He was anxious about a male backlash. I led a delegation to persuade him why it was necessary. We emerged victorious and Child Benefit was the result, a payment moving from wallet to purse.

The National Joint Committee met four times a year. It was a fundamental and crucial part of the social change agenda. The outcomes of its working groups, its documentation and booklets were highly valued by a range of women's organisations. It campaigned on employment and training, equal pay, women's health, abortion – the right to choose – and free bus passes for the elderly. Browsing in a second-hand bookshop I found a bound copy of its minutes for 1911 which I still have on my bookshelves. It sits along with some of their booklets on 'A Happier Old Age', 'Health Care for Women' and 'Women's Rights'. Every disadvantage women faced was considered. The committee even campaigned vigorously to remove VAT on sanitary towels and ultimately were successful in principle, in spite of objections from the Pharmaceutical Society.

Regrettably, in the mid-1990s the party decided for financial reasons that the women's officer could no longer be the committee's secretariat. The TUC were asked to take the committee over, but they said no and it closed down. A major link between women in the party and women in the trade unions was lost. I still believe it was a serious mistake.

⤙⤚

WOMEN ON
THE MOVE

The Tory recession of the early 1980s saw a growing number of women becoming unemployed. To publicise that and other restrictions women were facing I organised a women's rights festival in Battersea Park in London. It was held on 5 June 1982 under the banner 'Plan for Jobs'. It was a highly successful political and social event, publicising Labour's opposition to the Conservative government's policies for women. The rally was addressed by national and international speakers, and women's pressure groups and fringe organisations participated in the sixteen-policy forum. We distributed a wide range of leaflets and booklets, and there were 100 stalls offering various items for sale. Women's music and theatre groups provided entertainment. The brochure had a bright red rose on the front.

I was involved in so many activities at that time. I went on a vigorous organising campaign on the recognition of rape in marriage. Spousal rape was not made illegal by the courts until 1991 and not legislated against until as recently as 2003. I joined the women at Greenham Common, and worked actively with Women against Pit Closures during the miners' strike of 1984–5.

The highlight of the year was the powerful national Labour women's conference. There were lively debates as the delegates thrashed out the policies that the Labour Party should be pursuing. Held over a period of a week, it hosted delegations from the 1,500 Labour women's organisations across the country, the trade unions, socialist societies and the National Executive Committee. Many of today's well-known women started their political careers speaking on the rostrum at the women's conference. The conference programme included resolutions from the organisations represented as well as policy documents produced by the national women's committee. Importantly I reported on the responses to resolutions from previous years by the Labour Cabinet or shadow Cabinet and senior politicians in the party. They were well aware they could not ignore the issues raised by the women's conference.

My first conference in charge was in Folkestone in 1976. Although I had attended many conferences as a delegate, and sat on the platform as a member of the national women's committee, I found it very daunting to be in charge. For good or bad it was now my responsibility.

There were eighty-eight resolutions on the agenda. An important debate on the discrimination of women by Labour clubs took me back to my own experience of being refused entry to attend a party meeting held near Barnsley in South Yorkshire. It gained a sympathetic response from the executive of the National

Union of Labour and Socialist Clubs, which said that they would change the rules. They regretted that not all Labour clubs were affiliated to the National Union, and they could not determine the behaviour of those clubs, but they would do what they could to influence them. Eventually all Labour clubs changed their rules. Another success for Labour women.

The following year, in Harrogate, the main debate was the challenges that were being made by anti-abortion MPs to the 1967 Abortion Act, and the need to persuade Labour MPs to vote against any such proposals. Although the first anti-abortion Bill, a private member's Bill brought by William Benyon MP, was unsuccessful, the Labour government brought together a group of MPs to discuss a possible compromise. Jo Richardson was invited to attend the meeting, but she left when she realised that it was an attempt by a Labour government to water down the Act. The next proposed amendment, a private member's Bill introduced by John Corrie, nearly succeeded.

My aim as chief women's officer, working with a newly formed organisation, the Labour Abortion Rights Campaign (LARC), was for the party conference to agree a pro-choice resolution. My daughter Jeannette was an officer of LARC. I circulated constituency parties, requesting them to send pro-choice resolutions for the agenda of the 1977 national party conference. This resulted in seven resolutions, composited before conference into two. The one that called for support for the 1967 Act was overwhelmingly carried, and the policy still stands today. The second resolution, calling for a three-line whip for MPs, was defeated.

In their book *Abortion Politics*, David Marsh and Joanna Chambers record that I mailed MPs before each day's Commons debate during committee, and that I sat under the public gallery at report stage, in order to keep an eye on Labour MPs. Joanna says:

> Some members looked genuinely worried at the sight of her closely watching events as they knew that she would soon question them if they did not vote according to Labour Party policy, as passed at conference ... In fact she was a continual reminder to Labour MPs that abortion was party policy and this may have gone some way to sway waverers.

Tony Benn recalls the final vote in his diaries, and my counting through the Labour MPs as they went to vote. Mike Cocks, the Chief Whip, his deputy Walter Harrison and I met to discuss how to handle any further private members' Bills. In the following years fortunately that never happened, although the rumours were strong in 1979 that one was planned.

This was the time when my marriage broke down. Kevin and I split up. Kevin had become a councillor in Camden, and our separate activities caused the divide. It soon became known by Labour MPs that I was no longer attached. After our meetings Mike and Walter and I would go down to 'the office', the Stranger's Bar in the Commons. It was amazing how many MPs wanted to buy me a drink and made suggestive comments. My worst experience was when an MP pinned me against the wall to tell me how I would enjoy going to bed with him. Stan Orme, who Jeannette worked for, saw my dilemma, went out, came back and shouted at me, 'Joyce, do you know that there is a taxi waiting outside for you?' I made my escape.

Hedley Taylor is a theatre buff and had a long list of friends. He bought two tickets for at least two performances a week, and then found out who could join him. I did on many occasions and was truly grateful to him, particularly so, when one evening at the Almeida Theatre, I realised that my back was resting on Peter O'Toole's legs. Hedley's invitations got me out of several sticky situations with lecherous MPs.

The women's conference that has gone down in folklore was the one held in Newcastle in 1982, chaired by Anne Davis. My original thought that year had been to go not to Newcastle, but to the seaside town of Whitley Bay. Marian Craythorne and I travelled up north and met the mayor to discuss arrangements. It was a farcical conversation. He couldn't comprehend the concept that this was a conference for women. He seemed to see it as a gathering of men, who brought their wives along with them. When he proudly told us that the council would arrange coaches to take the 'ladies' on trips, we decided to give up and leave. We turned to Newcastle as the venue. As well as its excitements, it was the largest women's conference ever held even to this day, attended by 1,200 women for a whole week.

These were the days of the so-called 'dungaree brigade'. They made demands that it was sometimes not possible to meet. On this occasion it began with complaints about the crèche. It was in a school across the road from the conference, and having to cross the road put the children in danger. They were also angry because I had felt that a boy of fourteen was too old to be in the crèche.

The women decided to hold a demonstration. They brought all the children across the 'dangerous' road and sat them on the press tables in front of the platform. I knew something was amiss when I saw all my staff, including Jeannette, who was working as a steward, suddenly appear and form a circle around the platform. They later told me that they were there to protect me from this group of outraged mothers. The delegates showed the demonstrators how ridiculous their behaviour was. Noisily they took their children back across the road.

Gwyneth Dunwoody MP came back to Westminster from conference regaling her colleagues with unfortunately true stories. Stories about this episode, but also that hypodermic needles had been left on the floors in the toilets and that the northern regional women's officer, Brenda Whittaker, had been propositioned in the toilets by another woman delegate. My anxiety was how the NEC might react. Would they stop further conferences? Fortunately they made no comment. Some members were horrified and others just amused. Many perhaps saw the women's activities as of no consequence. In spite of all this excitement we did get down to the business of the conference and debating its theme, 'Disarmament and Development'.

Over twenty years later when I was chair of the Women's National Commission, I hosted a party for Angela Mason OBE (now CBE) when she retired from being the equality officer in the government's Women and Equality Unit. I talked about my first meeting with Angela when she was the director of Stonewall, the UK-based lesbian, gay and bisexual lobbying organisation. In her reply she accused me of having a short memory and reminded me that she had been one of the 'dungaree brigade' who plagued me at women's conferences.

In 1983 because of the general election we held a one-day

conference in London. At lunchtime the Women's Action Committee (WAC), a women's pressure group in the party led by Ann Pettifor and Patricia Hewitt, decided that no men should be allowed in the conference. The wonderful Jo Richardson MP took the microphone and made it clear to them what nonsense that was. That afternoon Neil Kinnock, the party leader, would be attending the conference and addressing delegates. Jo made it clear to the WAC that our relationship with the party hierarchy was vital to our future. It was at that conference that there was an attempt to throw out a photographer on the grounds that his camera was a phallic symbol.

At the conference in Swansea in 1984, held at the height of the debate on feminism, a theme that ran through all the conferences in the early 1980s, I was woken up in the middle of the night by the police telling me that one of the trade union delegates had been found wandering the streets, completely blotto, and had decided that she didn't need to wear any clothes. Next morning I had to go and arrange her release from the police cells. At the same conference Anita Gale (now Baroness Gale), our Welsh women's officer, organised an evening entertainment. The all-women pop group she had arranged let her down at the last minute. Their replacement was three women in gold lamé with a male singer. Anita expected an outcry. Fortunately everyone including the feminists liked the act and went on to enjoy the evening.

I had the audacity at a conference in the late 1970s to compare Labour women's achievement with the jam making of the Women's Institute. As president of the WI, Norma Major sent me samples of their jam with a polite rebuttal outlining their many other activities. Since then I have collaborated with the

WI on a number of issues, most recently on the cuts to the legal aid budget and the consequences for women suffering domestic violence.

The following year in Bournemouth we changed the design of the conference, making it more stylish. This was a dry run for the revamped national party conference to be held later that autumn. It was to be my last women's conference as chief women's officer. Gradually, the conferences were downgraded and eventually abolished to save funds. I believe that was a great mistake. Today a one-day conference is held the day before the national party conference.

At my instigation, the national Labour women's committee followed the words of Margaret MacDonald spoken so many years ago, when she called on Labour women to give support to the many women who were campaigning in organisations such as Anti-Apartheid, Chile Solidarity and the African National Congress, and with women from El Salvador and other countries. All came to speak at our women's conferences. We offered support and lobbied on their behalf to government and to influence Labour Party policy. We kept contact with a number of women who lived in areas of conflict such as Ana Margharita Gateszora in El Salvador. She was later to have a great influence on me.

Although the NEC did not fully approve, the committee had kept contact with the Soviet women's committee. Its president was Valentina Tereshkova, the first woman in space. When the invitation arrived inviting a delegation of Labour women to visit the USSR, I had firstly to get approval from the party's international committee. I had conversations with Jenny Little, our international secretary, on how we would persuade them.

We successfully elicited the support of the chair of the committee, Alex Kitson. He and Jenny jointly persuaded the international committee members.

The 1981 delegation which I headed comprised Renee Short, a longstanding MP and member of the NEC; Saxon Spence, chair of the Labour women's committee; and Mary Cohen, a past chair of the committee. We landed at Moscow airport to be met by Valentina Tereshkova, a small, courteous, very smartly dressed, grey-haired lady, not the image I had imagined for this famous astronaut.

Our chauffeur-driven car awaited us. We accompanied Valentina to a tea party in honour of our arrival and to meet the officials of the Soviet women's committee and other senior women officials. Not a man in sight.

One of the queries that we had raised with the secretariat of the Soviet women's committee was what gifts we should bring. The response was bras from Marks and Spencer and chewing gum. Discussions then had to be had on bra sizes and other items of underwear that they might like. We did take more formal gifts, but it was clear it was the items from Marks and Spencer that were most welcome.

Throughout the ten-day visit we were provided with a car and driver and Ivanka, our interpreter and guide. We had to be careful about any comments we might make, as they would almost certainly be passed on to a higher authority. The driver probably spoke English but would never do so in our presence.

The schedule of visits had been well prepared. Its aim was to show us that there was no discrimination against women in the USSR and the wonderful education their children received.

I so enjoyed the beautiful and endearing demonstrations of song and dance by children in their local costumes. With the head of the schools and their teachers we discussed their curriculum and their impressive programmes for their development.

Not on our schedule, although asked for, was a visit to a maternity ward in a hospital. We had been to a health clinic, which was efficient and well run, but we wanted to see how this compared with the maternity services. Our insistence broke down their resistance. It became clear why they did not want this visit. There were no curtains between the beds, which were so close together there was no space for lockers or even a chair. What was extremely distressing was that a woman might be giving birth in a bed next to a woman who had had an abortion. This wasn't seen as a problem and I soon realised that abortion was very much seen as a form of contraception, something I personally oppose. Contraceptives were rare.

We were escorted at the hospital by their Communist Party representative. She was loud and scruffy, with uncombed hair and very long red-painted fingernails. When leaving the hospital the five of us got into a very small lift. It broke down between floors. Our escort promptly had hysterics and started screaming. Poor Mary Cohen, who had asthma, crouched on the floor of the lift in despair at the lack of air. We begged our escort to quieten down. Russian voices from above tried to assure us that they were working to get the lift doors open. Eventually they did. They lowered a short ladder for us to climb up to get to the next floor. As soon as they could reach us, one by one, we were dragged to safety. It was certainly a day to remember.

We were appalled at the state of the hospital and its facilities, as well as its dodgy lifts. We did, however, feel encouraged when we were told that there were more women doctors than men and that they received equal pay. I went on to discover that the men's pay had supposedly been reduced to match that of the women, not that the women's pay had risen to match the men's. I was shown the Soviet national constitution, which committed the state to providing equal pay. Lowering men's pay was not how I would have interpreted a clause to achieve parity.

We were then flown down to Tashkent in the central Asian republic of Uzbekistan to visit a farm which primarily grew delicious melons. I did not enjoy the fact that the toilet there was a hole in the ground. I was anxious as to what might crawl out. The melons were taken to the cities on unrefrigerated planes in long baskets holding eight melons each. I bought two of these baskets in order to carry home the many gifts I was given and the purchases I made: beautiful pieces of china, pottery, Russian dolls and bright, multi-coloured scarfs.

We met women from all walks of life including from the Supreme Soviet. Discussions were held on the health service, healthcare for women and children, particularly maternity care education, the employment prospects of women, childcare facilities and nursery education. We visited the Winter Palace in Leningrad and sat in the grand box at the Bolshoi Ballet. We had the opportunity to explore shops and visit markets and were invited by a private family to have a meal in a Russian home. On the table were their best plates and cutlery and the food was delicious.

Each night we stayed in a tourist hotel. On arrival back from Leningrad, however, there was a panic over our hotel rooms, which had been double booked. Instead we were given rooms in one of their luxurious private hotels. What a difference. The carpets were inches deep, and the crystal chandeliers lit up our very expensive and beautifully cooked dinner. All the other guests were senior and high-ranking officials, of either the government or the Communist Party. During dinner we were entertained by a live band playing dance music. Our interpreter advised us not to speak to anyone but what was I meant to do when a rather attractive man asked me to dance, on the small dance floor? I was a guest, it would have been rude to refuse. We chatted in his not very good English. We parted gracefully and I thought that was goodnight. But on going up to bed, he started to follow me up the stairs. When the four of us reached our floor, the woman who sat at a desk on the corridor just smiled. We stood by our bedroom doors, shouted 'Now', shot into our bedrooms and locked the doors. Soon my phone rang, but the words coming from the other end were in Russian and all I could do was say 'Niet, niet'. Eventually he gave up.

Regaling the story to Ivanka the next morning, I asked what was he saying. Her reply was, 'To get you into bed, so you would be compromised.' I was glad I knew at least one word of Russian. The next day we departed for home, seen off by party officials. At the airport Saxon was brusquely told, 'You are not allowed to take photographs of the airport.'

Arriving at Heathrow with all our luggage including the many melon baskets, we were looked at suspiciously. The officials made the mistake of picking out Renee to have her luggage inspected. Out came all her belongings, in which they found nothing unto-ward, but the official asked the wrong question: 'Why have you no cigarettes?' Renee was well known as fanatical anti-smoking campaigner. Her response to the affront was a tirade about the dangers of smoking. She was a tough, formidable woman, certainly not the person to challenge. Her belongings were packed carefully back into her case and we were free to go, but not until the customs official had been given leaflets on the dangers of smoking. I am sure that he was pleased to see the back of these strange strong-minded Labour women.

My own feelings were that the visit had been a useful and valuable but that many of their claims of equality for women looked good on paper but were not real. Women in the USSR had little power.

We were keen to reciprocate, so were delighted when the Soviet committee accepted my invitation to come to this country. The four visitors were taken to schools, hospitals, and to a factory in the West Midlands where a majority of the workforce were women. In London we took them round Parliament and to see a play at the Barbican. I wanted to show them 'God's Own Country' so took them on a visit to the Yorkshire Dales. A highlight for them was a visit to Marks and Spencer, going through the lines of bras and pants. They also went back with boxes of chewing gum of differing flavours.

Two years later, accompanied by Beryl Roberts and Joy Mostyn, officers of the Labour women's national committee, I again paid a short visit to the Soviet Union. On this occasion we concentrated on women's employment, visiting factories, schools and hospitals. The majority of the women we met lived in the enormous ugly blocks of flats one saw everywhere. Housing was a serious problem, particularly for young couples; women often had to live with their in-laws. One woman told me that she wanted to leave her drunken violent husband, but had nowhere to go, so stayed with him and his parents.

This involvement in international affairs was particularly new for me. It gave me the opportunity to travel and meet so many fantastic women. I became the Labour Party representative on the International Council of Social Democratic Women (ICSDW), the women's arm of Socialist International. In 1978 it changed to its present name, Socialist International Women (SIW).

SIW is the largest and oldest international political women's organisation in the world, established in 1907, and currently comprises 139 women's organisations from 114 countries. It was and still is a non-government organisation with consultative status at the United Nations Economic and Social Council.

The outbreak of the Second World War made its work very difficult. In March 1941 Mary Sutherland, the Labour Party's chief women's officer, organised an International Women's Day event where comrades of the countries under fascist regimes made speeches in their mother tongue. This was to be the last international meeting of women until July 1955, when an event was held in London chaired by Edith Summerskill MP.

Fourteen years later I attended my first ICSDW conference in Eastbourne. It was my first international conference and the first time I wore headphones. At first I found it a little bewildering, but I had enormous admiration for the interpreters and the speed of their translation. Next was a trip to Geneva, my first as a full participant. I went on to participate in a series of biennial conferences and seminars. I became a member of the bureau and ultimately vice-president of the SIW.

The role of the bureau was to prepare resolutions for the conferences and meetings to consider. These working meetings were usually held in Brussels over a period of three days. All resolutions to be discussed were translated into English, regardless of their original language. This meant long discussions on the meaning of certain words. When the bureau members were satisfied the resolutions were translated into French, German and Spanish, being the main languages spoken by the delegates. I was pivotal in those discussions as an English speaker and became chair of the resolutions committee. I checked that the English translation was correct and that the final version didn't in any way corrupt the intention. The sessions normally went on into the early hours. Gin and tonic became my staple diet. At an event held to celebrate my retirement as chair of the resolutions committee, the question was asked if anyone could guess the amount of gin I had consumed. It appeared that I was never seen without a glass in my hand.

I was very honoured to be the key speaker at the SIW conference in Vancouver in 1979. I read a paper on 'Institutionalised Violence against Women' with the sub-heading 'Respect for Human Rights, Development and Peace'. It took me a considerable time to write. I was very conscious of the quality of the audience I was addressing. It was there that I learnt how important it was that what I believed from my Western perspective had a different relevance to women from other parts of the world, who were facing very different situations.

In my address I posed the question as to whether or not women should be on the front line in armed conflicts. The delegate from El Salvador, Ana Margharita Gateszoro, explained that she had to be on the front line fighting against the junta in her country. It was not a choice. She was young, beautiful, clever and passionate. Sadly later she was captured, imprisoned and tortured for her views. At home the women's committee campaigned strongly for her release, and to our delight she was released. That experience in no way made her give up the fight. A few years later she was killed fighting for the cause she believed in. Her story was a salutary lesson which has never left me. Every time I recall it I feel very humble and a little ashamed of myself, that with my comfortable existence I had not fully appreciated the great risks being faced by women in other parts of the world.

On leaving Vancouver I travelled overnight as I had to be in London the next day for the NEC organisation committee. Anxious about my ability to stay awake, Ian Mikardo MP, one of our members of the Socialist International delegation said, 'Have a glass of wine, take this sleeping tablet and you will sleep.' I did and woke up to hear the air hostess saying twenty minutes to landing.

There was a series of trips abroad to bureau meetings, on study tours and to biennial conferences. Two conferences were held in the UK: in London in 1980 on 'Feminism and Socialism' and in Sheffield in 1984 on 'Disarmament and Power'. The subject of the Sheffield conference was chosen to follow through the debate at a conference in Hamburg, when I spoke alongside Professor Mary Kaldor on the question of disarmament. Organising these conferences took a great deal of preparation, assisting Vera Matthias, the SIW secretariat. One of the biggest problems was ensuring that the speaker systems were in place and the interpreters booked.

The importance of the SIW conferences was that they were held alongside the major gatherings of the Socialist International (SI). I went to them with Jenny Little as part of the delegation from the UK. These were major conferences that brought together the leaders of socialist parties, some of whom were prime ministers, others leaders of the opposition.

The president of SI for most of my period of involvement was Willy Brandt, a previous Chancellor of West Germany. Brandt was president from 1976 to 1992. He was a strong supporter of Britain having joined the European Economic Community, and was chairman of the Brandt Commission on Economic Development. Its renowned report, 'North/South: A Programme for Survival' argued that the rich north should help countries in the poor southern hemisphere. It had great influence in the future of Aids funding.

It was an enormous privilege to meet and listen to such powerful politicians, such as Helmut Schmidt, Shimon Peres, Felipe González and Olof Palme, a man noted for his silent diplomacy. Palme's special advisor Bernt Carlsson was the general secretary of SI for seven years from 1976 to 1983. It was a real loss and a tragedy that he was a victim of the Lockerbie bombing in 1988. The following year Glenys Kinnock established the Bernt Carlsson Trust, also known as One World Action, in his memory, to give support to third world countries.

Jean Corston, now my colleague in the Lords, reminded me of an occasion when I returned from an SI conference in great excitement. I told Kevin about all the 'famous' people I had met. He brought me down to earth by informing me that we had acquired a new secretary for our local ward party.

CHAPTER 8

THE BIG DIVIDE

I attended my first meeting of the NEC on 28 September 1975. I was thrilled to be sitting at the same table as these important persons who ran the party and the country. This for me was a new and exciting experience.

Even though I was aware of the serious political differences between the members of the executive, I had no idea of the way they behaved to each other. Any illusion I had that there was a degree of courtesy and comradeship was soon shattered. I had over my twenty-five years in the party listened to, and at times participated in, arguments and debates, with substantial differences of opinion. I had heard harsh words aired but I had never experienced this level of antagonism, or the degree of bitterness and vitriol that almost bordered on hatred. The petty comments and unfriendly banter seemed on occasions to descend into madness. There will always be different views and opinions in political discourse but I thought the public denouncement of a Labour government by senior and leading members of the party, based on personal attacks, completely unacceptable.

The decision-making process relied little on substance and

debate and more on conspiracies, slates and views taken at caucus meetings. It was spurred on by the number of warring left- and right-wing pressure groups within the party. Groups were set up to counter each other. The Tribune Group, the Campaign for Labour Party Democracy, the Rank and File Mobilising Committee, Trade Unions for a Labour Victory, the St Ermin's Group, Solidarity, the PLP Campaign Group and so on. It is almost impossible to convey the splits, cock-ups and stupidities. This lasted in differing and in varying ways almost until I retired at Easter in 1993. Which not by accident coincided with the last traces of the Militant Tendency being expunged from the party, which had been a creeping distraction within the party.

The National Executive at that time was equally divided between those on the right and those on the left of the party. Who attended the meetings of the executive and its committees was absolutely crucial. At a meeting held in 1977 following a bad, snowy winter, Dennis Skinner's vote was considered to be the decider so he had to attend, even though he had fallen off his bike in the icy conditions and suffered a hairline skull fracture. He became ill in the meeting and I was asked by Jim Callaghan to look after him and find a way of getting him home to Bolsover. Jim offered his own car and driver. Dennis was adamant that he would not in any way take a free ride. It took a long time for me to persuade him to accept the PM's car, which he did only as long as he paid for the petrol and the driver's time.

This was a rare example of respect for another colleague in spite of political differences. Eric Heffer's behaviour stands out as representing the opposite. At times it was irrational. He seemed to be permanently on edge and would lose his cool on a regular basis. What I found hard to understand was that he was aware of this erratic behaviour and had tried to control it without success. Eric had been a devout Christian since childhood, having been a choir boy in his local church, and would whisper in my ear that he had been to church that morning and prayed to stay calm.

There was a particular bitterness between Eric and John Golding MP, who had the capacity to wind him up. On one occasion after he had threatened to throw John out of a third-floor window at Walworth Road, Eric put his head in his hands and for all to hear said, 'This morning I went to church, I prayed to God that he would give me tolerance.' John Golding was a product of Old Labour, the political officer of the Post Office Engineering Union, and MP for Newcastle-under-Lyme. As convenor of the loyalist group on the executive he played a major part in the demise of the hard left, of which he was a fierce and tenacious opponent.

Eric believed that sucking mints would somehow help to keep him calm. I attempted to help him by keeping him supplied with Polo mints. They didn't work. At a well-reported policy sub-committee meeting, John Golding was deliberately delaying decisions being taken by speaking on every issue. Members became irritated at his behaviour. Eric was particularly frustrated and became more and more agitated. Eventually, he gathered up his papers and stood up to leave, saying, 'I'm fed up with this f****** idiot, I'm going.' Unfortunately for Eric the meeting was held in a room in the Commons we had not used before, and in his fluster he forgot which door was the way out. He opened one door which turned out to be a cupboard, then tried another, whereupon a broom fell out and hit him on the head.

'Oh f*** it,' he said, sat down and got re-engaged in his intem-perate way in the arguments going on around him.

My own experience of Eric's wrath came when the annual conference voted him off the executive committee. The party had purchased its first computer. I can still picture five of us standing in the finance department looking at this machine. It was a complete mystery to me how it worked but what I wanted to know was how we could use it to help the party's campaign-ing. I was enthusiastic about how it might be used even though I didn't understand how it worked. I supported Computing for Labour in its efforts to bring the party into the modern age. On retirement I became their chair and now I am a life member.

One of the ways I thought it would be useful at conference was counting the ballot for the election of the executive. At the time, each vote was recorded on large sheets of squared paper and totalled up manually. Our first attempt to use the computer was in 1983. We recorded the votes into the computer on the Monday night. The totals were not to be added up until the next morning in case of a leak of the result before it was officially announced. Unfortunately, a voluntary scrutineer had added the figures up, and informed the media of the result.

I was not at all happy, having been up most of the night overseeing the count, to be woken up at 6.30 a.m. by a scream-ing Eric Heffer who had just heard from the press that he had lost his place on the executive. He firmly believed that it had been leaked by a member of staff. It was all a right-wing plot, he told the next meeting of the executive, a view supported by Tony Benn. After the outbursts were over I informed the NEC that computers would continue to be used but that the count would take place on the Tuesday morning and the results immediately announced.

In one of our more amiable conversations Eric confided in me that he was a feminist. His explanation for this belief was that he did the hoovering for his wife Doris.

My colleagues and I discussed our thoughts in private. How do we handle the chaos surrounding us? At the end of the day, however, we had a job to do, so we put our heads down and got on with it. All we could do was to try to encourage party members to continue campaigning and promoting the party. The number of members willing to do that was diminishing. This provided the opportunity for the local parties, particularly in safe Labour areas, to be systematically targeted by the more extreme fringe elements in the party.

The NEC were made fully aware of the level of unrest but many members chose to ignore it. The trade unions attempted to be a stabilising force. Their great anxiety was whether the party had the capacity to fight a campaign and win the next general election. This prompted David Basnett, general secretary of the General and Municipal Workers' Union, to call on the NEC to examine the party's finances and organisation, a proposal that was rejected. In the words of John Golding, 'the NEC could hardly be expected to acknowledge its own incompetence'.

It was obvious to me that the party organisation needed a major overhaul, but every proposal that was suggested was treated with suspicion. Eventually David Basnett persisted and with the backing of all the major trade union general secretaries he persuaded party conference that a review be held under a commission of inquiry. This was supposedly another right-wing plot;

Tony Benn contradicts that belief in his diaries, however, in identifying the political breakdown of the commission members as ten on the left against four on the right.

David Basnett, Michael Foot and Eric Heffer were appointed as co-chairs of the commission of inquiry. The party's general secretary, Ron Hayward, and I were its secretariat. As so often happens, I as the junior member of the team ended up with all the responsibility. To be fair, Ron took no credit for the outcome. That is not always the case.

There were fierce rows over the membership of the commission. This was not helped by Sid Weighell, general secretary of the National Union of Railwaymen, who wrote in the *News of the World* of Tony Benn and Heffer: 'These men must go, they couldn't run a fish and chip shop.' Recalling Sid Weighell, however, takes me to the 1982 party conference, when he voted against the decision of his union on the membership of the National Executive Committee. He was expected to vote for the National Union of Mineworkers, led by Arthur Scargill, but Sid secretly voted for the Electrical and Engineering trade union (EETPU). When the result of the vote was announced there was bedlam in the conference. Sid came to the rostrum and blamed the staff who had counted the ballots. As I had been in charge of the counting of the vote I took it personally. Some of the scrutineers were in tears. When challenged and the evidence produced showing his change of vote, he was made to apologise and branded a cheat. Later he had to resign as the general secretary of his trade union.

Three working groups were set up, to consider finance, membership and organisation, and political education respectively. Clive

Jenkins, general secretary of the Association of Scientific, Technical and Managerial Staffs (ASTMS), chaired the finance group; Moss Evans, general secretary of the Transport and General Workers' Union (TGWU), chaired membership and organisation; and Tony Benn chaired political education. Some 2,500 pieces of evidence were received – I had expected a big response but not such an avalanche of documents. Conferences were held throughout the country, all of which I attended. After a year's deliberation recommendations on all these issues were arrived at. I would have liked to get the views and thoughts of the members for this book about whether or not the commission had any value, but every one of them has since died.

The NEC were not normally vocal in their thanks to the staff so I was very surprised to see the eulogy to me included by the co-chairs in the final report:

> The commission records its warm appreciation of the invaluable assistance given by Ron Hayward and Joyce Gould. In particular gratitude must be expressed too for the outstanding contribution made by Joyce Gould, who organised and collated the vast amount of written and oral evidence received at the regional conferences in such a way that the commission had a clear picture of the views of everyone who had taken trouble to give them. Without the hard work and efficiency of Joyce and her staff the commission could not possibly have completed its task in the time.

It was an enormous piece of work, on which I spent many hours of my time, evenings and weekends. One of the rewards was that every Monday, the chairs of the commission and I met for lunch in a very good restaurant in Soho.

On the surface, everyone seemed to be harmoniously working together, that was until we came to the discussion on the three constitutional issues: the election of the party leader, the mandatory re-selection of MPs and responsibility for writing the general election manifesto. These issues were seen by the left as the major reasons for having the commission, whilst others saw it as a means of improving the party machine.

On Friday 13 June 1980 we all met for a weekend at White-hall College, the ASTMS's training college in Bishop's Stortford. There was tight security with policemen patrolling the grounds. The college was very luxurious with a swimming pool and a sauna, and was situated in beautiful surroundings with extensive sweeping lawns. It is reputed that Clive Jenkins bought some goldfish for the water garden especially for the weekend. During the first break in our deliberations I went on writing my notes of the first short session, but a number went for a swim including Jim Callaghan. He no doubt needed the calm of the pool for the chaotic sessions that lay ahead.

Before the evening session, we had drinks and a merry time was had by all. The peace was not to last. The session, on the difficult subject of mandatory re-selection of MPs, started at about 8 p.m. The motion that all sitting MPs should face re-selection before re-election was moved by Eric Heffer. It wasn't long before the remarks became abusive; any attempt on my part to take notes was impossible, I would not have wanted to record the language used. Tempers flared, and Jim Callaghan's anger was evident. He picked up his papers and walked out and the session broke up.

I followed Jim out of the room and, finding him ready to pack his bags, realised that his intention was to leave. I persuaded him to stay. For him to leave would have been disastrous. On return the motion was carried.

The next morning, it might have been sunny outside but the clouds once again gathered in the meeting. This time the consideration was on the election of the leader of the party. There were two contradictory opening motions: Michael Foot for the status quo, selection by members of the Parliamentary Labour Party, and Jo Richardson for an electoral college made up of trade unions, party members and MPs. I sat there wondering what the electorate would make of it if they were in my position listening to these warring factions.

Jim's view was that 'if you make these changes, you will have a break with the Parliamentary Labour Party, there will be a wave of national resistance, we shall not win the next election'. Two and a half hours' discussion resulted in support for an electoral college but no decision on its proportions between the trade unions, constituency parties and MPs. There then followed another heated debate on which no decision was taken, this time on who should be responsible for writing the manifesto for the general election. It was left for the NEC to decide.

Finally, the next day the commission got down to discussing the recommendations from the working groups, which were all accepted. The most important of these were an increase in membership fees and a new method of controlling the party's finances. Recommended was a change to the constitution of the party to introduce registered Labour supporters, who would pay £1 a year without any membership rights. This proposal was later rejected by the party conference. It is ironic that the party conference in 2013 accepted that on a payment of £3, registered members will receive the right to vote for the leader of the party and be full participants at party meetings. I do not think I was wrong when I argued that this decision meant we could again be faced with the problem of entryism and division.

A full report of the weekend's findings was presented to the executive committee. They took the decision that the three controversial constitutional issues should be considered separately at conference, and not be part of the commission report. This meant that I ended up writing a rather bland, even boring document. Its twenty recommendations were put to the conference and carried with little dissent.

Conference was a battleground. There was a feeling of antagonism towards MPs, which meant providing extra stewards where the MPs sat. First to be discussed was the re-selection of MPs. The exchanges were bitter. Joe Ashton, MP for Bassetlaw, pointed out, 'If you sack MPs, they will fight back. They get £12,000 for standing and losing.' The most surprising speech was from Sam McCluskie, leader of the seamen's union, who started by giving the impression he was opposing the concept, but staggered everyone by concluding: 'But I will tell you, I am convinced now by the arguments that mandatory re-selection is the answer. It can control the arrogance of the MPs in their relations with the constituency party.' His comments caused great anger amongst the MPs in the hall. Mandatory re-selection was carried.

After a year's work and hours and hours of controversy, no agreement was reached on the proportions for the electoral college

Joyce in her straight-down dress with a young friend

As a teenager with best friend Pamela

The young couple

With daughter Jeannette, then aged nine months

Celebration of the
suffragettes in the
Co-operative store
in Leeds

The conference
platform 1981 –
Jim Callaghan
and Ron Hayward

The conference
platform 1984 –
Neil Kinnock as
the new leader

With Valentina Tereshkova in the Soviet Union

The Women's Festival 1982

Supporting the
miner's wives with
Glynis Kinnock,
Anne Scargill and Jo
Richardson, 1984

With Eric Heffer
in South Yorkshire
supporting the miner's
families, 1984

Working with Larry
Whitty, the general
secretary, 1985

Joyce and
her staff

At a party with
Jeannette, Michael
Foot and Stan
Orme, 1983

On the platform
the day John
Smith became
the leader, 1992

Joyce with Roger
Hough and the Big
Red Book at her
retirement party

'Witchfinder general' keeps low profile

JOYCE GOULD, who brought the charges against Dave Nellist and Terry Fields, is an unlikely "witchfinder general", according to members of Labour's National Executive Committee, which heard her evidence yesterday.

"She is pleasant and personable, decent and fair," one NEC member said.

"It's deceptive," said another Labour MP who has seen her in action. "She would have made a good QC and her cross-examinations are brilliant. She lets people think they are on top and suddenly the trap door opens. They hang themselves."

The party's national organiser rarely gives interviews. Paul Sharry, Mr Nellist's agent, said yesterday that he had not met Mrs Gould and would not recognise her in Walworth Road, the Labour Party's headquarters, where the hearings took place. He said she had not interviewed Mr Nellist in compiling the dossier of evidence against him.

Mrs Gould broke her normal anonymity by giving a short television interview after taking on the task of inquiring into the alleged Militant links of the two Labour MPs, which could lead to their expulsions from the party. The impression was of a party apparatchik whose time had come.

Tony Jennings, leader of Broad Left, which supported Leslie Mahmoud's rebel stand against Labour in the Walton by-election, said Mrs Gould had said very little when she carried her investigation to Liverpool.

"She came and took notes but I did not hear her speak," he said.

Mrs Gould's husband was a footballer on Merseyside, a connection colleagues say gave her a valuable insight for her inquiries in Liverpool and Birkenhead, which could continue for many months.

Dozens of photographs were taken by Labour campaigners in the Walton by-election of alleged Militant sympathisers in the party who went to Walton to support Mrs Mahmoud.

In her fifties, Mrs Gould is committed to Neil Kinnock's *perestroika*. Her daughter, Jeanette, works at the Commons for Kevin Barron, a progressive mining MP who was Mr Kinnock's parliamentary private secretary and has clashed with Arthur Scargill's leadership of the NUM.

"It was thought she only got that job because the NEC wanted a woman," one insider said.

The Witchfinder General

Labour Organiser
Issue 651 April 1993 Volume 69

The end of an era

Joyce Gould leaves Walworth Road *see page 9*

A farewell from the
Labour Organiser

Day of introduction in October 1993, with Jeannette and brothers David and Louis

Class of '93: the John
Smith nominees, Joyce
with Brenda Dean and
Simon Haskel

Tony Blair and the
government whips
in the Lords, 1997

As part of Margaret
Jay's team when
Leader of the Lords

Honorary degree day
at Bradford University,
with Chancellor and
friend Betty Lockwood

Section 28: the
winning score

At the United
Nations with
deputy secretary
general Asha-Rose
Misiro and jurist
Margaret Owen

Speaking at an
international sexual
health conference in
New York

On the Lords'
terrace with Betty
Boothroyd and new
MP Dr Peter Kyle

to elect the leader of the party. It was agreed that a special conference be called in January the following year. It was held on 24 January 1981 in Wembley.

Prior to the conference 370 organisations had sent in more than 200 differing proposals on the way we should elect our leader. Everyone had their own views as to how the conference should be conducted, David Hughes, the national agent, and I were given no real guidance, certainly not by the National Executive. The executive members continued to bicker amongst themselves, and the various factions and the trade unions argued on what was the best outcome for them. Conference had to decide between seven options but only three had any real credibility.

Each of the options was voted on one at a time. For me the day was horrendous. I had two jobs that day. The first one involved holding up a board giving the suggested proportions for the electoral college. I felt extremely stupid standing on the platform, board in hand. The votes of the delegates were collected by tellers, going through the hall with their ballot boxes. Then for my second job I went backstage to supervise the ballot boxes being emptied and the votes being counted by the scrutineers. This of course took some time. With no other business, the arguments and rows between the delegates continued. There was one time when the noise was so loud that I had to ask the chair of conference for a little quiet, but to no avail. Five minutes later the delegates had become even more rowdy and vitriolic.

In spite of the chaos, the conference did come to a decision. This gave 40 per cent of the total vote to the trade unions and 30 per cent each to party members and MPs. A proposal of one member, one vote (OMOV) was heavily defeated. It was eventually agreed when John Smith became party leader in 1992, as was the elimination of mandatory re-selection of MPs.

The outcome was the immediate resignation from the party of thirteen MPs followed by a steady flow of other MPs and peers leaving to join the Council for Social Democracy. On 26 May 1981 the Council for Social Democracy became the Social Democratic Party (SDP). My thoughts concentrated on how many others would leave and join this new mainly middle-class party. What became known after the event was that there had been detailed planning on the setting up of the new party by the 'Gang of Four', Shirley Williams, Roy Jenkins, David Owen MP and Bill Rodgers MP long before the special conference. It appears that their only dilemma was whether to split straight after that conference or wait until the national party conference later in the year.

Who else was going to desert the party? There were some surprises amongst the twenty-nine MPs who defected but none greater than Tom McNally, Jim Callaghan's political advisor. Speculation was rife, but the leakage stopped. The leadership of the SDP had underestimated the deep-felt loyalty and commitment to the party even from those such as Roy Hattersley, Bernard Donoughue and John Golding who supported their concerns.

Maybe my colleagues and I were a little slow in not taking sufficient notice of the 1979 Dimbleby lecture by Roy Jenkins when he advocated a re-alignment in British politics, through a new group as he said 'driven by European principles of social democracy'. The signs of a possible split were all there. They can be traced back to the ideological divisions of the 1950s, to the opposition to the perceived left-wing shift of policy and to the arguments that only a new type of politics would save the Labour Party. But I still find it difficult to understand how long-standing members could break away and attempt to destroy the Labour Party and form a new party.

Losing the 1979 general election provided another ground for the continuing battles in the party. It was my first general election as part of the national campaign team. I worked with the regional staff to develop the level of activity within the constituencies. One of my initiatives was putting extra resources and efforts into marginal seats and for the first time identifying different categories of voters. I and my colleagues had planned for an election towards the end of 1978. But Jim Callaghan chose to carry on into 1979. I assumed he hoped that the extra time would help him claw back the Tories' ten-point lead.

Jim indicated his intentions not to call the expected election at the TUC congress by giving a rendition of the song 'Waiting at the Church'. It wasn't, however, until his broadcast on 7 September that there was absolute certainty. My campaign team were devastated. The trade unions knew that difficulties were to follow.

As part of the development of the strategy for the campaign, I called a meeting of the regional staff, to be held in the East Midlands. I was driven up by my colleague Walter Brown. I never got there. Just outside Rugby the car overturned on the motorway. Walter came out unscathed but I suffered an injury to my back and was taken to hospital in Rugby. It was decided that as I was having my period I could not be X-rayed. The young doctor on duty suggested I be put on a train and sent home. Thankfully the sister said no. Ultimately the X-rays showed I had fractured two vertebrae in my back. I am grateful to the sister for her persistence. I do believe that I could have ended up being crippled for life had the doctor had his way.

Jeannette and Kevin came to visit as I lay on my back. I became more and more bored as the weeks went by. I could not be sent home, as the ambulance staff were on strike and were only dealing with emergencies, which I clearly was not. I appealed to Reg Underhill, the national agent, for help. He sent out a request: did anyone have a car with a front seat that went flat? My West Midlands colleague Wally Burley responded. I was laid flat in his car encased in cushions and we set off down to London in thick snow. At some point we had to turn off to find a garage to mend the windscreen wipers, which had collapsed under the weight of the snow. Lying there and being too low down to see anything was a hair-raising experience. Eventually we arrived at my flat in West Hampstead, and I was put into a bed which had been moved into our enormous front room. Kevin's mother Lily came down from Leeds to look after me. She made Wally a meal and gave him a bottle of whisky and he departed back to the West Midlands. The weather had got even worse and he drove all the way behind a snow plough. This was a real gesture of kindness on Wally's part. I returned to work after six weeks to find to my surprise that my staff had re-decorated my office. It was a huge improvement and a kind gesture which I fully appreciated.

I vowed not to travel with Walter Brown again. I did so only once. He drove me and David Hughes back from party conference in Blackpool. Walter had stayed up late the night before. We stopped at every service station and talked non-stop to make sure he stayed awake.

There was strike action over pay policy by lorry drivers, by ambulance workers, by health service staff and by refuse collectors, resulting in black sacks piling up in the streets. The tabloids reported that bodies were lying unburied in mortuaries, although there was no real evidence that that was true. We all still remember the lasting images of the 'Winter of Discontent'. David Blunkett recollected it, and I quote, 'with a shiver up their spine', along with Jim Callaghan's supposed reaction: 'Crisis, what crisis?', three words that it is alleged helped bring down the Labour government, even though Jim did not in fact say them. They were the words of a *Sun* journalist. What Jim actually said, on his return from a visit to Guadeloupe, was, 'I don't think other people in the world would share the view that there is mounting chaos.'

There were enormous bitter rows when it came to drawing up the manifesto for the election. I found myself sitting through meetings lasting until midnight and later. We ended with a manifesto that was acceptable to the Prime Minister, based on the government's record. To the left it was seen as a 'betrayal', resulting in a number of senior party members making speeches opposing their own government. They had no concern for the consequences for the party, its membership and supporters.

We still had hopes, somewhat misjudged, that we might scrape home. The Tories won with a majority of forty-three seats. It began eighteen years of Conservative government.

On election night, trade union general secretaries and other senior members of the party were invited to head office to listen to the results. I always seemed to have the responsibility to see that all went smoothly. It wasn't easy. We watched the results on the television and were hugely disappointed. Jim's team was due to come back from his constituency in Cardiff that night but we heard that they intended to stay in Wales. At 3.30 a.m. and being aware that they were leaving empty bedrooms at St Ermin's Hotel, we decided to take them over rather than trailing home.

I settled down into bed in my hotel room, which had been designated for Derek Gladwin, Jim's campaign manager. I was fortunate to have a nightdress with me, for at about 6 a.m. the door opened and in walked Derek. He had decided to come back to London on his own. We sat and talked until it was time for me to get up. I made him turn his back. I escaped to the bathroom, dressed, and we went down to breakfast together. The waitress clearly had her own views about us, saying rather snootily, 'I only have one person staying in that room.' She did help to lighten our gloom, Derek took great delight in telling his colleagues without explanation that I had a beautiful black nightie.

It was expected that Jim would resign having lost the election, but he stayed on as leader for some eighteen months, and suffered the wrath of those who blamed him for the loss. It was extremely uncomfortable sitting on the platform at the 1980 national party conference hearing the chair, Frank Allaun MP, declaring that the election was lost 'because the parliamentary leadership ignored the wishes of both the TUC and Labour Party conference'. Unheard of, but even Ron Hayward in a heated speech also put all the blame on the government. Those comments may have had to be said, but the where and when they were said mattered, and we still had a party to get into power.

A month later, on 15 October 1980, Jim resigned. The electoral college described above was not yet in force, so the election of the leader was still being decided by Labour MPs. For the following four weeks nothing else was talked about but who was going to stand. The favourite was Denis Healey, whilst on the left the speculation was whether Michael Foot would stand. He was persuaded to do so. On 10 November, he became leader and Denis his deputy.

I had hoped that the combination of Michael and Denis would bring some sanity to the party. Initially there was a period of calm, and a concentration of activity to challenge the Conservative government. I became secretary of a newly formed campaign committee with Joan Maynard MP as the chair. Its aim was to get our voice heard by the electors up and down the country. We held demonstrations, rallies and other public events. We also held policy action weeks throughout the country, using differing themes dependent on what was relevant to the area. Merlyn Rees, MP for Leeds South, took responsibility for a Festival of Labour event in Roundhay Park. I encouraged him that we should hold it in Leeds, so I could go back to my home city, bringing with me the Labour Party in a festive mood.

Major marches and rallies were held on unemployment in Cardiff, Glasgow and Birmingham, climaxing in a major demo of 150,000 in Liverpool. It was at that demonstration that I first met David Lea from the TUC. In exhaustion I shared his flask of whisky. I don't like whisky. To engage MPs directly I organised a demo led by Gerald Kaufman MP, our opposition spokesperson for employment. We walked from Westminster to the Department of Employment. Party members and supporters travelled by bus and special trains to take part. We set off with our banners, Gerald leading the way. A gold-braided policeman held up his hand and said to Gerald, 'Sir, do put down your banner. There is a restriction on demonstrating within sight of Parliament.' Gerald was not pleased and was not inclined to do so, but I told him it would not help our cause if he decided to be difficult.

I felt it was critical that the difficulties women were facing as a result of government action were highlighted. I organised a women's week of activity, a rally and a lobby of MPs. I persuaded the party to devote a party political broadcast on the growing number of women becoming unemployed. To encourage local parties to organise their own campaigns and events, with the help of my regional colleagues I held some twenty-two consultations throughout the country and held planning meetings at the party conferences in the build-up to the 1983 general election.

It was expected that the party would deselect the sitting Brent East MP Reg Freeson in favour of Ken Livingstone, but come election time I was in the midst of a six-month investigation into breaches of the rules by the local party and the NEC imposed Freeson. The media were so sure that Ken was to be the candidate that he appeared in some of their journals as the selected candidate. Many of the journals had to be re-printed.

I must have established my credentials with the NEC for they gave me the responsibility of leading a delegation to Jersey and Guernsey. I was accompanied by John Cartwright MP and Arthur Latham MP. They represented the differing political strands in the party, John on the right, Arthur on the left. The NEC had decided that they wanted to know more about the islands: the structure of their administrations, their economic bases, their policies on industrial relations, housing policies, social security and health as well as their dependency on services provided from the UK. They rather farcically decided that a future Labour government would remove the islands' tax haven status. How that was to be achieved was never discussed.

Working through the south-west region of the TGWU, I arranged visits in Jersey and Guernsey. We met members of the chambers of commerce, the directors of social services, health and education, and trade unionists. In Jersey we also met with the Jersey Democratic Movement.

The two islands were very different in style and culture. Guernsey was more similar to the UK, with a small number of Labour councillors, who were our hosts whilst we were there. Jersey, however, was very different. The tension felt by the islanders, as we stepped off the plane, was evident. This Labour delegation was here to remove their tax haven status. We were met by all the local media, and appeared on every news broadcast that evening. Nevertheless we were welcomed formally and with courtesy and all the requests I had made were met. We had no difficulty in meeting the senior officials, the police, and health and education staff. Whilst there were no Labour councillors in Jersey the left was represented by a longstanding Communist councillor.

I assumed I knew no one on the islands, forgetting that my friend from the past Harry Patterson (Jack Higgins) lived in Jersey. Harry had seen me step off the plane and immediately called my hotel to fix a time for us to meet, which we did. I enjoyed seeing him again and drinking gin and tonic by his pool. The second contact was someone my brother Louis had worked with, a very wealthy tax exile. He offered us the use of his helicopter.

Arthur Latham wanted us to take up his offer but I declined on behalf of the delegation. I could imagine the reaction of the media to this Labour Party delegation flying about in a helicopter belonging to a tax exile.

I wrote copious notes, as this was to be my first major report to the NEC. That time was wasted for the report was never completed. John Cartwright defected to the SDP and the mission to the Channel Islands turned out to be a pleasant and interesting busy holiday but nothing more.

By 1982, the political make-up of the NEC started to change towards the centre. But irrespective the battles continued to rage not least over the writing of the manifesto for the 1983 election, 'The New Hope for Britain'. It was famously deemed by Gerald Kaufman the 'longest suicide note in history'. The election ended with our worst defeat since 1931, with only 27.6 per cent of the vote. This followed a steady decline in Labour's vote since the 1970s.

The election campaign was dogged by an abundance of mistakes and a lack of coherence. We came back to our old headquarters in Smith Square for our campaign meetings, with sometimes thirty or more people round the table. Many efforts were made to have a small campaign committee established, without conclusion because of disagreements as to who should be on it. Eventually it was established but too late and too large to have any major influence on the direction of the campaign.

After one such meeting, in despair Gerald Kaufman and I went back with Roy Hattersley to his home nearby. We discussed if anything could be done to get some degree of professionalism and structure into the campaign. The only success I had was when I managed to get an agreement that we should concentrate on the marginal seats. The response was 'If you want to do that, get on with it', so I did.

Michael Foot spoke at a large number of public meetings, meetings that attracted huge audiences. Michael's passionate speeches were always worth listening to. The large numbers at these meetings were interpreted that we were doing well. My own interpretation was that it was Labour supporters gathering together for warmth.

Significant was the conversation I had with John Golding. He recalls in his book *Hammer of the Left*, and I quote, that one of his most vivid memories of the campaign was 'my telling her in a corridor that I would lose my seat if I did not get back to Newcastle [-under-Lyme] and into the clubs and on the streets'. That was the reality. Going through the archives in Manchester, I found a paper I had written following the election, in which I highlighted the defects in the campaign, the inefficiencies, the lack of organisation in many constituencies and the inaccurate canvassing returns. No wonder we got it so wrong.

I reported to the National Executive my thoughts about the campaign, and the changes that were necessary: a need for a training programme for voluntary organisations, brighter and more positive publicity materials, more local activity and involvement of members in the decision-making processes of the party. I touched upon the image presented by our national conferences. Seen as most controversial of all by my colleagues was my contention that we should employ part-time organisers to help build the organisation of the party, a view opposed by the National Union of Labour Organisers.

Prior to the election it was me and my staff who had initiated and driven our campaigning activities, with little interest from our employers. I was determined that we should keep on campaigning afterwards. Immediately after the election Jim Parish from the publicity department and I asked the executive if we could spend the princely sum of £10 on an old ambulance from a scrapyard, to use in a campaign on the need to save the NHS. The NHS was our only policy that we felt could influence the electorate. I think the executive were amused. We went ahead and bought our ambulance and did it up. That poor old ambulance travelled many miles as it went round the country.

I took a personal decision to visit ten seats where we should have had a better result, to find out what went wrong. I made my first visit to Leeds West, having previously worked hard to get Joe Dean elected. It was particularly distressing to see him lose to the Liberal Michael Meadowcroft. The meeting was held in Leeds Civic Hall. When I left I was nearly in tears. They had put out just one leaflet each week, Joe Dean had been out of the constituency for part of the time and the agent had taken a week off during the campaign. No wonder we lost.

In October 1983 Michael Foot resigned and the contest for our new leader began. There were four contenders, Neil Kinnock, Roy Hattersley, Eric Heffer and Peter Shore. Neil was the clear favourite. He won, getting 71.77 per cent of the vote. Roy, in second place with 19.28 per cent, became our deputy leader. They were the 'dream ticket' that was going to take the party into the 1987 general election and win. Neil then became the longest-serving leader of the opposition in British political history.

CHAPTER 9

<∢•⊶>

TURBULENT
TIMES

Things were about to change. Hopes were high. I am not
sure that the new leader and his deputy had fully appreciated the extent of the task or the enormous level of disruption
they were facing. The party lurched from one crisis to another.
Some party members on all sides of the debate did not seem to
care about the consequence of their actions. The desire to try
and make a difference and to begin a programme of change was
shattered. Margaret Thatcher was determined to close down coal
mines across the country. There was the fiasco that followed
the introduction of rate capping for local authorities and the
Tory introduction of the community charge (the poll tax). These
Tory policies should have provided Labour in opposition with
a golden opportunity, but each time they blew it.

How to react to industrial disputes has always been a dilemma
for the Labour Party. Getting it wrong could be electorally dam-
aging. In 1984 Arthur Scargill had been the president of the
National Union of Mineworkers (NUM) for two years. He firmly

believed that the fight back against the policies of the Conservative government would inevitably take place outside rather than inside Parliament. Scargill called the miners out on strike. Even though he supported the 'case for coal' Neil Kinnock made a public appeal for the NUM to hold a ballot. He did not make his criticisms public until after the strike was over. Then he said, 'The strike wore on, the violence built up because the single tactic chosen was that of mass picketing and so we saw policing on a scale and with a system that has never been seen in Britain before.' Neil went on to ask the question 'how did the position arise?' 'The man from the Lodge in my constituency said, "It arose because nobody really thought it out."'

Margaret Thatcher's initial plan was to close twenty pits. Scargill claimed that the government had a longer-term plan to shut down seventy. This was vehemently denied by the government, who claimed that Scargill was deceiving his members. In the end Scargill was proved to be right and the pits did close.

I was fully in support of the decision of the NEC that, throughout the dispute, it re-affirmed its support for the miners. It called on local parties to raise money, suggesting the introduction of a 50p minimum weekly levy. It seemed like a small amount but it did raise millions of pounds for the hard-pressed miners.

Stan Orme was Labour's shadow energy spokesperson. He was chair of the Amalgamated Engineering and Electrical Union (AEEU) group of MPs and later chair of the Parliamentary Labour Party. He was given the job of trying to establish a basis for discussions between the NUM and the National Coal Board (NCB). My daughter Jeannette was his parliamentary researcher and was with him throughout. She was fully involved in those negotiations, as she was with the discussions between Stan and the party leader. In Parliament Stan attacked the government for its outrageous handling of the dispute and worked valiantly to get Scargill and Ian MacGregor, chair of the NCB, to talk – but to no avail. It was obvious that the government were not prepared to consider any compromise settlement.

The confrontation at the Orgreave coking plant in South Yorkshire between 5,000 miners and the same number of police in the summer of 1984 broke into violence after police on horseback with drawn truncheons charged the miners. Fifty-one pickets and seventy-two policemen were injured. Although it was denied at the time, it was a premeditated and unprovoked attack by the police on the workers. Jo Richardson MP, when replying to the debate on the strike at the party conference, showed the pictures of a policeman on horseback, truncheon ready. I thought it was disgraceful that the media refused to show these pictures and tell the real story of what was happening in the mining villages. A cartoon of the incident was on sale. I purchased a copy which still hangs on my wall at home.

From the start of the strike, the women's organisation of the party worked with the miners' wives, who had established a network of support groups. We appealed for financial donations as well as practical support such as food, clothes and toys. The miners' wives organised thousands of collections outside supermarkets, set up communal kitchens, and held benefit concerts and a whole range of activities to raise money. Items displaying the symbol of the Miners Union were produced by companies who supported the miners, one of which was a full tea set, which

I purchased, and although I have never used it, it is a reminder of those strife-ridden times.

After discussion with the executive and the NUM, Audrey Wise MP and I met frequently with the support groups to look at ways we might give them more help. I regularly went up to South Yorkshire and I have a photograph of myself and Eric Heffer behind a table helping to distribute the goods that had been received. At Christmas we made a special appeal to raise funds for hampers and presents for the children.

The extent of the hardship suffered by the families was made worse by the government's inhuman and primitive treatment of the miners' families. They stopped £15 in social security benefits, denied discretionary maternity benefits for mothers and delayed the payment of supplementary benefits, and refused miners the support that they should have been able to expect from the statutory bodies. The government's bizarre reasoning was that they had received gifts of food and essentials and therefore did not qualify.

Along with Jo Richardson and Glenys Kinnock I headed a march across London, organised by Women against Pit Closures. We were joined by many thousands of women from all parts of the country. An important development for those miners' wives who had never before been in the vanguard of any such activity was that they learnt the ability to stand up and tell everyone what was happening to them and their families. Many became brilliant speakers on public platforms.

Slowly the miners drifted back to work and the strike ended on 3 March 1985, three weeks short of a year after it had started. The miners disunited had been defeated, and whole communities destroyed. In several pits on the day their wives organised the distribution of carnations at the gates as the miners marched back to work following the music of brass bands. The strike had two consequences, one negative and one positive. The former was the diminishing of the power of the trade unions and the latter was the growth in support for the party. Labour was well ahead in the polls, party activity was increasing and attendance at meetings was high.

Not all miners had agreed with the strike, particularly in Nottinghamshire. The Union of Democratic Mineworkers (UDM) was formed as a breakaway from the NUM. In November I went with Stan Orme to Sherwood to meet the UDM. We were joined by Willie Bach, now Lord Bach, the then prospective parliamentary candidate for Sherwood. It was an unfortunate and angry encounter. The UDM felt that their views in opposing the strike had not been listened to. Tragically, in 1991 the Tory government completed its ambition and closed down most of the remaining collieries, causing further hardship to families in those mining villages, from which many have never recovered.

The government then capped the level of rates determined by local councils. It gave rise to the biggest rebellion of Labour-controlled councils against the government. Inevitably it developed into a bitter battle within the party, between councillors who were initially prepared to break the law, in their challenge to this piece of legislation, and not set a budget for the financial year 1985/6, and those that fundamentally disagreed with not breaking the law.

Neil Kinnock was adamant that there was no way he could support illegal action. Meanwhile Sheffield City Council, at a meeting of Labour council leaders, adopted an attitude of non-compliance; in the words of David Blunkett, then leader of the council, 'collective action, achieving government retreat, not martyrdom is the objective'. The national party conference later that year agreed with illegal budgeting. This was despite an appeal by the leader not to do so.

There was serious dissent amongst the councillors in the fifteen Labour councils who were acting illegally. I found myself inundated by claims of disruption and hostility within their meetings. Gradually the campaign failed, and councils with a Labour majority accepted the introduction of a legal budget. It was no easy task attending Labour group meetings where disputes were raging. Not only were the meetings themselves unpleasant but to get to them very often meant pushing one's way through hostile demonstrators.

I don't think I will ever forget the farcical happenings in the London borough of Lewisham. The Labour group had an absolute commitment to a no-rate-increase strategy. One council meeting was invaded by a group of twenty trade unionists, and the meeting was abandoned. The Labour councillors withdrew to a separate room to discuss tactics, not noticing that the Conservatives had remained in the council chamber and had re-convened the meeting. That meeting passed the budget. The debacle caused the council leader to resign.

Two local authorities notable for standing their ground are Lambeth and Liverpool. The position Liverpool took and subsequent happenings I leave to a future chapter. Lambeth under the leadership of Ted Knight refused to concede and in June 1985 he along with thirty-four Labour councillors were surcharged and disqualified from being councillors. Three Labour councillors who opposed the strategy were removed from all council committees by the leadership, because of their disloyalty. I witnessed the uproar at the next council meeting. I felt real frustration as I could only sit in silence and watch as members of the Vauxhall Labour Party unfurled a banner from the public gallery behind the Conservative councillors. When a Conservative councillor tore down the banner, a Labour councillor rushed across the chamber to confront him, only to be held back in a headlock by another backbench Labour councillor. The meeting was adjourned. After twenty minutes, they returned and agreed a legal rate by one vote.

However, the internal battle in Lambeth raged on. I received continual complaints of intimidation and harassment. I reported to the executive that there needed to be an urgent investigation into the activities of the Lambeth Labour group. Business was being conducted against a background of personal abuse, disruption and threats of intimidation to individual councillors. The only dissenting voices on the NEC to an inquiry were Tony Benn and Dennis Skinner.

As the fight between local authorities and the Tory government over rate capping was at its fiercest, the government was considering a new form of tax to replace rates, the community charge or poll tax. In their book *Failure in British Government*, David Butler, Andrew Adonis and Tony Travers say that the fight and acrimony over rate capping helped to encourage the government, and Thatcher in particular, to support this change. The government Green Paper in 1986 which outlined the proposal to introduce the poll tax was not taken seriously by the Labour

Party. There was no reference to its possible implementation in the 1987 general election manifesto.

The poll tax was introduced in April 1989 in Scotland and twelve months later in England and Wales. The public vehemently opposed its introduction with rallies up and down the country, large demonstrations and widespread non-compliance. It forced the Prime Minister, John Major, who had succeeded Thatcher, to repeal the tax in 1993. We were delighted at the embarrassment this caused the Tory Party.

Before the poll tax was repealed there was further discord in Lambeth over the use of bailiffs to collect it. The Labour group was suspended, then re-formed but again found itself in breach of the rules for a differing reason. This was for calling a special council meeting, at the time of the Gulf War, to debate a strong anti-war resolution. This was not a matter germane to the functioning of the council in Lambeth. The Labour group meetings were conducted against a background of cries of 'Victory to Iraq' and 'Bomb Israel', and those that disagreed were subject to threats of intimidation, harassment and personal abuse.

The National Executive decided, with only Tony Benn (once again) and Eric Heffer dissenting, that 'the director of organisation [should conduct] yet another urgent investigation into the activities of the Lambeth Labour group'. I met the Lambeth Labour group, who declared, 'It was a witch hunt.' I was accused of working with the Labour Co-ordinating Committee (LCC), a 'soft left' organisation, who were in constant conflict with the 'hard left'. It was true that I did get information from their members in Lambeth, but I also received such information from others who had no ties with the LCC, all of which I took into account. I was also accused of not meeting with the officers of the Lambeth Labour group to hear their views. Of course I had met them. Everyone involved was given the opportunity to respond to the charges.

I was always prepared for a storm of such accusations. It only made me ensure that everything I did and said had absolute validity. I had to be certain that no one could justifiably question my integrity.

After nearly three months of talks I concluded that thirteen councillors had sustained a course of action prejudicial to the party. I presented my findings to a meeting of the NEC in July 1982. The thirteen were suspended from the Labour Party for differing periods of time. At the meeting there was concern expressed by Joan Lestor MP that we might be accused of racism as some of those named were people of colour. Having fought against any form of racism from the 1950s, long before it was popular to do so, I had no such concern. My view was reinforced by one of the interviews I held in my office with a woman councillor of West Indian origin who accused me of being racist. She was firmly put in her place by Bernie Grant MP, who was her witness. He said, 'Under no circumstances can you call Joyce a racist,' and explained to her my long history of campaigning against all forms of discrimination.

I wish I had added up the hours and days that I spent in Lambeth.

The policies and actions of some Labour Party local authorities and leading local government politicians became characterised as 'the loony left', a pejorative label invented by the popular press before and during the build-up to the 1987 general election.

It didn't help the efforts of my staff in their attempts to prepare for the election.

The vilification of Labour politicians by the media was not new. They described Ken Livingstone on his election as leader of the Greater London Council in 1981 as 'barmy' or 'loony'. After the party lost the 1983 general election Michael Foot, with his habit of swinging his walking stick, was referred to 'as being like an escaped loony'. *The Sun* had a headline 'Kinnock admits – I back Loonies' when he endorsed a rise in 1987 of 60 per cent in local council rates in Ealing, where he lived.

The Labour local authorities were the main targets. Jolyon Jenkins, a BBC journalist, reported that 1986 saw the climax of the 'loony left' campaign. He recorded that it was the year 'when *The Sun* announced that it was going to award a prize – a symbolic two-figure statuette to the "looniest" council of them all'. The *Daily Mail* and *Mail on Sunday* sent teams of reporters chasing round London boroughs in search of good (if untrue) stories. Even *The Times* used the term without apparent irony. Labour local authorities were accused of being irrationally obsessed with minority and fringe issues, paranoid about racial and sexual 'problems'. Conservative Party chairman Norman Tebbit decided this could be harnessed as a vote winner for the Tories.

To sections of the media, the truth of the stories mattered less than the effect they would have on the electorate and the consequent lack of support for the Labour Party. The press fabricated myths as instances of loony left activity. The media research group at Goldsmiths' College estimated that some 3,000 news items about the 'loony left' were circulated between 1981 and 1987, mostly untrue. There were stories such as the nursery rhyme 'Baa Baa Black Sheep' becoming 'Baa Baa White Sheep' and the re-naming of manhole covers and black bin-liner bags. Reports appeared in the press that London Labour councils had insisted that homosexuals be placed at the heads of waiting lists for council housing. Some of the stories were quite comical, such as when the *Mail on Sunday* carried letters claiming that black pudding was henceforth to be called 'green pudding'. On the same day, in October 1986, the *Sunday Times* letters column noted that blackheads could no longer be called blackheads. What I found disturbing was that the words 'loony left' or 'loonies' were used extensively by the senior members of the party, so giving credence to the media reports. The completely ridiculous comments of the Tory press went practically unchallenged.

Lambeth Borough Council banned the word 'family' from council literature because it was 'discriminatory' and police were banned from using council facilities. Lambeth Council's leader, Linda Bellos, claimed, 'I think the police are bent on war.' Whilst many such actions were indeed absolute lunacy, the use of the term 'loony' by party members only helped to reinforce the image presented by the media.

The loss of the Greenwich by-election in February 1987 was put down to the effect of the 'loony left'. A widely leaked letter written after the by-election to Frank Dobson by Patricia Hewitt, Neil Kinnock's press officer, was published in *The Sun* under the headline 'Gays put Kinnock in a panic – secret letter lashes loonies'. The words of the letter were: 'It is obvious from our own polling ... that the "London effect" is now very noticeable. The "loony Labour left" is now taking its toll; the gays and lesbians issue is costing us dear amongst the pensioners.' Nick Raynsford similarly ascribed the general election defeat in June that year to the 'loony left', having lost his Fulham seat to the Conservatives. The 'soft left' in the Labour Party blamed the perception of the 'loony left' for this third consecutive general election defeat.

There are some constituencies whose members seem to be permanently at loggerheads with each other. Often it is difficult to identify the cause, but open friction between personalities can play a significant role. This was the position I faced in dealing with the dispute in the St Helens North party in spite of the best effort of Dave Watts, then leader of St Helens Metropolitan Council.

The constituency party was suspended in the mid-1980s by the national agent, David Hughes. It was to be re-constituted in 1986, the day before he retired. David was horror struck at the behaviour of the members at the investigatory meeting, which descended into a brawl and verbal abuse. In a hysterical outburst one of the delegates accused the assistant regional organiser, Phil Robinson, of being a liar. One male delegate told a female delegate, 'Get your kecks off, you're only good when you're on your back.' Another woman was referred to as a 'wanker'. It was no surprise the constituency party continued to be suspended and disciplinary action was recommended against those who were most disruptive.

I then took over from David. I held a further hearing in St Helens Town Hall. There were clearly two distinct groupings, each as difficult as the other. It was ridiculous that to cover its 'secret' meetings one group said they were meetings of the Ferret Breeders Association. I wanted to be fair to them all, so I gave them the choice of being interviewed individually, accompanied by a friend or collectively as two groups. They chose the last. Two meetings were held on one day, one in the morning and one in the afternoon. During the lunch break I was surprised to bump into Dennis Skinner and Les Huckfield, the MEP for the area. Curious, I wanted to know why they were there. It was a Saturday, the council offices were closed and no other meetings were taking place. They gave an implausible response that they were there to meet someone. In my opinion they were there to give support to the members I was interviewing that afternoon. I finished the hearings, went home and wrote my report for the National Executive.

On the morning of the NEC meeting when I was to present my findings I had a phone call from *The Guardian*. The person on the other end of the phone told me that they had received a tape of the hearing held in the afternoon. He went on that it was such a poor recording that there were gaps, and could I fill them in? I was staggered and refused this request. I tried to discover who had sent the recording to *The Guardian* and found as expected that it had been sent anonymously.

I was very shaken, and went into the executive meeting extremely upset. Other members had also been contacted by *The Guardian* and were as perplexed as I was. When I reported this to the meeting, most members expressed their anger at such behaviour. At this point Dennis Skinner admitted placing a bug on the window sill of the meeting room so he could question my neutrality. I could not believe that he could be so devious. Led by Neil Kinnock, members expressed their absolute condemnation at such an action. No apology was forthcoming from Dennis Skinner.

In the past even when I had disagreed with Dennis I had respected him. On that day he lost my respect. My report was accepted and disciplinary action against several members of the St Helens North constituency party followed.

Les Huckfield was also involved in controversy over the selection of a by-election candidate for Knowsley North. By seeking nomination he was in breach of an assurance he had given that if he was elected as the candidate for the Merseyside East European constituency, as he had been in the 1984 European election, he would not seek to go back to the Commons until the next general election. The Euro constituency agreed to release him at an unconstitutional meeting. The item was not on the agenda. Following a protest my recommendation that he could no longer be considered for nomination in Knowsley North was accepted. He challenged the decision in court; the judge ruled as the by-election process was underway he could not intervene.

Another investigation, this time into the practices of the Knowsley North party, was undertaken by Phil Robinson and me. This resulted in the disclosure of evidence of a sustained and systematic abuse of party procedures. Three members were charged before the National Constitutional Committee (NCC) and subsequently expelled from the party.

I had the task of putting right this craziness that had engulfed the party. It caused me a lot of heartache and despair. I felt it was necessary if the party was to be restored to sanity. It meant I had to travel to all parts of the country, from north to south and from east to west, to investigate allegations made, and to check the evidence. I went to Coventry to investigate false applications for membership; to Swansea and the Wirral to interview candidates for local elections; to Nottingham because of claims of intimidation, rowdiness and bullying; to Sandwell and Spelthorne, where the party rules were begin ignored; to Dunstable over disputes arising from the poll tax; and to Warley because of disruptive action in meetings.

In London I went to Bermondsey to discuss irregularities that had taken place during the 1987 general election. The investigation was carried out to give the maximum opportunity for everyone wishing to do so to present evidence to me and John Howarth, assistant regional organiser from the southern region. As alleged we found evidence of a Militant take-over of the election campaign. Party members had been intimidated and frozen out of party activity. There were also financial irregularities. The result was that all relevant books, bank accounts and equipment were to be sequestered by the regional office. The party officers were suspended, and an outside auditor was brought in to check the books for the previous five years. When the party was reconstituted there would be supervision by the London office of all units of the Southwark & Bermondsey constituency.

The London office were also instructed to run the Peckham party in Southwark, which I had suspended. The disputes in Southwark Labour group climaxed when a number of councillors decided to form their own group. Within the rules they were automatically expelled. I re-wrote the rules for the remaining councillors in the Labour group. At an event many years later organised by Harriet Harman, I met many of those councillors, who told me they still worked to Joyce Gould's bible.

When I received reports of problems in the Birmingham Labour group, I was instructed to examine the procedures of the group.

My job was to advise on future practices, to monitor progress and to examine the actions of group members. I looked at the rules and standing orders, the relations with the local party and the incorrect use of 'the conscience clause'. This meant many visits to Birmingham. As always all had to be consulted and assured that their views would be taken into account.

The report I finally produced was received with reservations by some on both sides of the dispute. It was, however, finally accepted. I told them that 'if they were going to maintain control of the council, it could only be achieved by a united group' and that 'their unity relies on the cessation of disruptive behaviour, hostility between individuals, personal attacks and the acceptance of majority decisions'.

Elsewhere in Birmingham, mayhem broke out in the Small Heath constituency with the selection of Roger Godsiff for the 1992 general election. There were accusations of people improperly attending the selection meeting. I investigated; ultimately Roger accepted that he had acted 'unwisely' but his selection was endorsed.

Interviewing witnesses was often disheartening and at times it could be very unpleasant. I was always accompanied by a regional officer. I cannot forget interviewing a party member in the East Midlands who had been accused of intimidating other members and their families. I felt as though I was facing someone evil, as he tried to intimidate me by leaning closer to me over the table. I could feel the hairs on the back of my neck rise and my back curl. Nonetheless I could not let my reaction to him determine my decision. The evidence I was presented with made it clear to me that his behaviour was unacceptable. Days before his hearing and my presenting the case to the NCC, the final arbiter, the main complainant withdrew his evidence because of threats to his family. On the day of the hearing, with Dianne Hayter (now my colleague in the Lords) in the chair, the witness attempted to re-introduce his evidence. To me this was a brave act, but the NCC panel in its wisdom said it was too late to re-introduce evidence. I fundamentally disagreed but it was their decision. I did not lose my case, but after an eight-hour hearing the accused member received only a short period of suspension from the party. I was later sent a press cutting showing that he also faced charges by the police and was subsequently convicted.

In spite of the abuse I regularly received from those aggrieved and the inaccurate reporting by the media, only twice did I feel it necessary to take legal action. In both cases I contacted Geoffrey Bindman to act as my solicitor. The first occasion was when *Guardian* reporter Hugo Young accused me in an article in the newspaper that I had peremptorily attempted to change the nomination rules to suit a person's convenience. This was clearly a defamatory and untrue story. A week later *The Guardian* printed an absolute apology, Geoffrey received his fee and I received a cheque for £750.

The second occasion arose from a nasty experience when I had been instructed to look into *Socialist Organiser*, a weekly newspaper founded in 1979 and circulated within the party. This hard-left paper purported to be a broad vehicle of left unity. When it became known that the investigation was underway, I was inundated with evidence against the activities of those involved. I interviewed the editor and other participants as well as those who wished to give evidence against those engaged with the paper. Particularly important was evidence from someone who had been involved with it for a short while as a student activist. It was a brave decision on her part for which she was seriously vilified by *Socialist Organiser*. On receipt of my report the party banned *Socialist Organiser* from being sold within it. Following splits about its policy direction, the paper soon lost ground and ceased publication in the mid-1990s.

The inquiry continued over one individual, Lol Duffy, who it was alleged was associated with this paper. He had also applied to be a candidate in Wallasey for the 1992 general election. I agreed the timetable for the parliamentary selection in Wallasey in January 1992. However, because of the imminence of the general election, the executive decided that an 'emergency by-election panel' would be set up to interview potential candidates and draw up the shortlist. It was no surprise that Duffy was excluded from the list. The explanation given by John Evans MP, a member of the panel was that 'on almost every area Mr Duffy said that although he would campaign on agreed policies he didn't personally agree with them'. Angela Eagle was ultimately selected as the candidate for the general election.

The most ludicrous article about the selection appeared in *Private Eye*. Their first inaccuracy was that I was the north-west regional organiser, but even more ridiculous, they wrote that I had influenced the selection because I was Angela and her twin sister Maria's aunt, and further that the members at the meeting had not been informed of this relationship. On being challenged by Geoffrey Bindman, *Private Eye* made no attempt to justify the article but did apologise, saying that they 'withdrew totally any suggestion that Ms Gould acted improperly in any way' and 'any suggestion that Ms Eagle was party to any deception or impropriety'. Geoffrey secured £3,000 each for Angela and me. I bought a new and comfortable sofa which sadly three years later I lost in a flood in my Camberwell flat.

In reverse I was threatened with legal action and spent seven years with that threat hanging over me. This arose from the selection of Frank Field as the parliamentary candidate for Birkenhead. At the selection conference, held in late 1989, Frank was deselected to be replaced by Paul Davies, an official of the TGWU. On challenging the selection Frank was told by Neil Kinnock that he had to produce evidence of malpractice. On receipt of the dossier the executive took the decision that I should conduct a wide-ranging investigation into the party on the Wirral. The following month I presented an interim report which made it clear that not one of Frank Field's allegations relating to the selection process could be substantiated. The process had been overseen by Peter Kilfoyle, a regional officer who felt that Frank's allegations were a particular slur on his integrity. Four months later I presented a more detailed report, again reinforcing that there had been no irregularities at the selection meeting. Nevertheless, a re-run was ordered. The re-run selection was delayed as Frank continued to make further allegations, all of which I had to investigate, so it wasn't until June 1991 that the re-selection meeting was held. Frank was selected as the candidate with a 7.5 per cent majority of the vote.

I personally took responsibility for the arrangements for that selection, working with the new regional officer, Eileen Mirfin, Peter Kilfoyle having made his way to Parliament by way of the Liverpool Walton by-election following the death of Eric Heffer.

I spent many hours making absolutely certain that everyone attending the selection conference was entitled to do so and that no rules had been breached. This time it was Paul Davies who challenged the result, not through the party machinery but through the legal process.

From then on until 1998, the statutory time within which the case could be heard, he threatened to take the case to court. He never did but every now and then John Sharpe, the party solicitor, would ring me up and say that Davis's solicitor had rung with another query. Although I was not happy to be in this position at no time did I have any anxiety that a case could be taken against me. I knew there was no case to answer. I did feel, however, that keeping the case open whilst knowing he was never going to go to court showed the malevolence that lay behind Paul Davis's action.

I was reminded of the legal threat a few years ago as I sat next to Frank Field on a government committee on counselling for abortion. We had opposing views on the principle of abortion and a woman's right to choose. I was not able to restrain myself when he said that women who had an abortion were mentally ill not only at the time of the abortion, but for many years after. I argued strongly that he was talking nonsense, and that there was no evidence to prove his case. Shortly afterwards the committee was disbanded without conclusion.

CHAPTER 10

⊰⟨⋅⟩⊱

THE NEW REGIME

Since being elected to the National Executive in 1978 Neil Kinnock's reputation for being outspoken and tough had grown, as had his opposition to the 'hard left'.

Neil gained prominence in opposition for his attacks on Margaret Thatcher's handling of the Falklands War. It was his passion and his oratory that convinced the party members that here was a future party leader and a future Prime Minister. On becoming leader in October 1983, Neil was determined to transform the party into a cohesive, disciplined and highly managed unit. Hard choices had to be made. He broke them down into five key areas: policy formulation, organisation, our approach to the media, campaigning activity and parliamentary selections.

Neil's first act was to engage a public relations company to examine the structure and staffing of head office. Their recommendation was for a smaller and more close-knit management structure, with a general secretary and three directors to replace the team of department heads. There was great speculation amongst the staff as to who would be staying and who would be going. Who would get promotion? Who were going to be the new bosses?

All the senior management jobs were advertised and interviews held, and amongst the successful four were two newcomers. Larry Whitty, a researcher for the General Municipal Workers' Union, became general secretary, replacing Jim Mortimer. Larry's appointment was opposed by Tony Benn, Eric Heffer and Dennis Skinner. Peter Mandelson was the other newcomer, appointed as director of campaigns and communications. Geoff Bish became director of policy – both domestic and international. I became director of organisation.

I was told that when Marian Craythorne, then conference officer, was asked whether I would get the job, she said, 'Yes, of course, because she is too bloody good.' That was a real compliment from Marian. Richard Taylor, her deputy, told me of her great respect for me – recalling that at the 1986 conference in Blackpool she asked him to get a cab for me and accompany me to the Winter Gardens to make sure I arrived safely.

One of my first tasks was to determine the role, function and structure of the new directorate. Jean Corston, the assistant national agent, was given responsibility for elections and training. A team was brought together to look at the development of the party, with Anne Wilkinson, Sally Morgan and Virendra Sharma as officers for women, youth and students, and ethnic minorities respectively. I took personal responsibility for relations with the trade unions, the third section (organisations affiliated to the party), the party conference and the conference office.

David Hughes, the national agent, became the conciliation officer, dealing with some elements of rule breaches. On his retirement in March 1988 David said:

> I have spent thirty-eight years working in the party's organisation service with two Yorkshire women: the 1950s and '60s with Sara Barker and in my final ten years with Joyce. For me she has been the epitome of the real Yorkshire character – warmth, kind-heartedness and generosity of spirit. I shall take into my retirement a fondness for Joyce and a deep gratitude for all the support she has given me.

I am pleased that I still meet David at meetings of the H. S. Chapman Society, a group of organisers from all parties established in the early 1990s. Working with the Electoral Commission, it holds seminars to examine all aspects of elections. I am the society's current chair.

David and I also meet at the annual gathering of the retired party staff. These events are organised by Wally Burley. Wally came from the West Midlands as an assistant national agent, becoming secretary of the National Constitutional Committee before he retired. The retired staff members go to a different city or town each year for our annual reunion. We visit places of interest and meet members of the local party. Importantly we learn if we are to get a rise in our pension. Wally also runs Labour's Animal Welfare Society, of which I am a member. Affiliated to the Labour Party, it vigorously campaigns against cruelty to animals, and organises activities to influence government to introduce animal welfare legislation.

The next part of my re-organisation plan was to conduct a review of the regional structure, looking at its future development, the quality of the staff, and relationships within the offices and with party members. This was the first major review since the introduction of a regional structure in 1951. The review was not welcomed by all. The regional organisers valued their independence strongly and didn't appreciate this interference. Nevertheless, I visited every region, often accompanied by Roy Hattersley. We met with the organisers, and separately met their staff and the full-time agents. We also met local party officers and members to hear their views. It was an item on the agenda of each regional annual conference.

The review proved to be an exercise of great value as the old regime retired. The new team of regional organisers had great strength and determination to improve their role and the image of the organising staff. They did so as equal players in a powerful team, a team that gave me great support. This prompted Larry Whitty to say, 'The problem with the regions is they have too much power.' True – the power of determination.

But the review was only a part of the progress of building that team. A committee looked further at the development of the organising services at all levels, in preparation for the 1987 general election. I headed this team with a representative of each region and NEC members. The strategy document we produced, 'On to Winning Ways', outlined a future plan of work. A six-month study project identified our electoral prospects in individual constituencies. I visited constituencies, identifying the specific requirements, the popularity of the candidate and the strength of the opposition, and reported back to Neil.

I well remember the first meeting of the staff of the directorate. This for them was a new experience. I said a few introductory words about the new arrangements and asked for their views, thoughts and ideas for the future. I got absolute silence. I asked, did no one have any comments to make? Carol Linforth, later to become deputy general secretary, said, 'You are very nice but formidable.' I did not see myself as formidable, and over time they all – at least I hope so – realised that I was always there to listen, to give support and at the same time heed their advice.

My reputation as a caring boss grew and staff from other departments came to discuss their problems with me. One such colleague, John Turner, who with his son Alan drove the party van, was particularly anxious about his future. He said he was getting little support from his director, Mike Watts. (There was, incidentally, a rumour rife amongst the staff that Mike Watts had been parachuted into the post in order to keep an eye on Larry Whitty.) My advice helped him solve his problem. He was extremely grateful. It was tragic that shortly afterwards John died of a heart attack at the staff reception at party conference. Because of the close relationship that I had developed with his family and the support that I gave them the family asked me to speak at John's funeral and presented me with a beautiful jardinière.

I hope Larry agrees that he and I worked well together even though our styles were very different. I expected instant action and decision making whilst Larry would take his time to deliberate. There were times when we had differences but in the main we managed to sort them out, and I respected Larry for the strength and importance he gave to the job. Only on one occasion did we have a serious difference. This was over Larry's use of the word

'I' even when he had not been responsible for a piece of work. My frustration grew. One night I decided to write a 2.30 a.m. letter. I suggested that he acknowledged the efforts of others not by using names, but by using the word 'we'. The next morning I left the private and confidential letter on his desk. There was no response. Larry put it in his pocket and forgot about it, and then we broke for Easter. Once back at work, Larry rang me and said, 'We must talk.' We went off to a wine bar on the South Bank and spent the evening talking about his problems. I don't recall mine being mentioned but 'we' entered his vocabulary.

My direct line of contact with the leader's office was with Charles Clarke, Neil's head of staff. He had been the president of the National Union of Students and Neil's assistant when he was shadow spokesperson for education. Later following the 1997 election Charles would become Secretary of State for Education and Skills and Home Secretary. We met almost daily. We were also constantly in communication by phone. I was expected to discuss with Charles every document or paper that I wrote for the executive and its committees. Neil had to be happy with it. In his early days Neil didn't seem to trust anyone to present his views correctly. After about a year, the tight rope loosened, and I was trusted to get on with my job.

Charles could at times be a little arrogant and pompous, but we worked amiably together. Once in the middle of a telephone conversation, he put the phone down on me. I was furious. A very short while later my office door opened and Charles came in to apologise. There had been a crisis in the office, and Neil had demanded his instant attention. This little episode illustrated the pressure we were all working under.

In 1977–78 Charles had been the British representative on the Permanent Commission for the World Youth Festival in Cuba. Jeannette and I consulted him when we decided one year to go to Cuba for Christmas and the New Year. His advice was invaluable, not least in telling us that we should inform the Cuban embassy in London of our intended visit. The embassy gave me a phone number to call if we were in need of any assistance during our visit. Assistance was needed on our first day of arrival. The hotel was awful. It was pouring down with rain and the rain came through the roof. We went to the tourist office, but got no joy, no other hotels, no flights. So I rang the number the Cuban embassy had given me. It turned out to be the Communist Party headquarters. I didn't care. A man and an interpreter arrived at the hotel. We sat down and went through a schedule for the two weeks we were to be in Cuba. Phone calls were made and miraculously hotels had spare rooms and there were seats on flights. I was grateful to Charles.

It could have been a free trip but I was not going to be obligated. I did concede to visit a young crocodile farm, although I dislike reptiles of any sort, and more happily I agreed to speak at a meeting of the Cuban Women's Confederation.

Neil established the campaign strategy committee almost immediately on becoming leader. I was appointed its secretary. It was attended by the general secretary, the directors, senior members of the shadow Cabinet and members of Neil's office staff. We all reported directly to the leader. Separate from the executive, it became an important decision-making body, almost as a rival source of power to the NEC.

The determination of party policy was the responsibility of

the NEC and the Cabinet or shadow Cabinet through the so-called 'Clause 5' meeting, with endorsement by party conference. The Clause 5 meeting was held jointly between the Cabinet or shadow Cabinet and the NEC. Neil was determined, rightly in the circumstances, to take overall responsibility. He set up a policy co-ordinating committee and started the reform of party policy. His aim was to move the party to a centre-left position that was more acceptable to the electorate.

The most controversial policy was the party's stance on unilateral nuclear disarmament. At the 1986 Labour conference, Neil had stood firmly behind the existing non-nuclear policy, saying, 'I would fight and die for my country, but I tell you I would never let my country die for me.' Events during the 1987 general election made him re-think that policy.

There was a point during that election campaign when a poll showed the Conservatives two percentage points ahead. This stirred them to run a more aggressive campaign with the focus on unilateralism, and they produced a powerful poster showing a British soldier's arms raised in surrender with the caption 'Labour's Policy on Arms'. This was followed by a party political broadcast ending with 'I vow to thee, my country' and a Union Jack fluttering in the breeze. Speaking at a Conservative rally in Newport, Margaret Thatcher attacked Labour's defence policy as a programme for defeat, surrender, occupation and then prolonged guerrilla fighting. 'I do not understand how someone who aspires to government can treat the defence of the country so lightly,' she thundered from the platform.

The unilateral policy of the party was said to be the biggest area of dissent amongst the electorate. It wasn't long before a headline in *The Independent* read, 'Kinnock set to modify nuclear weapons policy'. They were right, the policy was changed and we became a multilateral party.

I personally was committed to unilateralism and found myself with a personal dilemma and contemplated resigning. I sought advice from Sam McCluskie, a confidant who like me had always supported the unilateral cause. His response to me was clear: 'Joyce, think with your head and not your heart.' Good advice, which I took. My years of hard work for the Labour Party continued. Sam McCluskie was leader of the seamen's union. He was a colourful and controversial character, and it is reputed that the KGB once attempted to recruit him as a spy, but he exposed them and their overtures toward him failed miserably.

Having voted in the 1975 referendum that Britain's place was in Europe, I was delighted that the party at last changed its European policy at the party conference in 1987. This was a major reversal in Neil's previous stance on Europe. At the 1971 special conference he was anti-Europe and campaigned for a 'no' vote in the 1975 referendum. In his leadership manifesto, however, Neil argued that withdrawal should be the last resort. Anti-Europeanism was still deeply rooted in parts of the Labour movement. Change came about by degrees, mainly because of the social dimension, the importance of the social chapter and the party's success in the 1989 European elections.

Another area which disturbed me was the sale of council houses. Initially, the party policy had been to oppose the Conservative policy on the sale of council housing. I was not happy about the reversal of this policy as it depleted the number of houses for those who could not afford to buy.

Geoff Bish, head of policy, suggested that there should be a general review of policy, taking into account how society had changed. His proposal was rejected. It was understood privately to be what Neil wanted, but only when the time was right. The same proposition was put later by Tom Sawyer, chair of the home policy committee, when Neil willingly accepted it. Policy development began with a series of consultations known as 'Labour listens'. A new statement of aims and values was produced. There was an unsuccessful attempt to alter Clause IV of the party's constitution. It had stood since 1918 and called for common ownership of the means of production, distribution and exchange. Clause IV was re-written in 1995 by Tony Blair, with an emphasis on equality rather than public ownership.

Seven policy groups were agreed by the National Executive, each chaired by a member of the shadow Cabinet. Tony Benn and Eric Heffer refused to participate. To them it was another right-wing plot. It was therefore no surprise to hear their reactions on the outcome from each review. Tony Benn said they illustrated T-shirt socialism, whilst Eric Heffer saw them as SDP Mark II. In 1990, to involve party members more directly, the Policy Forum came into being, made up of 190 delegates. It was the end of the 'resolution' era. This was not a position that was accepted by many local parties, who felt that they had lost a means of influencing policy and the purpose for discussing policy in their meetings.

Throughout the history of the party proportional representation (PR) had been on and off the agenda. Policy discussions on the issue went back to Keir Hardie, who believed it provided a solution to Labour's future success. That enthusiasm waned as

Labour began to win seats. However, the loss of the third general election in a row in 1987, and the third time the Conservatives had won their parliamentary majority on less than 5 per cent of the vote, brought PR once again to the forefront. Support grew in the party for the Labour Campaign for Electoral Reform and for Charter 88, a non-party campaigning organisation. One of its main objectives was PR for the House of Commons. At the time Neil Kinnock dismissed Charter 88 as chattering-class 'whiners and whingers', but sometime later he changed his mind and aligned himself with their policy.

Robin Cook MP was a great advocate of PR. He influenced Roy Hattersley to set up a commission in 1990 whose remit was to undertake a detailed study on the electoral systems for all levels of government – except the House of Commons. The review was chaired by Raymond Plant, professor of politics at Southampton University, now Lord Plant. He was a supporter of first-past-the-post. The work carried out by the Plant Commission represented the most serious examination of electoral reform ever undertaken by a British political party. As a member of the commission I was particularly interested in the consequences for the organisation and structure of the party and the running of the elections themselves.

The Plant Commission concluded that there was no need for uniformity amongst the electoral systems across the different institutions. Rather it was important to ensure that the electoral system is appropriate for the body concerned. This view was subsequently taken into account for elections to the Scottish Parliament, Welsh Assembly and the London Assembly.

Following the 1992 election and another Conservative

government the commission was reinstated. By now the majority of its members supported elimination of first-past-the-post. Raymond Plant himself became a convert and in 1993 was the international winner of the Champion of Democracy award, made by the Center for Voting and Democracy, a US body that advocates electoral reform. John Smith, who was then the party leader, remained unconvinced of the case for changing the electoral systems for the Commons. He did, however, pledge that a Labour government would hold a referendum on this issue in its first term.

The determination of policy was ultimately discussed in each annual party conference. It was invariably the trade union delegations that determined the result, having the largest share of the vote. A great deal of negotiation went on prior to conference by the leader's office to ensure that the right result was achieved.

It became very clear to Neil Kinnock that party conference was in need of review, as it was all too often shambolic and badly organised. This prompted Larry Whitty to call together all the staff who worked on the preparations for the national party conference. We sat around a table in his office to discuss what we did and to tell him how conference was organised. We realised how little we worked as a team. Larry was appalled at the lack of co-ordination between departments, and he instructed me to take on that co-ordinating role.

I wrote the 'conference war book'. For the first time all functions, responsibilities and roles were recorded. It was a big job, and to do it properly meant having discussions with everyone involved. The bearded and unforgettable Ted Higgins, who was responsible for the sales of *Labour Weekly*, our then newspaper, gave me a sound piece of advice. He said, 'Have faith and trust.' Wise words for in the main the staff involved were keen to do their jobs well. They strongly supported my efforts to run conference like a well-oiled machine.

Marian Craythorne left her post as conference officer in 1987 to be near her family in Blackpool. I appointed her deputy, Richard Taylor, to replace her. Richard originally had applied for a job in the party rather than go to college. As he says, not in his wildest dreams did he expect to be promoted. My decision was the right one: he became highly respected for the efficient and friendly way he carried out his job.

Security for the party conferences came within my remit. It meant meeting the relevant police officer, usually the deputy chief constable, to discuss the level of security that they recommended for each conference, a level that was considerably heightened after the bomb at the Conservative Party conference in Brighton in 1984. The decision on the level of security was ultimately the party's, but the police made it very clear to me that unless we accepted their guidance they would opt out altogether. Together we discussed the checking of delegates' credentials and bags as they entered the conference hall, and if it became necessary how to get the delegates out of the hall in a safe and orderly fashion.

At a pre-conference meeting in Brighton one year Richard was asked by the deputy chief constable, 'How do you like working for a woman?' His reply was short and snappy: 'Why would I not? She is a good boss to work for.' After I retired, whilst Richard was still in post he always made sure I had a reserved seat at conference. He has moved on but we still keep in touch.

Normally conference delegates were not made aware of any security problems which did crop up. On one occasion a disturbance was created when it was discovered that a man in a wheelchair had a gun under his blankets. It turned out to be a dummy gun. He had got into conference on a false visitor's ticket that Tony Benn had given him. Tony was sympathetic to the story he told and somehow got him a pass. Fortunately no harm was done.

Inspecting the conference hotel for the members of the National Executive and other 'prominent people' meant working with the hotel management. Sometimes this was extremely frustrating. Were there enough rooms? Could they deal with the security arrangements? Could they provide a private corridor for the leader and international visitors? These visitors brought their own bodyguards, and places had to found for them to do their job effectively. There were many other questions and details to be resolved.

NEC members were sometimes hard to please. On one occasion Eric Heffer changed his room three times at the Grand in Brighton. Equally difficult was organising room shares for the staff. Richard Taylor reminded me that in 1984 he was due to share his room with another male member of staff, who complained about his sexuality. Richard got a single room but there was a nasty piece in the *Daily Star* about a transvestite striptease artiste who worked for the Labour Party who asked for his own room. We never discovered who gave the story to the so-called popular press, but it was an example of the level of homophobia prevalent at the time.

In those days every constituency, trade union and socialist society could submit a resolution for inclusion on the conference agenda. To reduce the number of submissions to be debated on the same subject, organisations were asked either to agree a joint resolution by post, or to attend a compositing meeting on the day before conference. That was a long and arduous day, with delegates airing their views and strong differences of opinion. Small groups of delegates would gather together before the compositing meetings, arguing over the words they wanted to retain from the original resolution submitted by their organisation. They attempted to ensure that key words and phrases that emphasised their point of view were not lost.

My role was to organise the programme for the day of compositing. I had to ensure that people went into the correct meetings and that there was a staff member present to write the notes at each session. It was made easier when an organisation had prepared a draft in advance which was accepted by those whose points had been included. Before the days of computers we used to type five copies, five sheets of paper divided by carbon paper.

When the movers and seconders of the resolutions had been agreed, and their signatures obtained, I would send a copy of each resolution to the conference arrangements committee. It was their responsibility to draw up the agenda for conference. The booklet of the agreed resolutions was printed overnight. My working day moved into a working night, going to the printer at least three times during the early hours to check the copy, and to ensure that it was delivered in time for distribution to the delegates as they arrived the following morning. At about 2.30 or 3 a.m. I would have a meeting with Derek Gladwin, the extremely powerful secretary of the conference arrangements committee, along with Geoff Bish, policy director. We would

go through the resolutions. Whilst I was doing the preparatory
work for this meeting Derek would be attending many of the
social events. I didn't resent the lateness of the hour for Derek
always made sure that refreshment was provided. Derek and
I became good friends and I was delighted when he asked me
to be his sponsor when he joined me in the Lords. He died at
too young an age. I was proud but saddened to speak at his
memorial service.

It seemed that no conference could take place that did not
have controversy and conflict. In 1981, for instance, Tony Benn
challenged the incumbent, Denis Healey, for the deputy leadership. Tony Benn had declared his intention to stand in March of
that year on the grounds that he was opposed to Michael Foot's
actions against Militant. The next six months were dominated
by this challenge. Tony held meetings up and down the country.
He walked the corridors and tea rooms in the Commons to gain
support. His campaign was gaining momentum, whilst some
MPs opposed to him were vitriolic in their views of him. Denis
Healey's campaign was less vigorous. Denis in his book *The
Time of My Life* says, 'Those six months were the busiest in my
life. And all for the sake of a job which I found disagreeable.
I felt however that it was essential to deny it to Tony Benn.'
Denis scraped home in his own words 'by a hair of my eyebrow',
by 50.426 per cent to 49.574 per cent. A third candidate, John
Silkin, representing the Tribunite 'soft left', also stood but was
eliminated on the first ballot. It was alleged that Neil Kinnock
had effectively prevented Tony Benn from winning by first supporting Silkin and then urging Silkin's supporters to abstain
on the second ballot. Margaret Beckett, who was supporting

Tony, was so outraged that at a Tribune rally later that week she accused Neil of handing victory to Denis. Tony's supporters bitterly attacked the abstainers as 'traitors'.

It was upsetting to witness a slanging match at that year's conference in the Grand Hotel in Brighton between Margaret and Joan Lestor, an abstainer. Joan had resigned as shadow Education Minister over proposed cuts in education, and Margaret had filled the post. Joan's reaction was: 'I am not prepared to accept lectures about unity on the left from those prepared to go into office in the place of a fellow left-winger and implement cuts in education.'

The National Executive met the Wednesday before conference to have the first discussion on the agenda. This was always the easier of their two meetings they held. On the following Sunday morning they met to decide their response to the resolutions that the Conference Arrangements Committee (CAC) had placed before them. As might be expected the left/right divide on the executive meant the debate was heated and acrimonious. Their decisions were ultimately determined by a show of hands.

Speaking times at conference were determined by the CAC: eight minutes for movers of resolutions and five minutes for other speakers. At my second conference in 1976, such was the political divide between the National Executive and the government that Denis Healey, then Chancellor of the Exchequer, was begrudgingly given five minutes to put the case for an NEC emergency statement during a debate on sterling. The powerful CAC were also responsible for the order of the agenda. Early each morning a number of delegates queued up outside the committee's office, the 'Star Chamber', to complain about their resolution not being included or with an 'emergency' resolution they hoped would end up on the order paper.

The hall filled up and the NEC stood in line behind the platform waiting for me to send them on. The conference opened with the chair or leader of the local party welcoming the delegates. The chair of the conference then gave their opening address and the first resolution was called. The Tuesday afternoon session discussed internal party business matters such as its financial state. It was heard in private. The media were excluded. This practice ceased in 1978. Initially my role was as a small but important cog in the smooth running of conference, that of keeping delegates to time. This was done by pressing a green button when they were to start, a yellow button when a minute was left and a red button when time was up, each button switching on a light of the same colour. I once pressed the red button too early, after only five minutes, when Arthur Scargill was moving a resolution on behalf of the National Union of Mineworkers. He should have had eight minutes. I was mortified. He accepted the red light and brought his speech to a close. Amazingly nobody in the hall noticed. When I apologised to him later he was gracious in accepting my apology.

Conference procedures were very bewildering to new delegates, with emergency resolutions, composite resolutions, statements, NEC reports and so on. Votes were taken either by putting a card in the boxes sent round by the tellers or by a show of hands. It was usual for a card vote to be called for by the mover of the resolution when it was on a subject where there were differences of view and where the weighted trade union vote would determine the outcome. To help explain this complicated process I produced a document of explanation for new delegates.

The seating arrangements made it possible for the chair to know whether he or she was calling a trade unionist, a constituency party member, someone from a socialist society or an MP. Trade union general secretaries vied with each other to get to the rostrum, a farce because all that was usually arranged in advance. Women delegates were noticeable by their absence. In the trade union block that took pride of place in the centre of the floor, it was hard to find a woman's face. Few women were called. In order to encourage the chair to call women to speak and in an attempt to show his or her fairness I kept a tally over the week. The chair would announce the figures at the end of conference. The rules were ultimately changed; now if a constituency party has more than 100 members it can have a second delegate, who must be a woman, and the trade union section is now dotted with women.

It was some time before conference registered how Militant Tendency supporters kept being called. I discovered that they were all given the same speech on each subject, on the basis that at least one of them would get called in each debate. It was a ruse that worked. They were very assiduous. They would get to their feet quickly, determined to make their speech. They were recognisable once at the rostrum by the arm movement they all used as they called for nationalisation of the 250 monopolies.

My role when I became the director of organisation was being responsible for conference. This meant sitting next to the chair, advising and briefing the chair's agenda in great detail and making sure they kept to it. Each chair had a differing way of handling conference. Some called delegates on the basis of their own political views, others went for those that shouted the loudest or wore a funny hat. In his book *The Odd Couple*, Dennis Skinner refers to my sitting next to him and says, 'Joyce Gould, the party's chief organiser, would sit next to me whispering who should be selected on political grounds.' What a fantasy. Dennis knew who he was going to call on political grounds. Dennis Skinner wouldn't wear his pass and was nearly refused entry to the conference. When Lena Jeger was the chair she had to be barred from alcohol for the whole week. I had a rota of people to be with her at all times. Tom Sawyer left his notes on the table when due to speak at the rostrum. I took them to him and was rewarded with a big kiss. Most interesting was David Blunkett. For the first and only time delegates indicated in advance that they wanted to be called. They were called by name. I prepared the list and went through it with David, making sure there was balance. David would put the names in a tiny Braille machine ready to call them from the chair.

I sat on the conference platform for eighteen years. It was the tradition for the chief women's officer to be the timekeeper, so I was on the platform almost immediately on taking office. Each conference was different, each had its own excitement, disputes and tensions. This was the party's authoritative policy-making body, recognised by the media and the listening public, by those in the hall, by the demonstrators outside hoping to influence the decisions being made. In writing my memoirs I have relied heavily on the detailed NEC reports and the reports of conference. Unfortunately they are no more, making recent information hard to find.

Since retiring I have had the unique (for me) experience of being on the other side of the camera and commentating on the proceedings. Huw Edwards told me his mother enjoyed my comments. I am not sure about anyone else. It was amazing seeing my name as the credits rolled.

CHAPTER 11

<+>

ELECTIONS AND BY-ELECTIONS WON AND LOST

Parliamentary selections and the running of by-elections came next for review. Our record in by-elections throughout the 1970s was variable. The by-election to be held in Great Grimsby in April 1977 created by the death of Anthony Crosland, a seat with a majority of only 7,000, was almost given up as lost. It was held on the same day as a by-election in Ashfield, triggered when the MP David Marquand went to a well-paid job in Europe. Ashfield was a safe seat with a 22,000 majority. We believed it was a certainty for Labour.

Early in the campaign some of the staff working in Grimsby called the national agent to express their concern that things were not going well and that the campaign needed livening up. I was sent up to Grimsby to take over the organisation. This was the first time I had run a by-election campaign. The candidate was Austin Mitchell. I knew Austin well as he fronted

Calendar, a daily news programme on Yorkshire Television, whose transmission area included Grimsby. As our candidate was a celebrity I decided on lots of music, balloons and kissing babies. It worked. Labour won. I was so proud and excited but unfortunately on the same day we lost the previously safe seat in Ashfield. The electorate did not like their MP going off to take a lucrative job elsewhere. A few years later I was a member of a Fabian delegation led by Austin to the Nordic countries. I still have the certificate which records my entry into the land of the midnight sun, the Arctic Circle.

My second visit to a by-election as a national officer was in August of that year when I was sent to Birmingham Ladywood after it had been discovered that the agent for the by-election was a member of the National Front. I met John Sever, the candidate, and the party members to find a new agent, which we did. I spent the first night there with other members of staff in the most dreadful boarding house. The party had very strict rules on the amount that could be spent on staff accommodation. I went back to London and made it clear to the national agent that we would not continue to stay in a place where you walked sideways to get into bed and where you had make your own breakfast. Surprisingly the national agent agreed with me. The staff moved to better digs and the restriction on finance was lifted forever. This was another by-election we won although with a reduced majority.

There was a whole spate of by-elections in the following few years. Three of these became major media events, the first in Bermondsey. In 1980 Bob Mellish, the sitting MP, had been appointed the deputy chairman of the London Docklands Development

Corporation and appeared to be about to resign the seat. Peter Tatchell was selected by the local party as the by-election candidate. Bob, a stalwart right-winger, intervened and produced an article which Tatchell had written in which he called for extra-parliamentary activity. A question in the Commons about the article prompted Michal Foot to say, 'The individual concerned is not an endorsed candidate of the Labour Party as far as I am concerned.'

Tatchell's endorsement was the main item at the next organisation committee on 7 December 1981. I sat and listened to the farcical debate. John Golding MP told us that Tatchell had pin-ups of Lenin in his flat. How he knew I am not sure. Joan Lestor replied that she had had pictures of Castro on her walls because she thought he was 'dishy'. The meeting descended into chaos, and someone remarked sotto voce that as Tatchell was homosexual he was less inclined to support him. By a vote of fourteen to five, the decision to endorse was lost. I was sure this was going to cause fury in the party and of course I was proved right.

David Hughes, the then national agent, and I were inundated with protests at the decision. The debate raged. Through a slip-up on the part of his right-wing opponents Eric Heffer succeeded in getting it agreed that there would be a new selection with no bar on Tatchell standing again. A year later after his first thwarted selection conference he was selected. In January 1983, he was endorsed by the executive with Michael Foot's support. Without question the delay and the furore had made it impossible for the party to win.

The by-election took place on 24 February 1983. The day

before, at a seven-hour meeting the National Executive expelled John O'Grady for standing against the party. O'Grady was the leader of Southwark Council, the local authority that included Bermondsey. It was also the day of the hearings against the editorial board of the *Militant* newspaper. Even though I arrived very early to get into the building for the NEC meeting, I had to push my way through a horde of journalists and abusive demonstrators who were supporting Tatchell or Militant or both.

The by-election itself was a horrendous affair. Rumours, slanders and innuendoes were circulated anonymously. I and my London colleagues worked hard to prevent a loss but as we expected the party was overwhelmingly defeated. The Liberal Democrat Simon Hughes won the seat, which he held until the 2015 general election. A leadership debate started over this fiasco; should Michael Foot resign and, if so, who would replace him? However, when we won the by-election in Darlington later in the year he managed to get the breathing space he needed. He stayed on as leader until after the 1983 general election.

I understood the mistakes that Michael had made over the whole Tatchell affair. I had been a friend of his for many years. He took me out for dinner when I retired. As we discussed my future and what I might do with my time, I could not mention the possibility of my entering the Lords, as it was against the rules, and in any case Michael had a real dislike of the Lords. When it was announced that I was going to be a baroness, he sent me a beautiful card saying, 'You know I disapprove of the House of Lords, but if anyone deserves the honour you do.' It was a tragedy that such an intellectually able and decent man not only suffered at the hands of the media but was also stig-matised by some of his colleagues. Maybe it was a mistake for him to have become leader.

One of my next ventures was as a member of the head office team sent early in 1984 to organise the by-election in Chesterfield, caused by the resignation of Eric Varley. Eric had been a long-time treasurer of the party. I went with Mike Cocks, the Chief Whip; Richard Clements, the editor of *Tribune*; and Nita Clarke, the press officer. Our candidate was Tony Benn, who had lost his Bristol South East seat in the 1983 general election. Before going to Chesterfield we met Tony in Neil Kinnock's office to discuss the running of the campaign, a campaign that would be followed by an unprecedented amount of national press and media. It was four weeks of intense work, with visits from the leadership, the front bench and about 100 MPs. Tony Benn himself was not keen on knocking on doors; he preferred public meetings and street activity, which he did with great skill. It was a pity that public election meetings were no longer popular, and that party leaders and candidates had to be protected, so meetings became ticket-only events. Tony Benn accused me of having made that decision myself. It was completely untrue; however, I accepted that the level of response from the public had diminished, and audiences were small. Candidates were seen and heard on the media, and in some ways this replaced direct contact between the party and the electorate.

Halfway through the campaign, the press reported incorrectly that Peter Tatchell had visited Chesterfield and been sent away. The media made great play about this, reporting that Tony had supposedly said he was delighted about Peter's visit. Tony wrote in his own diary that he vigorously attacked the BBC's Vincent Hanna for his coverage of the by-election, saying that Vincent was acting as an SDP candidate for Chesterfield and wanted a Liberal victory. Tony said in his diary that I was in a panic because 'there was an unspoken alliance between Vincent Hanna and the [Labour] party officials and I was breaking it'. I do not recall the incident but I take Tony's word for it. Tony won the by-election with a small but increased majority.

The third significant by-election was held in 1987 in the marginal seat of Greenwich. It changed the way by-elections were run and candidates chosen. The by-election followed the death of Labour MP Guy Barnett and was fought at a time when the media was viciously anti-Labour. *Guardian* journalist Martin Linton predicted that the by-election would be dominated by the 'loony left' issue and the success of the campaign would depend crucially on the candidate chosen by the constituency party. Deirdre Wood, the Labour candidate, became known by the media as 'Dreadful Deirdre'. She had been selected by the local party against the wishes of the party leadership. It was alleged that she privately promised Neil Kinnock, 'I won't drop you in it.' Neil's reputed response was, 'It's not you, it's those bastards the press out there.' The press portrayed her as a radical extremist, 'a hard-left feminist, anti-racist and gay rights supporter' as the *News of the World* put it, and they constantly made reference to her age and her figure.

The media, believing that the Tories couldn't win in this normally safe Labour area, actively promoted the SDP candidate, Rosie Barnes – not on policy issues but on the grounds that she was not Deirdre Wood. She won with 52 per cent of the poll.

I found working in the campaign a nightmare. The press reports were repeated by people on the doorstep. This affected the morale of the workers in the campaign. The Labour vote was slipping away.

The tragedy of the Greenwich by-election was that it closely followed the Fulham by-election held in April 1986, which was won with a 7 per cent swing to Labour. I had insisted that the election agent for the Fulham by-election had to be Terry Ashton, the acting regional general secretary in London. This meant having to placating a very upset local agent. I was determined that we should base the campaign on new professional techniques using personalised electioneering, and specifically targeted areas with local messages. Unfortunately we lost the seat fourteen months later at the general election.

Following the disastrous result in Greenwich the NEC took the decision that they would in future be responsible for drawing up the shortlist of candidates for by-elections. I was appointed secretary of the panel with Roy Hattersley as the chair. The other members were two MPs, Joan Lestor and John Evans; and two trade union representatives, Eddie Haigh of the Transport and General Workers' Union and Tom Sawyer, deputy general secretary of the National Union of Public Employees. Neither of these trade unions now exist in their own right as they were combined with other unions to form Unite and Unison.

The panel met all the candidates who had been nominated by the party branches, trade unions and affiliated organisations. We would ask each candidate the same standard questions. Would they support the Labour whip in the Commons? What were their qualifications and experience of the party? What were their

subjects of interest? One question that was always left to me
to ask was the 'skeletons' question. 'Is there anything that we
should know that you would not be happy to see on the front
page of the *Daily Mail*?' As might be expected, the answer was
always no! The shortlist of names that the panel had agreed
upon was then presented to the local party for them to select
from. Usually the shortlist was accepted and the selection went
ahead smoothly. However, if that was not the case, the panel's
responsibilities went further. They could impose the candidate.
The 1989 by-election in Vauxhall, caused by the resignation of
the sitting MP, Stuart Holland, was such an example.

It was clear from the start that this selection was going to be
controversial. I and my regional colleague Terry Ashton agreed
the timetable with the officers of the constituency. They demanded
that a black candidate be selected. The front runner was Martha
Osamor, a Haringey councillor who at the time was in conflict
with her local leadership, opposing the cuts being made by Haringey Council. Other possible candidates were Russell Profitt,
a well-known activist in the black sections; Wesley Kerr, a journalist; and Kate Hoey, a Southwark councillor and previous
parliamentary candidate in Dulwich. Wesley was the only black
candidate included by the panel in the final shortlist. He came to
see me to say he felt he had to withdraw from the shortlist for
personal reasons. The claim was made that he withdrew because
he would not allow himself to be used as a token. That was
completely false. This left an all-white team, which Ken Livingstone promptly declared was a racist action by the members of
the panel. When the list was reported to the executive, someone
leaked the names of the shortlist to *The Guardian*. Tony Benn

proposed at the NEC that Martha Osamor's name be added but could only secure four votes in favour.

When Terry and I arrived at Lambeth Town Hall on the night of the selection we were met by regional TV cameras. Terry says he was literally my bag carrier that evening, but the Thames TV presenter Barbara Long's team of photographers automatically focussed on the bloke, until she shouted at them, 'Not him, her!' The meeting attempted to shout me down, as I stood on the platform trying to read out the shortlist agreed by the panel. I was not surprised when the names were rejected by thirty-three votes to ten.

The four potential candidates had been sitting in a back room waiting to be called to make their speeches if the shortlist had been accepted. Being a good organiser I had planned an alternative. At the back door of the town hall were two cars to take the four nominees plus Terry and me to a committee room in the House of Commons where Roy Hattersley and the panel were waiting. After the panel interviewed all four, Kate Hoey was declared as the Labour candidate for the Vauxhall by-election. Not surprisingly it was a difficult campaign, with some party members opting out. Others, although not happy with the candidate, felt that winning the seat was more important than boycotting the campaign.

This furore further heightened the demand for black sections. Over a number of years a campaign had been run for black sections to have full parity with youth and women's sections in the party structure. In 1980 Liz Atkins, the equality policy researcher, and I as the secretariat for the party's campaign committee produced the party's first report on race relations, 'Labour and the Black Electorate'. It was seen by some black members as pure tokenism. Trevor Phillips, a leading advocate of black sections, had earlier written in *Marxism Today* that 'Labour's black members are bruised and aggrieved by what they see as the party's indifference to them and their needs'. Their frustration, however, sometimes represented itself in making impossible demands. An example of that frustration was a meeting held prior to the election in 1983. The organisers expected Michael Foot to participate. Michael having agreed, I tried to find out the time he was expected. I was told he should sit outside and would be called in at their convenience. This for me was not the way to treat the leader of the party, so I declined the invitation on his behalf.

Black sections did not become official until 1990, after I became secretary of the first black and Asian advisory committee. Virendra Sharma, now MP for Ealing Southall, became the party's first ever ethnic minority officer. The argument then arose as to what was the definition of 'black' – should it be based on colour, or should it include all minorities such as the Irish? Trevor Phillips became the first chair of the equality and human rights committee at the same time as I chaired the women's national committee, established by Harold Wilson to bring the voice of women to government. This meant that after many years we were again working together, but this time on a more friendly basis.

Knowsley North was a constituency where there were constant conflict and disruptions. A by-election was held there in November 1986. After interviewing nominees, the by-elections panel imposed George Howarth as the candidate. George was the son-in-law of one of my colleagues, George Rodgers, who worked in the library at head office and had previously been the MP for Chorley. I spent a lot of time on the campaign, a great deal of it trying to keep the members of Militant from peddling their newspaper on the doorstep when canvassing.

The National Executive subsequently went one step further and agreed that even if a parliamentary candidate had been selected and a by-election occurred, the panel could draw up a shortlist for selection, minus the already selected candidate. The first instance was in 1990 in Eastbourne, not a seat we had any chance of winning and it passed almost unnoticed. When the following year George Buckley died in Hemsworth the reaction was very different. George had been due to retire and a candidate, Ken Capstick, vice-chair of the Yorkshire miners, had already been selected locally to replace him. The by-elections panel removed Ken from the shortlist and Derek Enright was selected instead, a decision unsuccessfully challenged by the NUM. Derek was elected on 7 November 1991. Unfortunately, almost exactly four years later he tragically died and was succeeded by John Trickett in another by-election. Derek was prone to wearing bright-coloured fancy waistcoats, which I suggested he toned down.

I shall always remember Derek's short period as an MP. He sang 'Yellow Submarine' in Latin in the Commons chamber. It was during a debate on the Education Reform Bill. Derek, a former teacher, said, 'To help my pupils discover what the optative and subjunctive are all about I translated Beatles songs into Latin.' Nicholas Fairbairn challenged him to sing a Beatles song in Latin, so Derek immediately stood up and did so.

The Brecon & Radnor by-election in July 1985 was used as

the backdrop for the Save Our National Health Service campaign. Its main thrust was to maintain a level of activity at local level against NHS cuts, hospital closures and privatisation. That was a by-election we felt we could win. Teams came from all parts of the country and the media were out in full force, but sadly it eluded us, resulting in a Liberal–SDP Alliance gain from the Conservatives.

Campaigning activity was continuing to build up the party's strength out in the country in preparation for the next general election. We had a bus that travelled up and down the country, providing a platform for key speakers, members of the shadow Cabinet and constituency MPs. Its sides carried the slogan 'Labour on the Move'.

Neil Kinnock launched the Jobs and Industry campaign in 1984 to present Labour's economic and employment strategy to the public, and to try and convince people that Labour could put Britain back to work. Local co-ordinators were appointed in each area to take responsibility for promoting the campaign across the country. I organised the production of briefing packs, charters and materials designed for specific target groups. This was followed by the introduction of the Fairness and Freedom campaign, to go alongside Jobs and Industry by projecting the concept that real individual freedom comes from a fairer distribution of the nation's wealth.

To promote early activity in the forthcoming county council elections I established a shire county group whose job it was to set the process of electioneering in these widespread areas. Thirty shire counties were twinned with Labour MPs. Campaigning visits were made by key party figures, concentrating on the key policies of the under-fives, transport, education and community care. My friend Josie Farrington, now Baroness Farrington of Ribbleton, was on the group representing Lancashire.

In 1985 Peter Mandelson was appointed director of campaigns and communications. He made no secret of the fact that he believed that everything that had gone before had been a waste of time. Having not been involved he had little concept of the struggles that had been made to keep the party from destroying itself, battles that were still being fought. The Labour Party was still suffering from its persistent image of extremism caused by the media's concentration on the so-called loony left and the growing entryism of the Militant Tendency. The party was still some way from recovery.

Peter brought a professionalism and polish to presentation. As part of his new communication strategy he introduced the red rose as the party symbol. Peter had enormous skill in handling the media, which was a key element of the 1987 general election. The Shadow Communications Agency (SCA) was established, under the guidance of Peter and Philip Gould. They both firmly believed that the national media would bring the party victory. Peter did not give the impression of being a team player, often illustrated at campaign meetings by his absenting himself from the discussion going on around him. It was clear to me and the other directors sitting round the table that the decisions on the strategy, the presentation and running of the campaign were being taken by the SCA and the leader's office. An example was when Larry Whitty and Geoff Bish drew up a manifesto which when presented to Neil and his team was said to lack punch and style. Bryan Gould and Gerald Kaufman were given the job of re-writing it, but even after attempts by these two seasoned politicians it was re-written again by the leader and Charles Clarke.

The consequences of this new regime were both good and bad. The good was clearly shown with their first party political broadcast, 'Kinnock: The Movie'. It portrayed Neil as a decent politician, which he is, a man who cared, and it said that the strong should help the weak. Neil's personal popularity jumped sixteen points overnight. For me personally the bad was the scorn that was heaped on those who believed that there was value in party members communicating directly face to face with the electorate. My years of experience had taught me how necessary local campaigning was if we were to succeed. Canvassing was a waste of time and a waste of resources, we were told. Only the media mattered, the media was the message.

Nationally and locally organising posts were allocated several years before the election, the target seats identified and work patterns sorted out. The development officers in the directorate worked out strategies on how to influence their respective targets: women, youth, students and ethnic minorities. The pre-election team I set up worked on providing support and advice to the key areas.

Retired staff and MPs joined the team at head office, including Ian Mikardo, the outgoing MP for Bow & Poplar. He was not happy with his parliamentary replacement, Mildred Gordon, and told me he was desperate to work on the campaign. I gave him a job going through the correspondence we received each day. Someone in the communications directorate at head office had decided that we should sell wine with a Labour Party label. They clearly hadn't tasted it. When Mik did he immediately went out and brought in a crate of acceptable wine to keep us going during the long nights.

Mik had been a longstanding left-wing member of the National Executive. He was not always popular with the party establishment, but he was a friend to me not least as he gave me support and confidence to take a major role in the meetings and conferences of Socialist International Women.

The election result was disappointing. We only gained twenty seats but what we did achieve was to dash the hopes of the SDP–Liberal Alliance. We retained our position as the main opposition party. Party members expressed their disappointment at the election defeat. At the moratorium held at the following party conference, the blame and the consequences were heatedly debated. That was in contrast to the 1983 election, when no such inquest was ever held.

For Neil Kinnock, as for all leaders, there were good times and not so good times. It was during one of the latter that Tony Benn decided to challenge him for the leadership and Eric Heffer chose to stand against Roy Hattersley as the deputy leader. They said they were standing in protest against the direction the 'dream ticket' was taking the party. They caused disruption when they had no prospect of winning. In *The Times* in March 1988, Neil called the contest an 'outrageous distraction' which would 'not be forgiven'. Robin Cook was Neil's campaign manager, effectively putting the case as why Neil should continue as leader of the party. My daughter Jeannette was Robin's able assistant in the campaign.

A Mori poll conducted that April showed that only 61 per cent of Labour supporters and 37 per cent of trade unionists were satisfied with Neil as leader. By June, eight out of ten Labour MPs believed he lacked authority and four out of ten did not want him to lead the party into the next general election. Nevertheless, Neil's popularity was shown by his overwhelming majority in the ballot held at that autumn's annual conference, giving him 89 per cent of the electoral college. He now believed he had the authority to lead the party as he wished, an authority he took upon himself. Neil heard the result of the ballot not only as chair of the party but also as chair of the conference. It was for me, and I am sure for most people in the hall, a unique situation for the leader to make three major speeches: giving the chair's opening speech, his leader's speech and the winding-up comments. It is the only conference I recall being so dominated by the party leader.

Almost immediately following conference the party suffered a devastating defeat by the Scottish National Party in a by-election in Glasgow Govan. It was caused by the nomination of the Labour MP, Bruce Millan, as an EEC commissioner. I visited Glasgow to discuss the campaign, which was being run by the Scottish office. The organisation of the campaign left me in despair. The SNP candidate, Jim Sillars, was an ex-Labour MP who used the by-election to campaign for non-payment of the poll tax. He ran an efficient and lively campaign as opposed to the rather dull and regular one we ran.

Neil had to face other challenges including falling party membership and the financial crisis the party was facing. By 1988 the party was £2 million in debt. A quarter of the staff were made redundant, and *Labour Weekly*, our newspaper, was closed down. It was replaced by the highly controlled *Labour Party News*, which ended up being more expensive. Three years later extra staff were brought in to prepare for the 1992 election, increasing the party's overdraft.

Increasing membership was seen as the answer. A membership development group was set up with Eddie Haigh of the Transport and General Workers' Union as its chair. There had been a slow but marginal increase in membership post-1983, but the decision on financial grounds to increase the subscription to £10 in 1985 saw an immediate drop. Neil launched a campaign to make one million members. I hoped but never believed that it could succeed and it didn't. It failed badly with only a 6 per cent increase in membership. It didn't succeed for a number of reasons. The support for Labour was not there. The party's initial membership figures were widely inaccurate. The system for processing new members was shambolic. Pre-1992 there was no national membership as such. Each constituency party was sent membership cards and returned those they hadn't sold to head office, who calculated the number of members from this accurate system. There was also a barrier put up by local parties who did not want new members. This became known as the 'Sorry, we're full' syndrome.

In the nine years from 1983 to 1992 the party was in a state of turmoil and disarray. Yet in spite of this by 1992 Neil had transformed Labour policy. The party had a more attractive image. The organisation had dramatically improved and there was a chance of victory. Alas it was not to be.

The lead in the polls in 1990 and Labour's successful European election results put the party twelve points ahead of the Tories except on the two crucial policies of economic competence and leadership. A great deal of that success was due to the election planning group, chaired by Jack Cunningham MP. Set up in 1989, its aim was to centralise the running of the European and local elections. It was opposed by some but got my absolute and full support. At our meetings we planned and plotted and succeeded. Jack took the team to dinner at the Gay Hussar in appreciation of our work.

In November 1990 Margaret Thatcher resigned and John Major became Prime Minister. If a general election had been called then the future might have been different. Neil defied John Major to call an election, but Major, correctly for the Tories, ignored these challenges.

During the 1992 election the SCA along with the leader's office continued to determine the national strategy. Peter Mandelson had gone up north to be the candidate in the Hartlepool constituency. Meanwhile I was continuing to battle to get support and funding for local activity, so we could put greater efforts into the forty-two target seats.

Earlier Philip Gould had produced a 64-page review of the party's communication efforts and made recommendations for the future. This became the basis for the campaign strategy. Philip's philosophy, which I fully supported, was that a strategy will only work if it is written down.

Each day I received reports of the reaction to the national press conferences being held in the regions as well as the response to Neil Kinnock's walkabouts as he toured the country. This was to be a people's campaign based on social issues. Neil even appeared in a pop video. The liveliness of the campaign had a positive effect on the morale of the party.

Bryan Gould had joined the national team as the parliamentary campaign co-ordinator. This meant at times that Bryan, Philip Gould and I would meet – three Goulds together but not a connection between us. Mine originated in Ireland from Kevin's father, Bryan was a New Zealander and Philip was from Woking.

On the eve of the election, the opinion polls showed us level with the Conservatives. I was meeting with Philip Gould to discuss the possible outcome and polling day tactics when he said to me, 'It is all up to you now, Joyce.' I am sure there was no malice in his comment, but after years of struggling to get local activity recognised, there was no ceiling high enough to gauge my reaction. Nevertheless I respected him and the crucial part he played in every general election from 1987 through to 2005. Sadly this nice man died of cancer in 2011.

The 1992 result was once again disappointing, even though it reduced the Conservative majority to twenty-one seats. Without the efforts put into the specially targeted key seats, it would have been worse. The hard work of our hundred-plus full-time organisers and the many, many voluntary party members resulted in a 1.6 per cent national swing and a 3.75 per cent swing in the key seats.

The influence of local campaigning has long been a subject of debate. This issue is covered in detail in *British Elections and Parties Yearbook 1994*, edited by David Broughton, David M. Farrell, David Denver and Colin Rallings. The analysis shows that local party membership can mobilise, stimulate and boost the vote of the Labour Party but does not have a similar outcome for the Conservatives. This was a very significant predictor of the Labour vote in 1987, and the book goes on to show that in

1992 there was a correlation between the intensity of the Labour Party's local campaigns and the share of the vote. The book also suggests that political activists and party managers are right to ignore conventional wisdoms, and that general elections are not exclusively won or lost at national level. I am always happy when I am proved to be right.

There are many theories about why Labour lost in 1992. Was it the *Sun* headlines 'If Kinnock wins today, will the last person to leave Britain please turn out the lights' and 'Nightmare on Kinnock'? Certainly the editor of *The Sun*, Kelvin McKenzie, thought so with his boastful front page the day after the election, 'It's The Sun Wot Won It'. Did the Sheffield rally have an effect with its 20,000 audience, the hall decorated with flags, or was it Neil's triumphalist approach? Dennis Skinner's comment was that eight years practising to be a statesman was lost when Neil said, 'We're alright!' Was it the issue of Jennifer's ear, which featured in a party political broadcast on the preservation of the National Health Service? This incident illustrated the differing experience of two little girls with blocked ear canals: one girl had swift treatment using private medicine and the other girl, using the NHS, had her treatment repeatedly delayed. The broadcast had been badly researched and was wrong in its analysis. Roy Hattersley cautioned that we must not be so obsessed with glitz and glamour that the medium becomes the message.

An error was also made when the election literature about the NHS used a symbol very similar to that of the Red Cross. This inadvertently associated the Red Cross symbol with a political matter. The Red Cross had been afforded the symbol by law. As a consequence the Labour Party was prosecuted through

Larry Whitty, the general secretary. The prosecution was settled out of court.

Barbara Castle in her book *Fighting All the Way* had a different theory. 'The greatest mistake was that Neil's advisors would not allow him to be himself. He had been sanitised in case the press picked out of context a single phrase that they could distort.' She went on to say, 'The election rallies had no spontaneity, the order was fixed. Firstly the local candidate, then a celebrity and then Neil on his feet in time for the nine o'clock news to give his carefully prepared speech.' I must admit that as Neil's leadership went on, I began to support her view.

Meanwhile my team at head office had worked to the maxim that elections are won in years, not weeks, and had been developing and polishing new election techniques and skills. It was the first election in which we used new technology, sending to targeted groups one million letters from Neil. It was also the election where we introduced the concept of telephone canvassing. It was important that canvassers did not come over on the phone as automata reading from a script, but as genuine human beings. We did this by learning the skill in front of a mirror. If we smiled into the mirror the smile was reflected in our voice. Not everyone approved. Telephone canvassing does not replace face-to-face contact but does have its advantages. Party workers who cannot run door to door can be canvassers, and phone calls can be made from any part of the country.

It was important to me to make sure that the staff were happy in spite of the long hours, that they were kept fully informed of the strategy behind the campaign, that they were aware of each day's key event and that they all felt part of an important team, helping the party to win. They were a fabulous staff, who put aside any personal differences to get the job done for the party. I think I succeeded. The thirty members of my head office team all signed a thank-you card to me on the eve of poll, which read, 'Thank you for everything you have done to boost our morale.' For all the encouragement, biccies, tea and sympathy etc. My colleague Jean Corston wrote, 'Maybe women make better "directors"' – cheers, Jean. I was delighted with the comment from Paul Simpson: 'I have enjoyed working in the organisation directorate a great deal. This has been a great campaign, it will be a great government.'

That was not to be. It took time for us to realise how bad the result was. Maybe we ignored the fact that working people since 1979 had been slowly deserting the party for the Tories. Maybe there was fear about union power and a reminder of the 'winter of discontent', or maybe the decline in the level of voter registration arising from the poll tax was to blame. In the words of Roy Hattersley, we must not be so obsessed with the glitz and glamour that the medium becomes the message.

Standing on the steps of party headquarters in Walworth Road in the early hours of 10 April 1992 was one of the saddest moments I can recall. The media was out in force, and loyal party members had come to give their support and sympathy. There was a gathering of very disheartened staff and a number of celebrities, including Ben Elton and Michelle Collins. Our low spirts were made worse by cars full of young Tories going back and forth shouting, 'Four-nil, four-nil'.

We were waiting for Neil's cavalcade to arrive. To lose four general elections in a row was a serious blow. It was a major catastrophe to those party activists in the bedrock of the party who had given weeks of their voluntary time, canvassing, going from doorstep to doorstep, filling envelopes in committee rooms, and on the day getting every known Labour voter to the polling station to put their cross for Labour on the ballot paper.

Larry Whitty had been detained. I had to greet the defeated leader. I shall never forget walking down the steps to meet Neil as he got out of his car. Our embrace as we met was seen on television that night and has been shown at many other times. Three days later Neil resigned with the words 'My sorrow is that millions will suffer because of the election of another Conservative government'. How right he was.

The resignation of Neil, and Roy, was the end of an era, an era which transformed the Labour Party, an era that has a significant place in the history of the party. It saw substantial change in the image of the party, its professionalism and importantly its belief in itself. I am proud to have played a significant part in those developments.

CHAPTER 12

⊰⟨∙⟩⟩⊱

WITCHFINDER
GENERAL

The history of tolerance is something that we will defend
but there comes a time when you have to say that tolerance
when abused has to be spoken out against.

Tony Clarke (Lord Clarke of Hampstead),
1990 Labour Party conference

During the eight years that I was director of organisation I handled the most difficult and time-consuming disciplinary cases. I was wholly responsible for identifying evidence and implementing further action leading to the removal of the threat posed by the Militant Tendency. It often meant working eighty or a hundred hours a week. I learnt to have a broad back. It was eight years of vilification and threatening behaviour, abuse and violence.

How did I feel about the role? I was not always happy but I firmly believed it was necessary. Militant were not a party of the 'left'. This was shown so obviously by their attitude to policy issues which I supported – equality, individual human rights, reproductive rights and race relations – all of which they treated with disdain. Their response to these basic fundamental rights was always that it would all come right when the revolution comes. What some party members including members of the NEC failed to understand, deliberately or innocently, was that Militant were not a left-wing pressure group. Their definition of themselves was as a 'political entryist cadre'. But it was not political differences that determined my decisions. My actions were based on their disruptive behaviour, thuggery and breaches of party rules.

One of the names Militant gave me which I found most amusing, although it was intended to hurt, was Witchfinder General. I may have appeared to them as an uncompromising and evil reactionary figure but I found it difficult to see myself as the heavily fictionalised murderous figure of Matthew Hopkins, a seventeenth-century English lawyer. He claimed he had been appointed Witchfinder General by Parliament during the English Civil War to root out sorcery and witchcraft. In my case it was not sorcery or witchcraft that had to be rooted out but those whose aim and ambition was to destroy the Labour Party from within.

From a minuscule group with no resources, Militant became the most successful entryist faction within the modern Labour Party. Its rise had no parallel in the history of Trotskyist groups in Britain. Its stated aims were 'the winning of the most conscious, combative, fighting Militant sections of the working class'. Under Ted Grant, their founder and spiritual leader, they believed that that aim could only be achieved by the take-over of the British

Labour Party. When I read its 45-page bible, *British Perspectives and Tasks*, there was no doubt in my mind that with its central machine, its number of full-time organisers, its increasing membership, its own printing company producing its newspaper, *Militant*, and its fundraising activities, it was clearly a party within a party.

Militant targeted sixty constituencies, which they described as being made up of old men and women. They said, 'We must build in-roads into the wards and into these constituencies as we have in the Young Socialists.'

It was a particularly difficult time for my staff. We regularly discussed the state of the party at our meetings. I was told stories of party members being driven away by the disruptive and offensive behaviours by Militant 'members' and supporters. The information was reported to the National Executive but not acted upon. I was, however, astonished to hear the north-west regional organiser, Paul Carmody, boasting that he had no intention of going into Merseyside or getting engaged in Liverpool, which was the centre of Militant activity. He left his assistant Peter Killeen and the full-time agent in Liverpool, Wally Edwards, with the job of trying to stem the take-over.

Longstanding members of the party decided to stop attending party meetings and activities within the party. Others stayed active but appealed for help, appeals which landed on my desk. Meanwhile the NEC dithered and rejected the evidence, much to the hilarity of the Militants. Their glee was obvious as they continued their march forward, even more so when Andy Bevan, a well-known supporter of Militant, was appointed as the party's youth officer.

In 1975, Reg Underhill, the national agent, produced a paper analysing the role of the Militant Tendency and its entryism into the party. On its presentation to the NEC Eric Heffer promptly moved that the report should 'lie on the table' – a procedural motion that meant the matter was not discussed or voted upon. This was seconded by Dennis Skinner, who said, 'We should not spend time examining our navel.' The general secretary, Ron Hayward, said that 'we should not set up an inquisition'. Eric's motion was carried and the NEC went on to discuss other matters.

Tony Benn's reaction to the report was to claim that some of the information was sent in anonymously in brown paper envelopes by the security and intelligence services. They had broken into Militant offices to get the information. Other parts, he said, were forgeries parallel to the Zinoviev letter. He repeated these accusations to me when I was later presenting evidence against Militant.

After a long period of arguments and bitter rows, the Underhill Report was considered by a small committee of five members. The conclusions were a whitewash, a damp squib: the recommended solution was to have a membership drive and a programme of political education. The tenacious Reg Underhill, even though now retired and in the House of Lords, continued his lone efforts. In 1980, he re-submitted his report to Ron Hayward and the new national agent, David Hughes, who said, it is surprisingly alleged (but I doubt it), that he didn't have time to read it. Reg personally paid to print and distribute 750 copies. Like Reg, I was not thinking of expulsions being the answer to the problems created by Militant but action to curb Militant's activities. I soon changed my mind.

As leader of the party, Michael Foot too was opposed to expulsions but he agreed that some action had to be taken, after meeting delegations of MPs who expressed their concerns to him, including my friend Ken Woolmer (now Lord Woolmer of Leeds), who had been the leader of Leeds City Council. The real influence on Michael was, as he said, the concerns of people who marched with him at Aldermaston, people Militant saw as vicars or liberal middle-class trendies. Michael's proposal was that the general secretary and the national agent prepare a report looking at any breaches of rules by Militant supporters. Part of the vast amount of evidence was received from the regional organisers. The only exception was Jimmy Allison, the Scottish organiser, who according to his book *Guilty by Suspicion* refused on the grounds that he does not spy on party members.

There was nothing substantially new in the detail of the report. The recommendations, however, proposed the establishment of a register of non-affiliated groups, and further that Militant were not eligible to be on the register as they were in breach of the rules of the party. It was incredible for me to sit and listen to senior members of the party arguing in defence of Militant. Tony Benn referred to himself as an unregistered socialist and that he would not register. No one was asking him to.

It fell to the new general secretary, Jim Mortimer, to present the register to the party conference for approval. He concentrated on the role of the five members of the editorial board of the *Militant* paper.

Each conference has its share of excitement, level of disputes and tensions, but the 1982 conference was the worst I had ever experienced. It had its own brutality, its own level of venom in speeches from both sides of the argument. 'What they (that is Militant) do not have a right to do is to live parasitically. Parasites can live compatibly with some hosts, but some parasites kill the body they are in' – John Spellar MP. 'Are we going to engage in a game of Oranges and Lemons? If you are caught at being a Militant, here comes the chopper to chop off your head – chop, chop, chop, chop' – Muriel Gordon (Hendon South CLP).

To the media's delight the *Militant* editorial board were sitting in the gallery of the hall fully enjoying themselves.

This heated and acrimonious debate ended with conference voting by three to one accept the report. The implication of this decision was that members of the Militant Tendency were ineligible for membership of the Labour Party, an implication seen mistakenly by some as the beginning of the end of Militant's involvement in the party. Annoyingly, legal correspondence from Militant that told us that the register could not be a basis for expulsion, a view subsequently agreed by the party lawyers, on two counts: the rule book was deficient and there was no concept of natural justice built into the party procedures.

There was no strategy on how to progress. It was difficult to comprehend that after years of dithering and misguided attempts the only solution arrived at was unworkable. I sat through a subdued executive meeting as they agreed to send the *Militant* editorial board the 'motion' that the Militant Tendency was ineligible for affiliation to the party. It was accompanied by a request that they meet the executive. In protest Militant unsuccessfully went for an injunction from the High Court – in spite of their condemnation of the capitalist courts.

The five members of the editorial board arrived at head office

cheered on by a crowd of supporters that had gathered outside. I had to meet them and take them up to the board room.
Meanwhile Dennis Skinner had unsuccessfully moved that the
meeting not go ahead. The five made no attempts to respond to
the 'motion', rather relying on threats and assertions that they
had the support of the 'rank and file'. The meeting had to break
when Tony Benn spied someone on the roof. It was a reporter
complete with TV equipment. He was speedily removed, and the
meeting resumed. Questions and answers flowed. The members of
the editorial board then withdrew and sat chatting and laughing
outside the room. The NEC deliberated at length. Tony Benn and
Eric Heffer were defeated in their bid that no action be taken.
The editorial board members returned and were informed that
action would be taken to remove them as members of the party.
How that was to be done within the party rules took weeks of
deliberation by our legal team. Finally, a definition of Militant
membership was arrived at. This included providing financial
support, promoting Militant and participation in its activities.
A definition I was later to build on.

Wednesday 23 February 1983 dawned. The big day had arrived
for the hearings and possible expulsion of the editorial board.
Tension was high. I was greeted on the doorstep of party headquarters in Walworth Road by a barrage of slogan shouting and
banner waving, cheers for those people who it was assumed
would be supporting Militant, and boos and abuse for everyone
else. This went on for some time as the NEC started the meeting
on another subject, the decision to endorse Peter Tatchell as
the candidate for Bermondsey by-election. It was unfortunate
that all this mayhem was happening in sight of the Bermondsey

constituency, whose boundary was just across from Walworth Road. It was not the best image for a party embarking on its by-election campaign.

The NEC launched into its deliberations on how to handle the interviews, not without drama, in which Audrey Wise threatened to walk out of the meeting. Over two and a half hours later, at 12.53 p.m. I ushered the five into the board room. I had then to supervise the proceedings, included meeting their demands for breaks, usually on the pretext of requesting a toilet break when really they wanted to ring their lawyers for advice. Also I had to deal with their many requests for such trivial things as a pen or a piece of paper to write on. More difficult was having to work the rather ancient tape machine that was to record the meeting.

Throughout, the *Militant* board members indulged in bullying tactics. Their opening remarks were 'We are here under protest', 'It is the beginning of trouble for the NEC', 'There will be legal challenges', and 'There will be protests up and down the country'. Suddenly a solicitor's letter was produced challenging the NEC's right to hold the hearing. This meant another break whilst the NEC deliberated. The NEC disagreed with its content. The five *Militant* editors returned to inform the NEC that they were not worried about expulsion, as in future they would work through the trade union movement. At no time did they make a serious attempt to challenge the charges except to declare that they were not members of Militant Tendency, that the evidence was based on malicious gossip gathered by full-time officials and that no money was raised from mysterious sources as alleged.

The members of the *Militant* editorial board, Peter Taaffe, Ted Grant, Keith Dickinson, Lynn Walsh and Clare Doyle, were informed of the decision by the executive that they would be excluded from membership of the Labour Party, subject to their appeal to conference. They left the building shouting that it had been 'two hours of a show trial'. Standing on the steps, Ted Grant addressed the crowd, saying we had not heard the end of the matter and that there would be protests across the length and breadth of the Labour movement. These were sham protests for in spite of the decision by the NEC they knew that they had won this battle. Militant and their role in the party were safe. In their own words, 'Militant had won game, set and match'. They had won because no action was possible against the eight parliamentary candidates who had already been endorsed by the National Executive. I think John Golding was rather naive when he stated that the days of Militant bullying were over. It was my view that the battle had been lost but the war was still going on.

On the Monday afternoon at the 1983 party conference, standing orders were suspended to hear the Militants' appeals. Peter Taaffe went first. Each spoke without interruption, denying the accusations against them, and regaling conference with what they contributed to the party. Ted Grant was at his most defiant: 'We will be back, we will be restored, if not in one year, in two or three years. We will be back.' When all five had been heard conference adjourned for ten minutes. This was to give time for the trade union delegations to decide how to vote. All five were expelled by a margin of four to one. The result was greeted by a combination of hand clapping and barracking.

The next episode of this long saga was initiated by the actions of Liverpool City Council. Liverpool was a city of political conflict, going back to the days when Bessie and John

Braddock ran the city. They had previously been members of the Communist Party, then moved to the rigid right and ruled Liverpool with an iron hand. It was a city that was ripe for a Militant take-over.

By 1982 the Liverpool Labour Party was indeed under Militant control and had adopted the slogan 'Better to break the law than break the poor', which had originated in Poplar Borough Council in the East End of London in 1919–20. In 1985, rather than face immediate confrontation with the law by passing an illegal budget, the Militant-controlled Labour council decided on the 'tactic' of issuing 99-day redundancy notices to its 3,000 workforce. In his biography, Derek Hatton, the council's deputy leader at the time, acknowledges that this was an enormous mistake from which the council never recovered. This view was supported by Ted Grant, who saw it as 'a major tactical error'. The council admitted that they had had no intention of following the sackings through; it was a tactic to try and get greater government funding. At the same time it was alleged that they were negotiating a big loan from a Swiss bank.

All this provided the catalyst for Neil Kinnock's famous speech at the party conference in 1985:

> Implausible promises don't win victories. I'll tell you what happens with impossible promises. You start with far-fetched resolutions. They are then pickled into a rigid dogma, a code, and you go through the years sticking to that, outdated, misplaced, irrelevant to the real needs, and you end up with the grotesque chaos of a Labour council – a *Labour* council – hiring taxis to scuttle round a city handing out redundancy notices

to its own workers … You can't play politics with people's jobs
and with people's services or with their homes.

Eric Heffer walked off the platform. It was not unusual for him to walk out of meetings but this was real drama. Bedlam followed. Derek Hatton and his colleague Tony Mulhearn shouted 'Liar, liar' at Neil, whilst others jeered. Many delegates sat stunned.

In his book *Labour's Future*, Heffer blindly says Liverpool was not controlled by Militant, that it was a left-wing purge, a Neil Kinnock offensive against Liverpool City Council. It was, however, a watershed moment for the party. Letters poured in from major trade unions and party members in Liverpool outlining irregularities of the Liverpool District Labour Party and Militant's destructive influence throughout the city.

Not everyone in Liverpool supported the council. In October 1985 thousands of people gathered at the city's Pier Head for a Liverpool against Militant demonstration. They released an anti-Militant record. Neil Kinnock made the apposite comment at this stage that 'a church with open doors is still a church; a church without walls is an open space to be trampled on … We will not buckle any more than the people of courage who told the truth about Militant in Liverpool buckled to threats.' At a small seminar I recently attended on the provision of contraception services, the chair sounded as though he originated from Liverpool. At the end of the afternoon I asked him if he did. 'Yes,' he replied, 'and I was one of those people who received my redundancy notice by taxi.'

The Liverpool district party was suspended. An inquiry team was appointed to look at its the practices and procedures.

The evening before the first day of the inquiry I arranged for the eight members of the inquiry team, the general secretary and myself to have dinner together. I chose a round table, believing it might help to a get a feeling of co-operation. Indeed sweetness and light reigned as we spent the evening listening to Audrey Wise explaining to us how she recycled everything including the water she boiled the potatoes in. That period of calm did not last. We went into the first hearing the next morning with Charlie Turrock in the chair. The other members of the panel – Tony Clarke, Margaret Beckett, Tom Sawyer, Betty Boothroyd, Eddie Haigh, Neville Hough and Audrey Wise – settled behind a long table. Sixty gruelling hours of discussion, questions and debate began. Some 120 members were interviewed and 106 written pieces of evidence were read. I was the person dealing with the unruly mob that regularly gathered in support of their Militant comrades. It is impossible from the final report, 'Investigation into the Liverpool District Labour Party', to get any sense of the atmosphere in which the inquiry took place.

The interviews were long and arduous and sometimes incomprehensible. The tactic of constant demands for breaks was again the pattern. Now they demanded to see the charge sheets against them, they conferred with each other or used the telephone to get advice from their lawyers or their leadership. Derek Hatton loved this ploy. I had the unenviable job of accompanying him to the office where he could use a phone. He had this unfortunate habit of constantly winking at me; what that was meant to achieve, I had no idea. It certainly had no effect on me. Eric Heffer came to the hearing as his 'friend'. He had on occasions to be told he was not there to speak, something he found difficult not to do.

At 8.30 on the first night Hatton decided he was going home. He left to applause and loud laughter, arrogantly stating that if the inquiry went on in his absence he would go to the High Court. He didn't do that but the next day he turned up accompanied by his barrister. As the days passed witnesses on both sides were interviewed. There were contradictions and exaggerations. At the end of it all the panel concluded 'beyond reasonable doubt that the concentration of power and decision making is largely dominated by the organisation of the Militant Tendency', and further that all the rules of the Liverpool district party had to be re-written, that every unit of the party in Liverpool had to be reformed and that to enable that to happen a full-time organiser had to be appointed.

The panel split over the action to be taken against individuals. Six members supported the recommendation that sixteen members of the Liverpool party be investigated by the executive committee. Margaret Beckett and Audrey Wise opposed and wrote a minority report which was published at the end of the main report. Tony Benn's reaction to the conclusions was that he was not going to support police tactics: 'I shall fight like a tiger to prevent expulsions and proscriptions.' The redoubtable Joan Lestor retorted that he had a lot to answer for because of his failure to repudiate Militant's intolerance.

On 26 March 1986, Militant took the party to court, the day before the hearings of twelve of the sixteen members was due to take place. I went to court with Derry Irvine, our senior barrister, later to become Lord Chancellor; Alan Wilkie, now Sir Alan Wilkie and a High Court judge; and John Sharpe, our solicitor. Tony Blair, although not present, was the junior member of the legal team.

I had never been in a court room. I felt both anxiety and expectation. Derry's first words to me were: 'We have lost the case, we have a "natural justice" judge.' I was stunned. The case hadn't even started. But he was right; we did lose the case. Lord Justice Browne-Wilkinson's judgment was that the party had to modify its procedures in order to accord with the court's conception of natural justice, adding that the party's National Executive could not be both judge and jury. He ruled that the eight members of the inquiry panel could not take part in the disciplinary hearings, and that certain stipulations would have to be taken into account when considering requests for witnesses and legal representations. I worked with our legal team on the drawing up of the new procedures and the conduct of future hearings.

The first attempt to hold a hearing of the Liverpool Militants without the inquiry panel members had to be abandoned. Seven members of the NEC walked out, making the meeting inquorate. The twelve due to be interviewed arrived and were put by someone in Larry Whitty's outer office. They took great delight in opening the window which overlooked the street, posing so that the photographers below could take their pictures. They also took delight in receiving expenses for their journey, which Larry had agreed could be paid. They left the building to chants from their supporters of 'Liverpool, Liverpool, Liverpool – twelve-nil – here we go'.

Eventually the cases were heard. Tony Mulhearn was the first. His tactic was again to keep asking for breaks. He had to consult to determine if he should have a legal representative with him. He made phone calls asking for advice, and unbelievably was allowed a break for a fish and chip lunch. And so it went on. In my copious notes I recorded Mulhearn's comment that 'time passes quickly when you are having fun'. The day wore on into evening. At 9.15 p.m. Derek Hatton went home. He instructed his solicitor to make an application for an injunction. The hearings had to be adjourned until 11 p.m. At some time after midnight the case against Mulhearn was found to be proven. The next day saw another long hearing, three cases and one expulsion.

A month later five more cases were heard, including that of Derek Hatton. He was not present as 'surprisingly' special meetings of Liverpool council committees had been called. A motion by Tony Benn and Eric Heffer that his case be not heard in his absence was defeated by twelve votes to six, so it proceeded. On a ballot he was expelled. As deputy leader of Liverpool Council Hatton enjoyed playing games and shouting the odds, but he didn't stand up to face his critics. To me it was unbelievable that David Blunkett and Michael Meacher should propose that he be removed from office and candidature but not expelled from the party, as though that would have stopped his antics.

Three further hearings resulted in two expulsions and one case being withdrawn. The case against Felicity Dowling, the district Labour Party secretary, was deferred until October. All those who had been expelled were given the opportunity to speak for five minutes to the party conference. None turned up.

Following the judge's ruling the party had to review its disciplinary procedures. The National Constitutional Committee (NCC) was established. It meant that in the future the NCC would take the final decision on disciplinary matters. Not only had the role of the NEC changed but mine had too. I received all alleged complaints of breaches of party rules, whether initiated locally or by the National Executive. Together with the relevant regional organiser I would investigate their validity. I interviewed the complainants and those complained against. If I felt it was justified I would present a 'prima facie' to the executive. It was their responsibility to decide if they agreed with my findings. If they did I then became the 'prosecutor' putting the case before the NCC. If the case was proven they determined the disciplinary action that should be taken: expulsion from the party, suspension for a period of time or no action at all.

The hearings were mini-courts, with cross-examination of both the person against whom the case was being taken and their witnesses. There was also cross-examination of me on how I came to my conclusions and on the validity of my evidence. Sometimes it meant being questioned by the accused's legal advisor. I was never accompanied by a lawyer. I personally conducted the cross-examination of the person charged, their witnesses and my witnesses. I had to be confident. So I did an enormous amount of preparation to make sure that my evidence was solid and sustainable. I was determined to try not to lose a case.

The number of cases I had to 'prosecute' was extensive. I sometimes spent many hours working, well into the night. I worked with our legal team, examining every aspect and detail of every case. This meant the writing of many affidavits and reports. Derry Irvine had taught me the real meaning of natural justice, a concept that governed all my actions through these tumultuous years. Derry once asked me why I had not joined the legal profession; all I know is that I could not have been as successful without the advice and support given to me by him and John Sharpe.

There were those who believed that the establishment of the NCC was a path to making expulsions easier. How wrong they were. It provided natural justice for all involved and the opportunity for each person charged to challenge the evidence.

Peter Kilfoyle was appointed as the Liverpool full-time organiser. Peter, a Liverpudlian, had spent time in Australia but had now returned to his home town. In his book *Left Behind*, Peter gives a full description of living in Liverpool. He covers the years from 1986 until 1991, when he became MP for Liverpool Walton. He refers in the book to Larry Whitty as 'reluctant to engage in "witch hunts" and that it was when Neil Kinnock and Joyce Gould got the bit between their teeth that effective action began'. So began my personal Liverpool experience. Taking the train to Liverpool two or three times a week, I attended party meetings and held interview after interview. I discussed the situation in the city with many different individuals with many differing views. Peter was clear that my national role and my constant presence was vital in sorting matters out. His relationship with the north-west regional office was at times fraught, not least because he had a direct line to me, but also because overall the staff in the office were aware that I felt strongly that they were not on top of the situation and relied on him.

There was nothing regular about which days in the week I went on these journeys but somehow Militant always knew. I later discovered that one of the guards on the Liverpool train was one of their number. For my security I had to be met at the station by Phil Robinson, the north-west regional organiser, and another volunteer colleague. Phil had to pay someone to stay with the car to stop it being vandalised.

Irrespective of the threats of violence, including knee-capping, and the harassment, I refused to be intimidated. It was not easy. Most of the meetings I attended did not follow any form of procedure. The members talked across each other and were generally disruptive. 'Hatton's army', the static security force sitting in the front row, was a serious attempt to intimidate me. None of them had a right to be there but it would have been ridiculous on my part to suggest they leave, as it would without doubt have led to a serious fracas.

In desperation members were prepared to speak out against these political bandits. John Hamilton was the leader of the council, but in name only. He was a Quaker who enjoyed being the leader but clearly had no authority. He was constantly ignored and slighted. He was not even told about the redundancy notices fiasco before they went out. In one incident I was speaking to him before a group meeting when Derek Hatton pushed his way between us and said to me, 'You don't talk to him without me being present.' John Hamilton decided the time had come to expose the Militant role in Liverpool.

For me it was a most stressful time. In a note to me Richard Taylor sums it up:

> I do not think anyone who was not around at the time could realise the task you took on – it took tremendous courage dealing with some very difficult people! I remember you coming back to Walworth Road after being in Liverpool for the weekend and clearly exhausted but straight to your desk and on with the job.

> I recall Marian Craythorne saying Joyce looks like she has done
> three overnight NEC counts, she needs to rest.

It took time but the final reward was seeing Militant lose its control of the Liverpool party.

Peter Kilfoyle and I had respect for our different roles and supported each other's efforts and only on one occasion does Peter say in his book he 'got a rare roasting from Joyce'. It was the time of the Ribble Valley by-election, in March 1991, and I had instructed him to go to the by-election. He was not keen on the idea. Our candidate was my close friend Josie Farrington. Peter, however, acknowledges he enjoyed working with Josie, even though victory was never on the cards.

In the Walton by-election four months later, held following the death of Eric Heffer, Peter faced opposition from a Militant standing as Real Labour. During the campaign he was subject to death threats by telephone. He took my advice to record the messages. The police then stepped in and intercepted all his calls, but no one was apprehended.

Liverpool was not the only area where Militant was in the ascendant. However, tackling Liverpool gave other party members the impetus to build up cases against the Militants in their constituencies. I received all their findings and checked their evidence to determine whether their allegations were justifiable, and if so presented them to the NCC. Across the country expulsions went ahead. Others were sent back as spurious and not acted upon.

I was instructed by the National Executive to investigate three other Militant hotspots, Bradford, Glasgow and Brighton.

There had been a long history of Militant activity in Bradford. As far back as 1976, Harold Sims, then the Yorkshire regional organiser, berated head office for its inaction on Militant entryism in Bradford. Pat Wall, a long-time senior Militant figure, became the MP for Bradford North in 1987. This was after two unsuccessful attempts by the National Executive not to endorse him as a candidate. Wall moved from Liverpool to Bradford in the early 1980s, to introduce Militant there. Popular, with a regular job as a hardware buyer for a mail order firm, he was seen as the acceptable face of Militant.

After the 1987 election, complaints were received of Militant activity in Bradford during the course of campaigning. Accompanied by the regional organiser, David Robertson, I conducted sixty-five interviews before I concluded that the allegations were justified. The NEC agreed and charges were brought against nine members, including John Ingham from Leeds West. Ingham had not had any success in his own constituency so concentrated his efforts in Bradford. Some were suspended or left the party. Ingham was expelled.

From Bradford I went to Glasgow Pollok to begin another investigation, and another round of long and at times tedious interviews, sitting with Jimmy Allison, Scottish party secretary. In order to get back to London in time for my other responsibilities I liked to stay at a hotel near the station. Jimmy was keen to save the party money, so always booked me into small cheap hotels. One time he made a mistake. The hotel entrance opened onto a flight of stairs, with a desk half way up and my room at the top. I quickly realised this was a hotel where prostitutes took their clients. I shot into my room and locked the door.

Next morning at six o'clock, I belted down the stairs past a woman at the desk, who was clearly waiting to take her cut. I was relieved to be out of there.

Tommy Sheridan was the key figure in Militant's disruptive activities in Scotland. He was an attractive, charismatic young man. Through the Anti-Poll Tax Union, a Militant front organisation, he used public platforms and the media to discredit Labour. It was raining when I arrived to present the case against him. The media were out in force. The evening news broadcasts portrayed me arriving under a bright multi-coloured umbrella. After a ten-hour session, the NCC expelled him. Sheridan later spent six months in jail for non-payment of poll tax but such was his profile that whilst in jail he was elected as a councillor to Glasgow City Council, standing as Scottish Militant Labour. He was later to become a member of the Scottish Parliament. When the Jenkins Commission visited the Scottish Parliament, I found it disconcerting to be sitting in the gallery directly above the man I had expelled from the party.

I never thought during the many hours I spent in Brighton gaining evidence of Militant activity, accompanied by Tony Beirne, the regional organiser, that I would end up living in the area and become friends with people who I had interviewed and who had condemned my actions at the time. Many of Militant's leading cadre were recruited whilst students at Sussex University. Brighton became second only to Liverpool in its importance to Militant.

It was the same story there as elsewhere, complaints received and investigated. I declared six councillors ineligible to stand again as candidates for the local authority, and imposed their replacements. I suspended the Brighton Labour Party. It was yet another long investigation, Tony driving me day after day from Brighton station to the Hove Labour Party offices. We were termed in an article by Militant as the 'Joyce and Tony show'. Such was the intimidation that pervaded the area that the names of those who had complained were kept secret. The inquiry recommended a number of suspensions and two members were expelled after hearings before the NCC. The two constituencies in Brighton worked as one unit, which made it easier for Militant to take control, and my final action in the town was to reinstate them as two separate units. Both of these constituencies elected Labour MPs at the next general election in 1997.

The final decision by the executive committee was to bring charges against two sitting MPs, Dave Nellist in Coventry South East and Terry Fields in Liverpool Broadgreen. Both were alleged to be members of Militant. I conducted two very long investigations. These were the big cases. Taking action against an MP was a major event. On receiving my evidence the National Executive invited both MPs to attend a meeting on 25 September 1991, so they could justify why disciplinary action should not be taken against them. The meeting had been called to determine whether there was a case for referral to the NCC. It was chaired by Tom Sawyer. Only Dave Nellist turned up. Tom asked me to make a statement outlining the case against him arising from my investigation. I was cross-examined by NEC members, and Nellist then spoke at length. The outcome was that I was instructed to prepare charges for presentation to the NCC. Terry Fields did not appear. His solicitor attended to read a statement. After consideration, the same decision was taken that charges be laid.

The advice of our barrister, Derry Irvine, was that the charges and the conclusions against the two MPs should follow the same pattern. I spent many hours preparing the cases. I did most of the work at home and if the weather was good in my garden in Tooting Bec. I put stones on the great piles of paper to stop them blowing away in the breeze. I had to collate each case. They each covered some 125 pages of evidence.

I arrived at head office on the morning of the NEC meeting to present my findings, only to discover someone had submitted a last page changing the charges against one of the MPs. It was being circulated to the meeting. Feeling extremely tired and fraught, I stormed into Larry Whitty's office to learn that it had been written by Neil Stewart, then head of Neil Kinnock's office. Neil Kinnock arrived for his pre-briefing meeting, and saw how upset I was. He threw Larry out of the office whilst I explained. He made it clear he knew nothing about how it had happened. At the NEC meeting, John Evans, a prominent member, announced in all innocence that there was a new version to one of the conclusions. Neil immediately told him to tear it up as the meeting was going to support the original words written by the director (me). At Neil Kinnock's insistence the two Neils travelled back to Westminster on their own. Later that day I received a phone call from Neil Stewart saying the leader had instructed him to take me out for an expensive lunch as a way of an apology. We went to the restaurant at the Tate Gallery.

The hearing against Terry Fields was heard on 5 December by the general secretary and resulted in expulsion. Larry followed absolutely the evidence that I had prepared so that there were no discrepancies between the two cases. I presented the case against Dave Nellist at a six-hour hearing two days later in West Bromwich. Dennis Skinner was a key witness on behalf of Nellist. Dennis believed in the importance of conference decisions, so it was easy to point out to him that supporting Nellist's action was in breach of a decision of conference. This was the higher profile of the cases and it attracted a great deal of media interest. Both MPs were accompanied by their legal advisors. It is alleged that Terry Field's legal bill was £1,500, and that of Dave Nellist £1,980. Both were expelled from the party.

A statement was made to the press by Jack Cunningham, the party's campaign co-ordinator, that the MPs were no longer members of the party. It was encouraging that my part in these events was recognised, and I quote from Betty Boothroyd's auto-biography: 'Joyce Gould had played a crucial role in bringing the evidence together, in seeing that the NEC's decisions on expul-sions were carried out – a difficult task in which her knowledge of party strictures helped enormously.'

I was amazed to find in my papers a letter written in June 1991 by Chris Patten, then chair of the Conservative Party, declaring that both MPs had expounded Militant policies and spoken on Militant platforms, with the rather threatening statement 'Unless you act swiftly to expel them from the party your commitment to rid Labour of its hard left element will be revealed for what it is, a total sham. I challenge you to make clear today what you are going to do about this important matter.' To me such inter-ference was totally unacceptable.

By early 1993 all the known cases of Militant activity had been resolved. Militant decided to abandon its entryism strategy, made possible by the support and determination of the leader Neil Kinnock, those party members and my colleagues who supported me through those years; members and staff who were determined to bring sanity and unity to the party and make it electable. It is ironic that Ted Grant, their spiritual leader, who was opposed to the change of strategy, was himself expelled by Militant – his second expulsion.

CHAPTER 13

◄◄◄►►►

EXODUS

The leadership election to find a successor to Neil Kinnock was between John Smith, who was the shadow Chancellor, and Bryan Gould, who for a number of years had been a prominent member of Neil's shadow Cabinet. Robin Cook MP and my daughter Jeannette led John Smith's campaign team and delivered 90 per cent of the vote to him, a leadership victory that was seen as a model of its kind.

Three candidates stood for the deputy leadership, Margaret Beckett, Bryan Gould and John Prescott. Margaret Beckett was elected with over 50 per cent of the vote. Bryan resigned from Parliament and went back to New Zealand to resume his academic career.

John Smith continued the process of change. At the 1993 conference he supported the demand for 'one member, one vote' (OMOV) in all party elections. This followed my initiative in encouraging constituencies to carry out their own ballots prior to voting for the NEC. This practice became mandatory in 1990. The outcome was that delegates voting on the election of the members for the NEC changed dramatically. Gerald Kaufman was in 1991 the first person for fifteen years on the right of the party to be elected as a constituency representative on the NEC. I was reminded of his success in an article he wrote about me on my retirement in which he says: 'I rang Jo [Richardson], who was sick in her hotel room to say how sorry I was that my victory meant her defeat. The person who answered the telephone was Joyce. She was there looking after Jo. That was absolutely typical of her.' Two years later he was followed by Gordon Brown and Tony Blair and then Harriet Harman.

John Smith believed that party members had the right and the ability to make policy for the Labour Party, but that decision was contentious. The outcome depended on the attitude of the trade unions. Most unions had determined their attitudes in advance of conference but the Manufacturing, Science and Finance Union (MSF) were undecided. My friend Ann Gibson, now Baroness Gibson, was influential in persuading them to vote in favour. John Smith took the clever decision of asking John Prescott to wind up the debate. So OMOV was introduced after twelve years of campaigning by its supporters. Another crucial change was the abolition of the mandatory re-selection procedure.

The party lost a great leader and the country a potentially great Prime Minister when John died two years later on 12 May 1994. It was a terrible shock to me, having heard him speak at a dinner the evening before. My daughter had joined John's office and rang me early the next morning to let me know the sad news. I went straight to the office to be with his team. John had qualities that impressed the public. He had been an MP for twenty-four years and had the ability to savage the Tories. His famous one-liners included his references to John Major as 'the devalued Prime Minister of a devalued government' and to Major and Norman Lamont as the 'Laurel and Hardy of British politics'. John's sincerity shone through in his statement 'The opportunity to serve our country that is all we ask'.

The House of Commons adjourned for an hour before the tributes, in respect for a man of great integrity, honesty and decency. Margaret Beckett through her tears said, 'I have never met anyone who was so certain of himself, of what he could do.' After the tributes the House adjourned again. I went to the Commons to be a part of that momentous day.

On 20 May, I travelled to Edinburgh for his funeral along with the 900 mourners in the church and the 600 gathered outside. At the wake I went to speak to John Major, standing on his own. He was isolated from our feelings of loss but as he said he came out of respect for a great politician.

This was almost exactly a year after I had retired from working for the party, having been on the staff for twenty-four years. Twenty-four years which had given me opportunities that I would never otherwise have experienced. I was told that the staff were shell shocked on hearing I was leaving. I could have stayed another five years, but I think I knew when it was the right time and I was sure my time had come. The very capable East Midlands regional officer, Peter Coleman, replaced me. The staff were delighted, saying to me, 'He was a safe pair of hands to continue your good work,' and so he was.

I worked with and met some fantastic people, people whose views I shared, with aspirations to improve the lives of all people, to make the party electable and once again to achieve a progressive Labour government. I thank them all for their support and co-operation and hard work for the cause we all believed in. My leaving coincided with the end of the in-fighting in the party. I was sure that Labour's prospects for returning to power were better than they had been for a very long time.

I was gratified if a little surprised to read some of the comments that appeared after I announced my retirement. Michael White and Patrick Wintour said in *The Guardian*:

America's General Colin Powell is not the only top military person thinking of stepping down. Joyce Gould, Labour's veteran director of organisation, known by the left as the Witchfinder General for her role in expelling Trotskyists and trouble-makers, told John Smith last week she plans to retire at sixty – in April.

Also departing in the current shake-up at Walworth Road is Geoff Bish, director of research since 1974, who helped to draft no fewer than five Labour manifestos, ranging from Bennery ('the longest suicide note ever written') to Kinnockery (the second longest?). Holding down one of the toughest jobs held by a woman anywhere in British politics, Ms Gould leaves satisfied in the knowledge that her team delivered large swings to Labour in the key marginal last year. The likelihood that the once entryist Militant Tendency will set up its own party in England next month is also something for which she can take credit.

She has prepared a valedictory, discursive paper for next week's National Executive meeting. As she explained yesterday: 'We must now rebuild from the base again and adopt a more open attitude to party membership. We should be less bureaucratic and realise party members are volunteers.'

Shortly before I retired, one Saturday afternoon I was sitting in my garden in Tooting when I received a call from Tom Melia of the National Democratic Association in the United States. He asked me if I would join a team of four Americans that had been established to advise new democracies in eastern Europe on their new constitutions, on the organisation of their first democratic elections and on civic and voter education, to provide advocacy and importantly to help citizens to engage in the political process.

My immediate reaction was to ask the question 'Why me?' Tom's reply was a surprise: 'Peter Mandelson recommended you.' Thanks to Peter I then experienced three fantastic years, travelling back and forth to eastern Europe.

My first visit was to Bulgaria, a country I returned to a number of times. I bought new clothes. I wanted to look smart and authoritative when I met my American colleagues. I arrived in Sofia, and was driven straight to a rally in the centre of the city. It was hot and the crowd was large and noisy. Ferried to the front of the platform, I collapsed to the ground in a faint. It may have been the heat, the noise or hunger. I came round to voices screaming at me, in a language I did not understand. For an instant I panicked with no idea where I was, but after a little while I recovered sufficiently to make a short speech.

There were so many interesting incidents. We met many senior dignitaries before travelling out of Sofia to meet the mayor of a small town. The Town Hall was many storeys high and made of green marble imported from South America, with a fountain flowing down the walls. The mayor was a nervous little man who gave us a lecture on democracy. I could not resist asking him what had changed him from being a communist to a democrat;

putting his arms in the air, he said in a loud voice, 'I had a reve-
lation'! I felt sorry for him. After other interviews with people
who were excited about the future and those organising elections,
I returned home. The visit did not end happily, for on my return
journey my suitcase was stolen and I lost all my beautiful new
clothes. Fortunately I was insured.

I went back to observe the election campaign. It was not perfect,
as it involved some bribery, the main bribe being a bag of sugar.
Overall, however, I felt it had been free and fair. At the meeting
of all the observers after the election, a Republican from the
United States complained that the rosewood floor of a school had
influenced the vote. The rose is the national flower of Bulgaria,
and to him it was a left-wing symbol.

In Romania, I wore three layers of outer clothing to keep out
the cold. I had to take them all off on an overheated train and put
them all back on before stepping out into the cold. The avenue
that swept up to Ceauşescu's palace in Bucharest was magnificent
in comparison to the areas of great poverty. Here the idea of free
elections was not accepted by all. There was particular objection
to the presence of the Americans. This was exacerbated by their
active working to get involved in industries and commercial
ventures in the country.

There was a different attitude in Poland. Young entrepreneurs
were working vigorously to get involved in the development in
this new country. It was in Poland that we called together representatives of the seventy parties that were putting up candidates,
all suspicious of each other. We had requested three delegates from
each of the parties and stipulated that one had to be a woman.
I was annoyed that the only party not to send a woman was the

Social Democrats. I separated them into cross-party working groups. They refused to speak to each other. They said it might give secrets away about their respective campaigns. I gave them a lecture on the meaning of democracy. I had to explain to them that in a democracy we had different philosophies and policies but we did speak to each other. There were times when the arrogance of one of the Americans shone through: he was the expert; only the Americans knew how to run democratic elections. At one point I was to buy a T-shirt which said 'I am not an American'!

The concept of the third sector was completely alien to the establishment in many of these countries. We made a special visit to Slovakia and the Czech Republic, where the few charities were in despair. Our aim was to try and convince the establishment in those countries that they should work with the charities and not reject them. I think we were partially successful.

Moving from Eastern Europe we went to South Africa and held many training sessions. I had a private meeting with aspiring women candidates from the African National Congress (ANC), who had come together from across the country. I gave support and comforted one woman who was crying for home. She had never left her village before. She was nevertheless determined to be elected, staunch in her belief that the ANC would improve the lives of black women. We discussed how to ensure women became candidates. They asked, should they demand a quota? They suggested 30 per cent, but I suggested they go for 50 per cent as they were sure to get less than they were asking for. I was delighted when I heard they asked for – and got – a 50 per cent quota.

The Westminster Foundation had sent me to the Soviet Union as part of an all-party delegation, with Chris Rennard (now

Lord Rennard) representing the Liberal Democrats and Geoffrey Harper from the Conservatives. Now at Tory head office, Geoffrey was originally an election agent from Leeds, so we knew lots of the same people and reminisced about our time in the city. The meetings held with would-be parliamentarians were often cantankerous and difficult. But part of the job Geoffrey and I had was making it clear to Chris that we had many years of experience in running elections.

I knew that I was to return from South Africa to my retirement party, held on 1 April 1993. On the night I realised how hard the organisers had worked in my absence. I am sure they were assisted by my daughter although she denies it. How do I describe the evening? I could never do it justice. I could not believe the scores of people who were there, all my national and regional colleagues, NEC members, shadow ministers, MPs and general secretaries of trade unions, along with personal friends.

There were paper hats, balloons and decorations and masses of food and drink. Roger Hough, one of our computer team, was the master of ceremonies and started by putting on a video which showed my antics sitting on the platform at conference. He accompanied it with a witty and sometimes rude commentary. Joyce drinking water, Joyce eating a chocolate biscuit. She is now straightening her hair, now shuffling papers. Someone had watched the video and lip-read my comments: 'Now that's a good-looking man', 'I had the fish, yes, lovely', 'What does it say on that T-shirt?' and so on.

I was then given a massive framed poster from the film *Gone with the Wind*. Instead of Vivien Leigh gazing into the eyes of Clark Gable, there was I looking lovingly into the eyes of Derek

Hatton! Members of the staff gave comic readings about their life working with me. Then came tributes to my work for the party. Reference was made to my international role, to my development of the women's agenda and my days of touring the country cleaning up the party.

Next out came the red book in the style of *This Is Your Life*, titled 'A Work's Life for Labour'. It was narrated brilliantly by Roger, who paused to ask me rather impertinent questions I had to answer. 'Tonight's guest is Labour's well-known director of organisation, Joyce Gould.' It started with my biography from *Who's Who* and the nicest photograph of me I have ever seen. I don't know where they got it. Roger moved on to my voluntary work in Leeds and then to my appointment to the Yorkshire office. There were photographs of activities I was a part of, extracts of interviews with newspapers and articles I had written. There were lots of photographs of my many friends and, to be treasured, a picture of all my staff. My days in Liverpool could not be ignored, and the book ended with an advisory memo:

> **Private & Confidential**   NEC 1st April 1993
>   DO/26/3/93
>
> Joyce Gould – director of organisation
>
> It has been noted that the above person has conducted a campaign (along with the National Executive Committee) of
>   a) Sorting out the party in Liverpool
>   b) Attempting to get rid of the nasty element in Liverpool
>   c) Stopping the Liverpool Labour group being held to ransom by unrepresentative cliques

   d) Interviewing lots of 'headbangers' for endless hour upon hour as part of another tedious investigation

   e) And generally being a pain in the arse to those elements in the party who have a hidden agenda.

In this respect it is recommended:

   1) That Joyce Gould be suspended from holding office, delegation or representation under Clause 18(2)(h)(ii) of the Constitutional Rules, pending further investigation

OR

   2) That Liverpool DLP [District Labour Party] be reconvened and Joyce Gould be made lifetime secretary and the organisation have no quorum

OR

   3) Alternatively she have a long and happy retirement and never have to bother with Liverpool again.

The presents and flowers piled up. I was absolutely overwhelmed, and gave my thanks for them all, and thanks to my colleagues for their friendship and support over the years. I thanked everyone who had worked to make this a most wonderful and memorable evening, albeit tinged with the inevitable sadness that I was leaving a job that I had loved. My thoughts turned to what lay ahead for me and the Labour Party. One thing I vowed was that I would never look at a party rule book again. My friend from Leeds Hedley Taylor had a van which he filled up with my gifts and took me home in. I never looked back; for me, an era was over.

Will we ever replace her?
Gerald Kaufman MP

Joyce Gould, the director of organisation, retires in April. Here the Rt Hon. Gerald Kaufman MP pays tribute to her and her work for the party (March 1993)

A few months ago Joyce Gould gave me a telling off. It was over a minor matter, but she was absolutely right. At the time I was a member of the shadow Cabinet and even more important to Joyce as a member of the body she was responsible to the National Executive Committee. Yet the posts I hold did not prevent Joyce from telling me exactly what she thought. She respected everybody, but she bowed the knee to nobody. That is exactly how a good servant of the party should behave.

And a good servant of the party is exactly what Joyce has been. How could it be otherwise for someone who started her party activities in Leeds (as naturally I was)?

For Joyce it has been the party and not any particular individual that have counted. If that makes her sound like some grey Stalinist apparatchik, then I am expressing myself badly: for Joyce is a democratic socialist to her fingertips and has a sly sense of humour as well.

What I mean is that she can intensify about the Labour Party, wants it to win and wants it to retain its integrity. Party rules are there to be observed and Joyce was going to make sure that everyone observed them, whatever position they held in the hierarchy and whatever position they occupied in the political spectrum.

Some have distorted her interpretation of her duties in order to misrepresent her as a witch-hunter of the left. Nothing could be more mistaken! I do not know Joyce's personal politics within the party are though, am sure they are nearer the left than the right. But she was determined that nobody would on any side of the party be described as a better socialist than someone else. For her the rules of the party were her Ten (or more) Commandments and nobody, Militant or about-to-desert-the ship Social Democrats, was going to get away with violating them. Her recommendations to the National Executive, during my membership, were models of impartiality and rectitude.

All this may make her sound like some remote Goody-Two-Shoes, if so I am getting it wrong again, Joyce was always accessible. Joyce was always ready to laugh at a joke or to make a joke herself. She was human and kind.

No individual in our party is indispensable, and Joyce will be replaced. It is no reflection whatever on her successor to say that, even so, Joyce will leave a gap that cannot be filled. We will miss her. We wish her well.

CHAPTER 14

◄‹›►

BEING A
BARONESS

On 13 October 1993, I crossed another threshold. I entered the House of Lords accompanied by my two sponsors, Betty Lockwood and Merlyn Rees. When I asked Merlyn to be one of my sponsors, his good advice was 'Don't forget to put your bum on a seat in the chamber or you won't get your money'.

Before that momentous day I paid the statutory visit to the College of Arms to meet Garter, Conrad Swan Esq. His first question was 'What do you want your title to be?' I said, 'Joyce-Gould' but he told me that hyphens were no longer allowed. My geographical area of choice was, of course, Potternewton, where my political life had started. Out came the big book to check such a place existed. He couldn't find it. 'Tell me, my dear,' he asked, 'if I was in a car in the centre of Leeds and wound down my window and asked the way to Potternewton, would someone be able to tell me?' I replied, 'There is Potternewton Lane, Potternewton Park and a military hospital.' After turning the pages of his big book he realised that he had used the wrong spelling of Potternewton. Next he asked, 'How do you wear your hair? We don't want your hat to fall off.' I assured him it would be short and tidy. His last comments were to invite himself to my pre-introduction lunch and read out my full title, 'Baroness Gould of Potternewton in the City of Leeds in the County of West Yorkshire'. My title prompted an article in the *Yorkshire Evening Post* with the headline 'The Lady sticks to her roots'.

The introduction went smoothly and I nodded my head in the right places. I doffed my hat three times and it didn't fall off. My robes were fastened up with safety pins to stop me tripping on the steps. My colleagues who kept score gave me nine and a half out of ten. Shaking hands with Derry Irvine, the Lord Chancellor, he whispered, 'Who would believe we would meet again in this august way?'

As I sit on the red benches in the Lords I look around and I see a snapshot of my sixty-three years in Labour politics, many of my colleagues sitting nearby. Looking across the benches there are faces that take me back to Yorkshire, and to the early days on the party's women's committees. To mention some but not all names would be invidious, and there are too many to mention. I am reminded of Neil's leadership, members of his staff, members of the NEC and its multifarious committees, not forgetting deputy leaders and general secretaries. There was a time when there were enough of us to actually have an NEC meeting: members from constituencies, the trade unions and affiliated organisations. But most of all I see around me colleagues who at one time were on my staff. So I arrived amongst friends.

My 80th birthday was a special occasion. Jan Royall put on

a drinks reception and Josie Farrington arranged a special curry night. So many of my friends came, it was a great evening.

I sat in the chamber for two weeks trying to get used to the strange language and procedures. I was dreading the day I made my maiden speech. The debate was introduced by Garry Runciman detailing his report on prisons. I chose to speak on women in prison, which hadn't received a mention in his report. I worked hard on my speech, getting help from Andrew McIntosh, who gave me advice on length and style. The women in the women peers' room were very supportive and wished me well as I walked into the chamber. I was number six on the list of speakers, following five eminent judges. I didn't allow my nerves to take over. I got through it. I was so relieved when I received letters of congratulations, from all sides of the House.

Three weeks into being a baroness, the Chief Whip, Ted Graham, asked me if I wanted to be an opposition whip. 'You will get a desk.' For the desk if nothing else I said yes. Getting a desk was a real bonus, they were like gold dust. It was only a desk, not an office, which I shared, but the beauty of the building made up for it. I love showing people round the magnificent royal gallery and Queen's robing room.

Ted Graham was replaced as Chief Whip by Denis Carter, who I met weekly, mainly to discuss the political situation. His daughter Catherine had been a member of my staff. Catherine was blind and when I appointed her I met some resistance from one or two of the staff: 'Where will the dog go?' or 'How much will the new equipment cost?' Unfortunately, Denis told me that Catherine was being made redundant when the party was making cuts in the number of staff. She did get another job but a few years later she sadly died, as did Denis, but I still keep in contact with Teresa, his wife.

Standing at the despatch box to make my first speech on behalf of the party, I was both proud and terrified. Fortunately it was also the first time for the government minister Doreen Miller. We welcomed each other across the chamber as sisters. The next day I received a letter from Doreen: 'If you were anywhere near as nervous as I was it certainly didn't show – you were excellent. Here's to both of us, Doreen.' Simon Haskel, Brenda Dean and I were planning a drinks party for the intake of 1993 from all parties, but tragically Doreen died and we cancelled the event.

It was important for me to develop two skills, to both write speeches and to stand on my feet and make them. I attempted to speak at least once a week. I attended the peers' Labour group every week in bewilderment. Not only did the Labour Party never get a mention but there was nothing to tell me about who did what and when. As a typical organiser, after a while I suggested to Ted Graham it would be a good idea to have a handbook for new peers. He wasn't keen but said, 'OK, go and write one,' which I did. Although it is now considerably updated, we still have that handbook.

I soon realised that being a member of the Lords provided other opportunities to be involved in organisations engaged in issues that I was interested in. I was elected by the peers' Labour group to the Council of Europe and followed Betty Lockwood as the chair of the equality committee on the Council. The highlight was to head the Council of Europe delegation to the 1995 United Nations Women's World Conference in Beijing. Betty and I had a holiday seeing the sights in China before the conference.

We went to an evening entertainment in Xi'an. We arrived late, the room was dark. When the lights went up, facing me across the table was my colleague Margaret Prosser, who was also taking the opportunity to take a holiday before the conference. After two weeks, Betty departed for home and I went to my hotel in Beijing.

The receptionist at the hotel demanded to see my conference credentials. I had not had time to get them. It was certainly too late that night – it was ten o'clock. I was told, 'No credential, no room.' After going from one manager to another, I told them if there was no room available I would sleep on a couch in the foyer. They could not let that happen. Eventually they gave in and I was escorted to my room. A knock on the door, a basket of fruit; a second knock on the door, a bouquet of flowers; and then a third knock on the door to check if the television worked. It didn't. In came the ladder, up to the ceiling, and wires were adjusted. Finally I could go to bed.

Over the next two weeks, there were many late nights going through the papers with my delegation. The longest night, however, was spent with an international working group to produce and acceptable form of words on reproductive health. Words that gave the women the right to contraception and the right to choose.

The venue for the women's non-governmental organisations was some miles out of Beijing. Women from all parts of the world had set up their stalls and exhibitions and played their music, to promote women's rights. I daily made the journey by taxi down a road lined with white houses. I was told that only the fronts of the houses had been painted to give a good impression.

Before leaving I went on my own for a walk in a park and sat down on a bench next to a middle-aged Chinese woman. She worked in a hotel, so had a little English. We chatted. It was one of the memorable moments of my month in China.

Shortly after returning home, on the day after my birthday Jeannette became ill. Betty and I had been invited to a Fabian reception but decided instead to have a drink in the peers' guest room. We had just settled down when I was told that there was a phone call for me in the whips' office: Jeannette had been taken to St Thomas' Hospital. Betty and I rushed there. I wanted to run over the bridge but Betty rightly insisted we got a taxi. Jeannette was unconscious and very ill. I rang Kevin and my brother David. She was dashed to the National Hospital. My sister-in-law drove us there behind the ambulance going the wrong way down one-way streets. Jeannette had suffered a subarachnoid haemorrhage. I sat, I paced anxiously in the waiting room, with Kevin, Betty, David and my sister-in-law Hilda. After many hours a nurse came and told us they had managed to stop the bleeding. Jeannette was in hospital for many months. Kevin and I spent every day at the hospital. She averaged twenty visitors a day. I was overwhelmed. I kept a book so that when she came out of her coma after five weeks she would know who had visited her.

I can never express my feelings of appreciation for the level of support I received from Jeannette's friends and mine. Isabel Larkin, now at the TUC, came every evening to take Kevin and me home. At weekends Sally Morgan organised a rota of car drivers to take us to the hospital and bring us back. Colleagues and friends brought me food to make sure I was eating properly. I did not go to the Lords for many months, nor to my mews house in Brighton, and my thanks go to Molly and Tony Beire, who looked after it for me.

There was great excitement one day amongst the doctors, nursing and hospital staff when Tony Blair paid a personal visit to see Jeannette. Everyone knew he was going to be the next Prime Minister. To my amusement, the staff stood in a line to shake his hand. Neil Kinnock and John Prescott were regular visitors. All the members of the shadow Cabinet came. Mo Mowlam ignored visiting times but somehow always got in.

At Christmas the cards poured in for Jeannette, including one from John Major. The word went round: a patient has had a card from the Prime Minister. How did it happen? Mo Mowlam had told him she had a dear friend very ill in hospital and it would be nice if he could send her a card and he did. Jean Corston, the chair of the Women's Parliamentary Labour Party, kindly invited me to a dinner the women MPs were having at the Red Fort restaurant. It gave me a rare social evening. Although she did not say so explicitly, this was to give me a break. To give me some respite, again although not said as such, Brenda Dean invited Betty Lockwood, Muriel Turner and me to spend an enjoyable weekend at her home in Falmouth. I cannot forget such kindness.

There was a real buzz of excitement as we returned to the Lords after our victory in 1997. The party under the leadership of Tony Blair, branded as New Labour, returned to government after eighteen years, and went on to win the two following elections. It was a strange feeling sitting on a different side of the chamber and looking at the different designs on a different wall.

Following the 1997 election I agreed to become a government whip along with my colleagues Josie Farrington, Simon Haskel,

Doug Hoyle and Larry Whitty. Government whips in the Lords hold the title Lords and Baronesses in Waiting to the Queen. They are members of the royal household, and take on duties on behalf of the Queen. The five of us had to go to the Palace to be approved. We went together but my colleagues left me to do the talking. We discussed the role of computers in our work, and heard from the Queen that the grandchildren were teaching their grandfather how to use a computer. We were approved as members of the household, and I took the first month's duties.

My first engagement was to have breakfast with Nelson Mandela at the Dorchester, before he was to see the Queen later that day. I had met the great man previously when he came to meet the Anti-Apartheid members, but this was a very special occasion.

Two other particular memories stay with me. The first was a memorial service for the former Lord Chief Justice Lord Taylor of Gosforth. The other official guest was the newly appointed Home Secretary, Jack Straw, whom I met on the steps of St Paul's. It was magical. I enjoyed the moment we bowed to each other. 'Good morning, Home Secretary.' 'Good morning, Queen.' Jack went in and I followed, accompanied by the Dean of St Paul's. I was seated in a chair at the front, all on my own. All the clergy formed a semi-circle round me and bowed, I bowed my head in response and hoped that was the right thing to do.

The second event, the visit of the King and Queen of Sweden, caused me some awkwardness. They arrived at Waterloo Station and proceeded to the escalator. I suffer from vertigo and do not go down escalators. Embarrassed, I uttered my apologies to the Queen. She insisted on accompanying me in the lift, saying to her husband, 'We will meet you down below.'

When Margaret Jay became leader in the Lords, our first leader in government for eighteen years, she took over from Ivor Richards, who had the post in opposition. During the summer recess we discussed how to improve the relationship between the front and back benches and how backbenchers could be of greater assistance to ministers. We came up with the concept of department liaison peers (DLPs), whose role was to work with the minister, build a team of backbenchers on each piece of legislation, and keep the team informed on the minister's views. The role was different to that of parliamentary private secretaries in the Commons in that DLPs could, and did, participate in the relevant debate. Bruce Grocott when he became Chief Whip was not overkeen on the system and it gradually faded away. Eventually I was the only one left, continuing with the job under the next three leaders, Gareth Williams, Valerie Amos and Cathy Ashton.

Jan Royall took over from Bruce for only a few months as Chief Whip before becoming leader of the Lords in 2008 when Cathy went to become a European Commissioner. Steve Bassam took over as Chief Whip. For almost seven years they ensured that the Labour group of peers were effective firstly in government and then in opposition. Jan resigned in 2015 and was replaced by Angela Smith, who had been the MP for Basildon for thirteen years before losing her seat in 2010.

Gareth was an exceptional person. He was clever, funny and a brilliant speaker. He would say to me, 'Come in in fifteen minutes.' The fifteen minutes was to cool a bottle of white wine, so I could have a drink whilst we talked. What a shock it was to receive a phone call from No. 10 early one Saturday morning in 2003. Sally Morgan gave me the sad news that Gareth had died.

I was asked to tell no one else as his death had not yet been announced. I had to tell someone, so I made the half-hour walk to Jeannette's, only to discover she was out. I had to cry on my own.

As Margaret Jay's backbench assistant I had the responsibility for briefing our backbench team on the clauses of the House of Lords Bill as it was going through the House during 1999. It removed all but ninety-two of the hereditary peers from the Lords. A great deal was made by the hereditary peers of their heritage, but the best speech in reply was made by Gareth Williams. He detailed his heritage coming from a mining family in Wales, a heritage that had made him what he was. He was someone who had come into the House of Lords in his own right and not because of who his great-grandfathers were.

Within a year of getting into government, Tony Blair set up a commission on Commons electoral reform, which he asked me to join. It was headed by Roy Jenkins, by now Lord Jenkins of Hillhead, and its principal aim was to formulate the question for a future referendum on whether to change the voting system for the House of Commons.

After discussions with Tony and Jack Straw I agreed to join the commission. They said they appreciated that I would have to resign as a government whip in the Lords and therefore would lose the salary I was receiving. Promises were made that when the commission had completed its work, a job would be found for me, a commitment that was never honoured. I also had to explain to the Queen why I was leaving her household. I was summoned to meet her at 11.50 a.m. on 15 December 1997. It was an interesting twenty minutes. We discussed her views on proportional representation; I will not disclose her words but they were not supportive. I was constantly asked if I would return to the whips' bench. I constantly refused. One year, after I had again said no, the No. 10 website included my name on the list of government whips. This caused great embarrassment to both me and the person who filled the post.

No question was asked about my own views on PR. I believe I was asked because I had sat on the Plant Commission and more importantly because I would always take into account the electoral consequences for the party of any proposed system. Working with my friend David Lipsey was invaluable, for his level of expertise was far greater than mine. It was a formidable group. Apart from Roy himself, we were joined round the table by Conservative peer Bob Alexander and John Chilcot, whose tough reputation in dealing with the IRA was well known. Roy's skill showed in the way he brought us together even though there were major differences of view.

We travelled the country and listened to the views of others, some sane, others tinged with eccentricity. We went to Germany to look at the additional member system, to New Zealand to examine the mixed member system and Australia for the alternative vote system. We investigated in detail the consequences of the differing systems they used.

Our travels also gave me the opportunity to meet old friends. In New Zealand I was pleased to have a private lunch with the leader of the opposition, soon to be Prime Minister, Helen Clarke. She is now administrator of the United Nations Development Programme, the third highest position in the UN. We had been colleagues on the Socialist Women's International Committee. The delegation also had dinner with Bryan Gould. A weekend break in Australia gave me the opportunity to catch up with my nephew Nick, his partner Liz and their two young children, who lived on the outskirts of Sydney.

Following the commission's conclusion in favour of the 'alternative vote plus' system I spoke at many constituency meetings up and down the country explaining our conclusions and the basic elements on which our decision had been based: the importance of maintaining the constituency link; that stable government was assured; that the overall result would reflect the broad choice of the electorate as a whole as well as proportionality of representation. The promised referendum on the election of the Commons was not held. In 2011, a referendum was held on AV (not AV+), which resulted in a big fat 'no'. For me it was an intellectually interesting time but one without a conclusion.

I took on a number of other jobs. Besides the Jenkins Commission, I became vice-chair of the Hansard Society, chair of the All-Party Group for Sexual and Reproductive Health, president of my women's centre in Brighton and Hove, and chair of the All-Party Group for Epilepsy, a group I reinstated after becoming president of the British Epilepsy Association (BEA). The BEA is based in Leeds and I was delighted to open their new premises in my home city. This was a new experience for me. It gave me the opportunity to meet many brave people who lived their lives with this problem. I was proud to be awarded the Dods' Champion Charity Award 2011 for my report on living with epilepsy. Then, after hearing a speech by Waris Dirie on her experience of suffering female genital mutilation (FGM), I became president of Forward, which is a leading organisation working on countering FGM.

In 1997 I followed Margaret Jay and Philip Hunt as president of the Family Planning Association (FPA), a post I still hold. At the Labour Party conference in 2005, the FPA's 75th birthday, the FPA had a large cake on their stall, which Cherie Blair and I were invited to cut. Cherie was accompanied by a horde of journalists. The FPA had been told by the party staff to cover up the word 'sex' on a banner above the stall. What they did not see was the bowl of condoms on the table. Cherie picked one up and handed it to a young journalist with the words 'You have more use for this than me!'

Being the chair of the All-Party Parliamentary Group for Sexual Reproductive Health, previously known as the All-Party Parliamentary Pro-Choice Group, gave me the opportunity to continue my commitment to ensuring the women had proper access to the best contraception services and the right to choose. The group continues to flourish and is a valuable means of keeping MPs and peers in touch with those working in the field of sexual health.

In 2003 I was asked by Hazel Blears, the public health minister, to apply to be the first and ultimately the only chair of a new quango, the Independent Advisory Group on Sexual Health and HIV. It was to be set up to implement the recommendations of the first ever review of sexual health. The review had been initiated by Tessa Jowell, the first minister for public health, and chaired by Professor Mike Adler.

I wanted the All-Party Group to give evidence to the review, but I wasn't sure of the process. I took advice from Jane Mezzone, an expert and official in the Department of Health who lives in Brighton. We had lunch and have been friends ever since.

Before my interview I wrote masses of notes. There were aspects of sexual health and HIV that were new to me. I had to read up about the number of people with HIV, chlamydia testing programmes and where people went to receive treatment for sexually transmitted diseases. What would I be asked? The review had produced thirty-eight recommendations which broken down came to over a hundred. I was interviewed by Kathy Hamlyn, Jane Mezzone's boss, and Jane. I got the job.

The advisory group was a big committee, consisting of twenty-eight experts covering every aspect of sexual health ... and me. I went to the first meeting with trepidation. How would I cope if they got technical? They didn't, they were supportive and excited that the committee had been established. What was evident was that the sexual health and HIV services were badly neglected, a Cinderella service.

To learn more, I visited contraceptive, GUM and HIV clinics and spoke at many meetings and conferences. I was overwhelmed by the dedication of the staff I met. Professor Mike Adler became my advisor. He had hoped to become the chair. He told me later that because of my close connections with health ministers, I could open doors he might not have been able to, which had proved invaluable. One of my successes was getting £300 million for sexual health services from John Reid, then Secretary of State for Health. It was disappointing to find after doing a survey that a great chunk of that money had been used by the primary care trusts for other services.

A major achievement was getting a ruling that clinics had to provide 48-hour access to patients. Duncan Selbie was the official responsible. He told me later that he had worked it out on the back of an envelope; that I did not believe. Duncan is now the CEO of Public Health England. He moved to Brighton as CEO of the Hospital Trust and he continued his interest in sexual health. I went with him to open the newly refurbished clinic he had provided.

A chlamydia screening programme was rolled out nationally, and 48-hour access to services was introduced. We also gave consideration to sexual health and sport. I persuaded senior NHS officials that the group should be responsible for initiating a sexual health agenda up to and covering the Olympics and Paralympics. I led a delegation to the Football Association explaining the need to raise awareness of HIV/Aids when the World Cup was held in South Africa. We met with David Triesman, the FA doctors and other senior staff. I was staggered when I was shown their briefing for people travelling to South Africa: 'Boys beware!' Apparently only boys go to football matches. It was also implied that as people didn't die of HIV what was the problem? I explained that HIV was a transmissible disease.

Our successes showed how it is possible to make real progress through team working. The stakeholders on the group, the public health minister and the Department of Health worked together. For over eight years we calmly and steadily made progress. I was proud of our achievements. In 2010 the group was disbanded by the coalition government without notice along with many other quangos. It was replaced by a Department Sexual Health Forum, which I surprisingly was asked to co-chair with Gabriel Scally, regional director of public health in the south-west, whose experience was invaluable as the new public health and NHS structure came into place. This, however, has now been abolished too, and the services have been fragmented. Sexual health is now the responsibility of local government working to Public Health England. There is virtually no ministerial accountability.

The complexity of the service now, caused by the changes made in health and social care, is having a drastic effect across the NHS. It is alleged that the proposals for these changes were put to Margaret Thatcher, who refused to implement them.

I took responsibility as the unofficial whip when we discussed in the Lords subjects not whipped such as Section 28 and the age of consent. When opening a gay health clinic in Manchester I was asked what I did in the Lords. Without thinking but much to the amusement of the audience I said, 'I am the sex whip!' It took me a long time to live it down. I made another mistake when I met Simon Stevens, now head of NHS England, then Tony Blair's health advisor at the time of the re-organisation of the primary care trusts from very small trusts into bigger units. I said I didn't know who had ever thought up the idea of having so many small trusts, and in reply he said, 'I did.' There wasn't a hole in the floor I could sink into.

For me my biggest success was to organise the campaign in the Lords to get Section 28 removed from the statute book. I was so proud when, on 6 November 2006, I handed the result to the Lord Speaker and the victory was announced. I had many letters of congratulations, but one in particular stays with me: 'Justice will prevail, but sometimes it takes a little organisation. Well done and thanks from lots of people who you don't know but who owe you a lot.'

After speaking in New York to the international conference of the British Association of Sexual Health and HIV (BASSH),

I accepted an invitation from the chair of the conference, Professor Jonathan Zenilman, to lecture at Johns Hopkins University in Baltimore. This was out of my comfort zone but surprisingly I thoroughly enjoyed it. I was delighted that one of the students had an article printed in a major US health magazine based on my recommendations on sexual health services.

I am proud that I was made an honorary fellow of the Faculty of Family Planning and Reproductive Health and the British Association for Sexual Health and HIV. I also received two further honorary degrees from Birmingham City and Greenwich universities, to go with the one I already had from Bradford. During this time I became patron of a number of HIV organisations including Yorkshire MESMac, HIV Sport and the Sussex Beacon. I continue to work closely with the key HIV organisations, the Terrence Higgins Trust, the National Aids Trust, Halve it, NAZ and many others.

Because of my level of activity on HIV, in 2013 I was asked to give the annual Windsor Ethics Lecture at Cumberland Lodge in Windsor Great Park on thirty years of HIV. I was anxious, as there were guests from Windsor Castle. I referred to and was critical of a speech made by Princess Anne, which showed her misunderstanding of the issue. However, during conversation over drinks, it was clear that at the time the castle staff had been unaware of her lack of understanding.

One day I received a phone call from the man who owned the golf course at the bottom of my garden. I had complained about the height of his leylandii trees, which were stopping the sun coming into my garden. His opening comments were 'You and I have something in common'. Nonsense, I thought, I don't play golf and know nothing about trees. Lawrence Boon then explained that his full-time occupation was as a condom manufacturer. He came to see the trees, but the time was spent discussing our joint involvement in sexual health. The trees were cut back. We still discuss our mutual interest.

In 2006 I became the interim chair of the Women's National Commission (WNC), shortly afterwards being appointed chair, replacing Margaret Prosser. The WNC came into existence on 24 October 1969. It is reputed that Marcia Falkender whilst Harold Wilson's assistant threw a loaf of bread onto the Cabinet table and asked how much it cost. Not one of the men round the table could tell her. She pointed out that they needed the advice of women who knew the price of bread. And so the WNC was born. Its first historical meeting was addressed by the then Lord Chancellor, Lord Gardiner, when he proclaimed himself to be a strong supporter of women's rights. For the next forty-one years, all governments had a direct line to the voices of women.

Initially the government chose the membership of the commission. In 1997, Joan Ruddock and I, as part of the equality team, started changing the structure, opening it up to all women's organisations. The change was completed by Margaret Jay, who I also worked with. I was the only person to see the re-structuring through from start to finish.

The new WNC heard the voices of over 600 women's organisations. The twelve commissioners were representative of the differing voices of women. We had enormous support from a dedicated team of officials, the director, Barbara-Ann Collins, and her deputy, Susan Rogers.

The WNC became noted for its campaigning on violence against women, working alongside the Metropolitan Police. We established the Muslim Women Group and a gender expert group on trade. We played a major part in the preparation and promotion of the Equality Act 2010. Many meetings were held with our partners on the direction of the Act. We discussed the views of the many women's organisations who were part of the WNC with the relevant minister, Harriet Harman, and organised joint activities. A great deal of the success of the equality agenda is owed to the years of persistence and years of advocacy.

Every four years the government presents a report on its progress on gender equality to the United Nations' Convention on the Elimination of Discrimination against Women committee. Ministers are questioned by jurists appointed by the UN. The WNC co-ordinated the views of its members and presented a shadow report, which the minister was questioned on. This report outlined the progress that the government should be making.

Each year, the commission organised a delegation to attend the annual session of the UN Commission on the Status of Women in New York. This was my opportunity to meet women from around the world and attempt to influence UN officials on the improvements that were still needed to better the lives of women. I had meetings with UN deputy secretary general Asha-Rose Misiro to discuss the introduction of the UN Women Organisation, which took many years to achieve.

Barbara-Ann Collins and I made several trips to the UN. The last one started in Washington with visits scheduled to the West

Wing at the White House, to the Office of Public Engagement to meet President Obama's Council on Women and Girls, and to other senior officials.

The officials were in a flap. It seemed that President Obama's long-awaited healthcare reform summit with Congress was due to be held that day. Could we come earlier, use a different entrance to the West Wing? Of course, we said. Problem was, all the perimeter roads were closed. Our taxi driver put us out in the snow, and waved us airily in the direction of the White House. There was a full-scale demonstration on the President's healthcare reform programme. We wove our way through the crowds. I started to negotiate with the policeman blocking our way. He accepted we were indeed there officially, but he had to do his job and stopped us going further. Time was getting on, and we were perilously close to missing our appointment.

Suddenly another policeman started re-arranging the barriers to take the growing crowds. We saw our chance and according to Barbara-Ann's blog pounced like a pair of gazelles. Within seconds we were free and I smooth-talked our way through White House security, who were clearly impressed by our tenacity. This delay meant that we missed the President as he had just walked over the road to address the summit in the Blair Building.

We had over an hour's fascinating discussion about equal pay and violence against women. We heard about the President's vision for gender mainstreaming, and about the machinery of government and how it worked in a federal system. I gave them an overview of our priorities and the breadth of our activities. We were not then aware that the WNC was soon to come to an end.

We thanked them, and came out to bright sunshine. As we made our way to the security gates, we suddenly saw him, accompanied by his two minders. He was making his way indoors with a jaunty stride, as cute in the flesh as in his photos. There was no mistaking Bo. We gave him a stroke and went on our way.

Before leaving Washington we visited a women's collective which focused on marginalised and older women living with HIV/Aids. We also went to the Rape, Abuse & Incest National Network, a nationwide on-line support service with more than 1,100 local rape treatment helplines. How amazing it would be to have that level of support in this country.

The WNC was another victim of the coalition government's bonfire of the quangos. The only discussion about our future was a fifteen-minute conversation with the equalities minister, Lynne Featherstone. She rang me to break the news. I suggested that she might attend the last meeting of the commission to explain the decision to the commissioners. She agreed. I had to stop them walking out when she indicated that she had only looked the WNC up that morning, and had not realised what an impressive group they were. The Independent Advisory Group on Sexual Health and HIV also went into the fire. The two committees that had brought together my lifelong interests were slashed.

Speaking to 4,000 people at a conference in Paris on the plight of women in Iran was a unique experience. Fortunately with an audience that size you cannot see all the way to the back. One event I particularly remember was a human rights visit I paid to eastern Turkey. I went with Lord Avebury and Lord Hylton. The conditions that some of the Kurds were living in were appalling, with few toilets and no running water. My pack of cleansing wipes was my treasured possession. There were tanks and armed soldiers at every corner. We got arrested and spent some hours in a police station for having a poster of one of the official candidates for the forthcoming elections. I tried to express my disgust to a Turkish delegate to the Council of Europe and was very abruptly told, 'Don't talk to me about them, they don't deserve anything better.' I got a very different response to the breach of human rights when I had lunch with the Dalai Lama – 'Love and peace' was his response.

When it was proposed I become a deputy speaker, I was sure that I would not be able to do it well. But with Betty Lockwood's encouragement and advice I held the post for ten years. It had its tricky moments but I soon came to realise that there were two things I had to do: firstly, to prepare for every possibility and secondly, to sound confident, even if I didn't feel it. Although I enjoyed being on the Woolsack I resigned after ten years, for I felt I could no longer do the late night shifts. That would have been unfair to my colleagues.

Over the years I have been kept extremely busy with my outside committees and have been fully involved in the business of the House and its committees. I have tried to give my time to helping organisations that work with the most disadvantaged – women suffering from domestic and sexual violence, trafficked women and those from the BME community. Following my participation in the Equality Bill moving amendments in support of the transgender community, I re-established and chaired the parliamentary committee for gender identity. This was another new experience. I learnt of the discriminations that trans people face and the support that is needed to counter their problems.

A constant theme throughout since entering the Lords has been the campaign to make sex and relationship education along with PSHE statutory on the school curriculum. I talked to every education Labour minister on the subject only to have it related to other subjects such as geography, which are not statutory. I thought that progress was being made when I launched the PSHE training academy with the then education minister, Andrew Adonis. At the very end of the Labour government it was included in an Education Bill. Too late. It will at last be included in the next Labour election manifesto. The campaign continues, spearheaded by Doreen Massey, who has been fighting the cause for a great number of years.

I moved to Brighton and Hove in 1993 but spending all my time in the Lords made it difficult to participate in local activities. I became chair of the women's refuge fundraising committee and I recently became a trustee of Brighton and Hove Age UK, becoming chair of its governance committee, a role I thoroughly enjoyed but after two years of having to travel down to Brighton and back on the same day I had to resign. I was exhausted. I have, however, retained my presidency of the Brighton and Hove Fabian Society and attend whenever I can. I have been patron of the Brighton Women's Centre for over ten years, which has grown as a real force in the area, working on behalf of the women of Brighton and Hove. In spite of my decision to not be too active in general elections as I was retired, at the request of the regional director I took over the running of the election in Hove in 2005 and we won. Unfortunately we lost Hove in 2010 but re-gained it at the last election. Peter Kyle is now our new MP, one of only two red spots on the south coast, the other being Southampton.

It gave me great pleasure to be asked to sponsor eleven friends on their introduction into the Lords. This meant that I met the then Garter, Peter Gwynne Jones, on many occasions. He was a nice man and we got on well, but I gave him no hint, so I was staggered when he asked if he could take me on the London Eye. I didn't want to be rude but excused myself on the grounds of my vertigo. He was very persistent, not least because he got encouragement from some of my colleagues. He told Doug Hoyle that I had refused even though he would take a bottle of brandy. Doug's reply was 'Take champagne, she would prefer that'. I never went. Garter and I had absolutely nothing in common: he was Eton educated and went game shooting in Africa for his holidays as his father had done before him. I knew this because he asked my advice when Eton College wanted permission to discard the animal heads his father had presented to the college. He had nowhere to put them, so I suggested he agreed to their disposal. On the day of the last Queen's Speech before he retired, he found me in a crowded Prince's Chamber and publicly gave me what I thought was a goodbye kiss. I was surprised to receive a letter from him asking if we could meet. I politely declined.

I have a steady stream of visitors to the Lords, very often from the many outside and charitable organisations I support, to discuss how I can help them. I thoroughly enjoy showing family and friends round this magnificent building. It may have limited working conditions but I still find it amazing to be able to call it my workplace. I get irritated when people, particularly MPs, fail to appreciate the value of the Lords' role in revising legislation or to recognise its ability when in opposition to challenge and defeat the government, and when they ask me 'How often do you go to the Lords, does it meet every day?'

Time passes so quickly I find it difficult to believe that I have been a baroness for twenty-two years. A quarter of my life, which started the day John Smith said to me, 'Would you like to go into the Lords?'

EPILOGUE

Those who forget the past are doomed to repeat it.

Philosopher George Santayana

As I re-read my memoirs I reflected back to myself as a young girl, a second-generation immigrant who set out on a political journey. A journey that would not have been possible without the guidance of the many, many people who saw some ability in the young girl from Potternewton and who nurtured and encouraged me to take the next step. People committed to the Labour Party, who were elated when the party was successful, when seats were won, but who were saddened when from time to time, as with all political machines, the party lost its way.

Throughout those years, society changed and life has become more impersonal, people have become more acquisitive and overall we live in a more insular world. It was not possible to have foreseen that society as I knew it could undergo the phenomenal transformation that has taken place in recent years.

Thirteen years of Labour government came to an end in

2010. The general election resulted in a country divided, none of the three major political parties achieving an overall majority. The Conservatives as the biggest party chose the Liberal Democrats to be their coalition partners, and so together they began the process of cuts to public services. The word 'austerity' entered the vocabulary as the coalition reduced the levels of public expenditure and invaded the hard-fought-for provisions of the welfare state.

I personally found it distressing to see Liberal Democrat peers whom I had respected going through the lobbies with the Conservatives to support policies that disadvantaged people with disabilities and drove families into poverty, giving little concern for the human cost. They were policies they would have opposed if they were not so committed to being a part of government. I will not forget, when making a speech on the consequences for women and families of these draconian policies, I referred to the problems caused by the reduction of benefits of some £30 or so a week. I watched the faces opposite. One Tory peer looked at me with a smirk on his face as though I was mad. Thirty pounds to him meant no more than a couple of drinks in the bar. I tried, I know unsuccessfully, to explain in more detail how much food that would have put on the table. There was however one bright spark, the introduction of same sex-marriage, expanding on the Labour government's civil partnership legislation.

As the 2015 election approached, the pollsters were predicting that the Labour Party could be the biggest party, with Ed Miliband the Prime Minister. How wrong they were. Ed decided to resign immediately after Labour's defeat, meaning we were once again faced with another leadership contest, a contest that lasted for three long months. There were of course many theories as to why we lost so badly but the immediacy of the leadership contest did not give time for any debate about our terrible defeat. There is no doubt that we failed to present the electorate with a clear coherent message, not helped by the trashing of the record of the Labour government in other quarters, with little recognition given of its achievements.

The media were at their most vicious, a reminder of 1992 and their attacks on Neil Kinnock. Policy was rarely mentioned; they preferred to attack Ed personally rather than politically. Their favourite picture of him eating a bacon sandwich was the highlight of the media's political comment. A piece of advice I always gave candidates was never to be seen eating whilst on the campaign trail.

The new rules on voting procedure for the leader and deputy leader of the party provided the media a chance to report negatively about the 'hundreds' of new entrants to the party. My sympathy was with the general secretary and his staff, having to sort out who was entitled to vote and who should be excluded. Jeremy Corbyn's victory with 60 per cent of the vote gives him an overwhelming mandate from party members but has left him uniquely facing opposition in policy terms from the majority of Labour MPs, a swathe of his newly appointed shadow Cabinet and his deputy leader.

There are difficult and rocky days ahead; there are red lines to cross, many flashpoints and crunchy policy issues to be resolved, policy not imposed but determined by party conference, resolved through an open policy-making process engaging all party members, I can only hope that the current tension in the party does not develop into trench warfare, to a period of splits and squabbles, with outside groups established explicitly to meddle with the internal workings of the party and dictate its policy. I may be being optimistic but fear that it is already happening. The party has a tradition of fringe groups across a range of views, but just as the intention is that the party should be more open and democratic, the same should apply to any such group by declaration of its membership, its organisational structure and its funding.

This I believe will not detract from our vigorous opposition to the Conservative government, a government with no compassion or care, whose brutal austerity measures are driving millions of working families into poverty, creating a society where food banks are for many the only way to feed their children, where the number of people sleeping in the streets is increasing, where our National Health Service has been depleted to make way for private companies to make profits, with a staff that is demoralised about its future, and where the floodgates have been opened after fifty years to the return of selective grammar schools.

The outcome of the elections in May 2016, in Scotland, Wales and London and for local councillors across the country, will be a defining point. The electorate will give their verdict on the new Labour regime and its record. That regime must present a coherent, alternative agenda, showing that we still are a party that defines fairness, equality and justice. In the words of Denis Healey:

> There are far too many people who want to luxuriate complacently in moral righteousness in opposition. We are not just

a debating society. We are not just a socialist Sunday school. We are a great movement that wants to help real people at the present time. We shall never be able to help them unless we get power. We shall never get power until we close the gap between our active workers and the average voter in the country.

INDEX